THE RED HOT TYPEWRITER

The Life and Times of JOHN D. MacDONALD

Also by Hugh Merrill

Esky:
The Early Years at Esquire

The Blues Route: From the Delta to California,
a Writer Searches for
America's Purest Music

THE RED HOT TYPEWRITER

The Life and Times of JOHN D. MacDONALD

Hugh Merrill

Thomas Dunne Books/St. Martin's Minotaur
New York

THOMAS DUNNE BOOKS.
An imprint of St. Martin's Press.

www.minotaurbooks.com

Photograph of John D. MacDonald facing the title page is
from AP/ Wide World Photos.

Book design by Diane Hobbing of Snap-Haus Graphics

Library of Congress Cataloging-in-Publication Data

Merrill, Hugh.
The red hot typewriter : the life and times of John D. MacDonald / Hugh Merrill.—1st ed.
p. cm.
ISBN 0-312-20905-3
1. MacDonald, John D. (John Dann), 1916-1986. 2. Detective and mystery stories,
American—History and criticism. 3. Novelists, American—20th century—Biography.
4. Detective and mystery stories—Authorship. 5. Fort Lauderdale (Fla.) in literature.
6.McGee, Travis (Fictitious character) 7. Private investigators in literature. I. Title.
PS3563.A28 Z73 2000
813'.54—dc21
[B]   99-462151

First Edition: August 2000

10 9 8 7 6 5 4 3 2 1

For JACINTA

and also for

JIM O'KON

and

CAROL O'KON

ACKNOWLEDGMENTS

The Red Hot Typewriter would only be tepid without the help of a number of people during my research and writing.

Stuart Towns, chairman of the Department of Communication Arts at the University of West Florida, was generous in granting me time off to do research and writing, as was Martha Saunders, acting dean of the College of Arts and Sciences at UWF. Sarah Russell, my graduate assistant during part of the work on this book, did valuable and essential research. The book would not have been possible without the dedication and help of the librarians and staff of the special collections department at the George Smathers Library at the University of Florida. Peter King, the author of the Gourmet Detective series and now the president of the Liar's Club in Sarasota, gave me copies of a history of that organization. Leigh Patmagrian, then of the Ringling School of Art in Sarasota, now of New College, was gracious in her help in collecting data on that institution and on Sarasota in general. Walter and Jean Shine provided invaluable aid in helping me find John D. MacDonald manuscripts that were almost impossible to get, and Leona Nevler, MacDonald's editor at Fawcett, provided assistance in understanding the publishing world MacDonald knew so well. I must also thank Ruth Cavin, who edited *The Red Hot Typewriter* and provided the help and insight that have made this book what it is. Jane Dystel, my agent, stuck with me all the way, providing moral support as well as leading me through the maze of the commercial publishing world. Moral support and occasional trivia answers were provided by Pat Murdock, Julie Hairston, Jim O'Kon, and Carol O'Kon. Of course, the book could never have been written without my wife, Jacinta, who helped me with my research and provided criticism and support throughout the whole research and writing process. And then there's the Queen of the Blues. She made it all happen.

THE RED HOT TYPEWRITER

The Life and Times of JOHN D. MacDONALD

CHAPTER 1

From the 1950s through the 1980s, John Dann MacDonald was one of the most popular and prolific writers in America. He was a crime writer who managed to break free of the genre and finally get serious consideration from critics. Seventy of his novels and more than five hundred of his short stories were published in his lifetime. When he died in 1986, more than seventy million of his books had been sold.

But it was not just sales figures that made MacDonald important. London *Times* critic H. R. F. Keating selected his 1979 novel, *The Green Ripper*, as one of the one hundred best mysteries of all time. That same novel won him the American Book Award for the best mystery of the year. His books were translated into Afrikaans, Czech, Danish, Dutch, Finnish, French, German, Greek, Hebrew, Icelandic, Italian, Japanese, Norwegian, Portuguese, Spanish, Swedish, Turkish, and Serbo-Croatian. Eight of his novels were made into motion pictures, including *The Executioners*, which became the critically acclaimed *Cape Fear*. Kurt Vonnegut said of MacDonald, "To diggers a thousand years from now, the works of John D. MacDonald would be a treasure on the order of the tomb of Tutankhamen." The author and critic Stephen Vizinczey said MacDonald sketched "the laid-back life of golf, boating, long cool drinks, the peculiar callousness bred by hot climates and luxurious comfort, better than anyone else since Graham Greene."

As a master of detective fiction, MacDonald adapted a uniquely American hard-boiled style that influenced writers around the world. In 1995 the Library of America canonized this tough direct prose when it published a collection of the writing of Raymond Chandler. What was once dismissed as cheap literary entertainment now has a place beside Hawthorne and Faulkner. But hard-boiled literature is no museum piece. It began in the 1920s with the novels of Dashiell Hammett and the stories by other writers for *Black Mask*, the best of the thousands of pulp magazines of the era. The hard-boiled style continued with Raymond Chandler in the 1940s and redefined itself in the 1950s and 1960s with the novels of Jim Thompson, Ross Macdonald, and John D. MacDonald.

Some purists believe the style eroded with the grotesque, comic-book-like, violent novels of Mickey Spillane and his imitators and then vanished forever. It did not. John D. MacDonald returned hard-boiled writing to the realm of literature and pulled it from the sewer of sadism where Spillane had dragged it. Because MacDonald's early career was as a paperback writer, it was a long time before he was taken seriously by most critics. However, beginning in 1953, Anthony Boucher became his champion in *The New York Times*. "[His] writing is marked by sharp observation, vivid dialogue, and a sense of sweet, warm horror," Boucher wrote. He also called MacDonald "the John O'Hara of the crime suspense story."

In his Travis McGee novels, MacDonald gave the hard-boiled tradition something new, a likable hero. Both Chandler's Philip Marlowe and Hammett's Sam Spade were failed policemen who lived alone, had no friends, and went to the office every day. Hammett's other detective, the Continental Op, didn't even have a name. These hard-boiled heroes had small, lonely apartments in the middle of the city and ate greasy diner food. Travis McGee, on the other hand, lived on a houseboat in the Florida sunshine, drove a Rolls-Royce pickup truck, had lots of friends and scores of women, ate good food, and worked as little as possible. Millions of readers wanted to be Travis McGee, and after MacDonald's death in 1986 other writers— Jimmy Buffett and Carl Hiaasen, for example—created heroes in McGee's image.

And yet McGee was more than a detective. He was the mouthpiece for MacDonald's diatribe against the spoiling of the environment and the corrupting of civilization.

"Far off on the north-south highways there was the insect sound of the fast moving trucks," MacDonald wrote, "whining toward warehouses, laden with emergency rush orders of plastic animals, roach tablets, eye shadow, ashtrays, toilet brushes, pottery crocodiles, and all the other items essential to a constantly growing GNP."

To understand John D. MacDonald, his writing, his life, and his rebelliousness against mainstream society, you have to go back a generation, to his father, Eugene Andrew MacDonald. A believer in the bootstrap theory, he was devoted to the juvenile novels of Horatio Alger, the Gilded Age dime novelist whose books taught boys that hard work, education, good manners, and a little luck could give them everything capitalism could offer.

Eugene Andrew MacDonald was born in 1888 in a house in Gildeas Alley, New Haven. His own father, Hugh MacDonald, had come to America from the suburbs of Glasgow. He was twenty when Eugene was born. Eugene's mother, Catherine King MacDonald, was seventeen.

Hugh MacDonald was a gardener and a handyman. He didn't make much money, but his desire to own property so possessed him that food and clothing for his family were secondary considerations.

He was overwhelmingly jealous. He constantly accused Catherine of having affairs with other men. He apparently beat her regularly, although Eugene MacDonald doesn't say so in his memoirs. His jealous rages became so bad that doctors advised Catherine that she would suffer a mental breakdown if she didn't leave her husband. Her brother, Edward King, worked in Washington, and he sent her enough money to come south and live. Bur he didn't send enough to bring her two children, Eugene and his younger sister, Lillian, with her. "She kissed us both goodbye and told us somehow, some way, she would secure enough money to come back to New Haven and get us," Eugene wrote in an unpublished memoir. But she never did.

While Catherine was in Washington, Hugh tried to put his children in an orphanage. Eugene remembered "a cold, snowy evening with my sister and I hand in hand, being led up to one orphan asylum after another. Each asylum told my Dad that they could not take us in because both of our parents were living." A few months later, Catherine and Hugh reconciled and she returned to New Haven.

Eugene was an excellent student. His teacher gave him copies of a few volumes of Horatio Alger's books to take home, along with *The Youth's Companion*. The books made a deep impression on him. "The stories gave me confidence, hope and ambition," he wrote.

In 1902, when he was fourteen, he put those lessons to work.

When he entered high school, he got a paper route to earn money for books. On the first Saturday he went out, he signed up fifteen subscribers to the *New Haven Union*. "I gave them a good story about wanting to stay in high school. It proved that Americans are always ready and willing to help the underdog." He was so successful that the *Union*'s rival paper, the *New Haven Register*, hired him away. But no matter how well he did, there was never enough money at home. He and his mother got work sewing hooks and eyes on cards, he added another paper route, he got a job as a lamplighter for the gaslights that dotted the New Haven streets. With it all he still managed to get good grades.

But there was another problem: Hugh was beating Catherine again. "I realized that unless I could get my mother and sister away from such unpleasant surroundings, they would sooner or later crack up," he wrote. "It was then I decided to work during the summer to build up a fund which some day I could use to start life anew somewhere with my mother and sister."

One of his paper route customers was a foreman in the cartridge department of the Winchester Arms Company, and he helped Eugene find a job polishing .22 caliber cartridges. He took the new job but kept delivering the papers and lighting the lamps. By the end of the summer he had saved $66. Still there was not enough money. Congressman N. D. Sherry, one of his paper route customers, told Eugene he wanted to nominate him to attend West Point. "I was flattered and thanked him profusely," Eugene writes. "But financial and home considerations were such that I could not accept."

Another customer on his paper route, a professor at Yale, arranged for a college scholarship. Again Eugene thanked his benefactor and refused. "After the first of the year, I noticed that my mother was failing in health. The doctor advised us that she would never be herself again until she was relieved of the mental strain she was experiencing." In June 1906, on the night Eugene was to graduate from high school, Catherine was rushed to the hospital in critical condition. She was not expected to live. Eugene made his graduation speech and then hurried by cab to his mother's bedside. "The doctor told me they had done everything known to medical science to improve her condition without success." But four weeks later she showed some improvement and was discharged.

Soon after she arrived home, there was a telegram from her brother, Edward, in Washington. His wife had died. Edward had a nine-year-old daughter and a thirteen-year-old son and needed someone to take charge of his household. Could Catherine and the children come as soon as possible? The three of them began counting the days.

On the first of August, Eugene resigned from his job and booked tickets to Washington. Catherine left a letter for Hugh. It was a bleak, gray day. "With fear and trepidation in my heart, I was not relieved until the train pulled out of the depot," Eugene wrote. Nine hours later, the three MacDonalds arrived in Washington in a heavy rainstorm.

Eugene went to work at the Bliss Electrical School, keeping the books for $25 a month. Life certainly seemed better than it had been in New Haven, but then Uncle Edward decided to remarry and the MacDonalds had to move out. Eugene changed jobs and went to work for the Potomac Telephone Company; Catherine repaired old rugs and carpets for $5 a week.

MacDonald's first assignment for the Potomac Telephone Company was cleaning out old phones in a brothel. "They assigned me to the red light district with instructions to call the office every half hour . . . I took [the first phone, a heavy coin-box phone] from the wall and laid it against the stair post with the [large] transmitter sticking out. One of the girls of the house, dressed in a funny gown and half awake, came down the steps and hit the set and bruised her toe. I never heard such a string of foul oaths in my life, not even by a man. I was so embarrassed I sweated like a horse, and the job, which ordinarily took ten minutes to do, took me one half hour, fortunately in time to put in my first report call."

A few months after Eugene's whorehouse job, he was reassigned to the White House, where he accidentally listened in on President Theodore Roosevelt. "What's that? Somebody is listening on this line," he heard the President say. Fifteen minutes later, Eugene was arrested by the Secret Service. Potomac Telephone cleared him, and he was assigned permanently to White House duties. Even so, telephone work didn't seem the way to success. Times were better for the MacDonalds now— Eugene was making more money, his sister, Lillian, was working as a telephone operator, and his mother was able to quit her job.

Then Eugene was befriended again by N. D. Sherry, the congressman who had offered to nominate him for West Point. Sherry got him a job mailing the *Congressional Record* along with garden seeds to his constituents. The pay was $75 a month. But Catherine fell ill again and was advised to get out of Washington; the heat and humidity were killing her. Luckily, Eugene found work at the Winchester Arms Company in New Haven.

"My mother occasionally questioned me about the future, and insisted that I must look around for someone to marry, someone who had a good business head and knew how to watch the pennies," he wrote. Most of the time Eugene was too busy working to pay any attention to girls. Then, in the Savin Rock amusement park in New Haven, he saw a redhead riding a white horse on the merry-go-round.

"That," he told a friend who was with him, "is a Wow."

The redhead was Marguerite Dann (called Margie, with a hard G), a secretary at the New Haven YMCA. Her mother had died when she and her sister were young children, and she had been raised by her father, Edward Odell Dann, and her mother's spinster sister, Emily Grace (Nana) Williams.

Eugene and Margie began courting in 1911 when she was eighteen and he was twenty-three. Before they were married, Eugene had been successful in helping to liquidate the assets of the Gotham Shirt Company for a New York bank and had moved to New York City. Here he was able to streamline the business offices of the company that made the Owen Magnetic, an electric automobile with an automatic transmission. The car sold well for a time, until it turned out that no one knew how to repair it.

In the midst of this business crisis, on June 21, 1915, Eugene and Marguerite were married. They moved to an apartment in the Bronx. Within a few months, Eugene's mother and sister took an apartment next door to the newlyweds. Again there was not enough money. Then Margie announced she was pregnant.

Eugene went back into the arms business. World War I had begun. His first job was supervising the manufacture of six-inch shells for the British navy. The MacDonalds moved again, this time to Sharon, Pennsylvania, where Eugene's employer had a plant.

On July 16, 1916, the same day the MacDonalds' furniture arrived on the train from New York City, Margie went to the hospital and began labor. It lasted for fifteen hours. It appeared that a cesarean section might be necessary, but finally the baby was born. It was an eight-and-a-half-pound boy. Eugene and Margie named him John Dann MacDonald. They called him Jack.

CHAPTER 2

Eugene MacDonald, born in a dingy dwelling in a New Haven alley, had achieved stability and financial security while still in his twenties. He was no longer the handyman's son. After years of working at odd jobs, taking correspondence courses, and inching his way up the social and professional ladder, he was respectable. It was within this cocoon of middle-class respectability that Jack and his sister, Doris, grew up.

During World War I, Eugene had prospered. Moonlighting as an accountant for an elderly businessman named Stevenson, he discovered that the man had overpaid his taxes by $100,000. The grateful Stevenson made him secretary-treasurer of the Standard Tank Car Company in Sharon, which he had acquired. At thirty, MacDonald was earning the handsome salary of twenty thousand dollars a year plus bonuses.

The MacDonalds moved again. For Jack MacDonald, who was only four years old, the best thing about the new house was a crystal radio set with earphones on which he used to listen to KDKA in Pittsburgh, the first commercial radio station in the United States. Jack's early childhood was the common one of a middle-class kid. He enjoyed the outdoors and sports—except for swimming. Three times he had to be hauled unconscious out of a pool or a lake. After the third time, he abandoned aquatic pleasures.

The family spent summers in a house they bought in Orangeville, Ohio, on the Pymatuning River, about twelve miles from Sharon. There Jack collected and mounted butterflies. "I sent away for a butterfly manual, a killing bottle, a proper net, instructions for mounting and identifying." The one he had called "the Zebra" was properly the yellow-barred Heliconian. "The Ghost" was *Claudius pernicius*, and the little lavender job was called the great purple hairstreak. In a speech to a group of Florida educators years later, MacDonald remembered that he "acquired and with great care cut up the colored plates of rare butterflies and pinned the paper images next to the

----

dead ones. The paper images were never as detailed as the ones which had been alive."

MacDonald was at the family's Ohio home when he celebrated his ninth birthday.

On the July evening, [Pa Dann, his grandfather] asked me if I would like to go down to Orangeville with him in the rowboat. I was very pleased whenever he asked me to go along. He was going into town to buy a new pocket knife. He always carried a pocket knife and he always kept it razor-sharp. We tied up at the lower dock and walked to the general store. My grandfather spent a long time studying the pocket knives, called pen knives then because, I suspect, they had been owned in a previous age to recut and renotch the nibs on quill pens.

He finally bought one exactly like his old one. My recall is precise and exact. It had two blades. The handle was slender and graceful, and made of a streaky graygreen substance, slightly translucent. The blades clicked into place with oily precision when opened. Set into that greenish stone-like substance of the handle, on one side, was a tiny shield-shape of silver metal. The knife came with a soft gray chamois case which had a brass snap and a black button on the snap.

Then he rowed us back up the river. It was hard work in the summer heat. The sounds were the creak and thunk of oarlocks, a bubbling of water around the blunt bow, an infrequent grunt of effort.

Halfway home there was a place where the river widened for a short distance, and there was a place near the bank where the current circled, where one could pull in and rest for a time, turning slowly, before contesting the current again.

As Pa Dann rested, he took the old knife out of his pocket. My heart jumped into my throat. My birthday was coming soon. He was going to give me his old knife. I *knew* he was going to give it to me. Why else had he asked me to come along with him?

He opened the blades of the old knife and closed them. They had been sharpened and sharpened again until they were narrow slivers of steel perhaps half their original length. I would treasure it. I would keep it as sharp as he had. I would learn how to keep it that sharp. He would teach me.

He said it had been a good old knife. He said he hoped the steel in the new one would be as good, but he doubted it. He looked at it and sighed, and I was ready to reach out from the broad seat in the stern so he could put the knife in my hand.

He flipped it over the side into the muddy river and picked up the oars and rowed the rest of the way back to the cottage dock.

He had no way of knowing. He was not an unkind man. I can still see that knife glint in the summer air and hear the little plop it made as it fell into the Pymatuning River.

I dreamed of it. I dreamed that a big hole had opened up and the river had disappeared, leaving black mud where I walked and walked, looking for the knife. . . . The knife is still there, forever turning and twinkling in the light of a lost July, falling, falling toward the greenbrown river.

In 1925, Eugene's employer, the Standard Tank Car Company, fell on hard times. The majority of stock was sold, and Eugene was elected a director and officer of the new company, but a year later, he was asked to come back to Savage Arms, where he had worked before. His present company was about to be taken over, and he could be without a job. The family moved once more, to Utica, New York.

As he packed for the move, Jack MacDonald began going though his various collections. There were ship models, balsa-wood gliders, crystal sets, bits of old clocks and watches, and all the stamp-collecting paraphernalia that was part of his current hobby. He came upon his butterfly collection. "The paper insects had curled their wings and faded to grays and pastels," he remembered later. "They had faded just as my trays of moths had faded. The butterflies were still vivid. . . . The pins had rusted. The wing scales had flaked off them." Jack threw the butterflies away. He was a stamp collector now. The family finished packing, climbed in the car, and drove out of town.

Utica was typical of upstate New York towns. If Ronald Reagan's nostalgia politics of the 1980s had any basis in reality, it was probably in Syracuse, or Rochester, or Utica. These were towns where almost everyone—certainly everyone of consequence—was white, Protestant, and Republican. Anything at all exotic was kept at bay—Negroes were in Harlem or Alabama, Italians were in Philadelphia, the Irish were in Boston, Democrats were in Chicago. This was the America of Norman Rockwell, a nation where young men who followed Horatio Alger would feel at home. It was the America that Hollywood used when it began its fabrication of the land Frank Capra would celebrate in his sentimental movies.

Jack attended John F. Hughes Public School. He was pressured by his parents into going to Sunday school and got medals for attendance. He was indifferent about summer camp. "I didn't especially like it or dislike it. It made me feel impatient, as though there were other things I would rather be doing, but I couldn't put a name to them," he remembered later. He fought with his sister, Doris, and was punished for tying her to the living-room drapes. "[We] could always trust [our] mother's understanding, but somehow Father just didn't seem to see things [our] way," Doris MacDonald wrote of her father's sternness.

When he was twelve, Jack developed severe headaches accompanied by a high fever. His tongue turned white and there were red splotches on it. He developed a body rash. It was scarlet fever, and in this case it was accompanied by mastoiditis, an inflammation of bones in the head. Today, scarlet fever would be treated with penicillin. But this was 1928, nine years before that antibiotic was discovered and another six or seven before it was used. Jack was put to bed. He stayed there for a year. Today, medical experts believe it was mastoiditis that kept him in bed for so long. Scarlet fever, even in those pre-antibiotic days, seldom lasted more than a few weeks. It was the complications—in this case, mastoiditis—that caused the long recovery.

During the year of convalescence, Jack MacDonald read. He read everything—Flaubert, Hemingway, Faulkner, Galsworthy, Upton Sinclair, B. Traven, Dorothy Sayers, Edgar Rice Burroughs. He read the classics. He read the pulps. And when he was not reading, his mother, Margie, read to him. That year was an immersion into the world of letters that would change his life—a baptism of literature. It was also a year of solitary confinement. "I entertained myself by exercise of imagination," he wrote later. After his recovery, he devoured the books in the Utica library. "I read my way through library shelves, one book after another, going at the rate of a couple a day for years, making myself astigmatic and myopic." He also became more of a loner. "He is a prolific reader and a deep thinker," Eugene wrote in a letter about his son.

Eugene MacDonald had become a gloomy man who lived a life of never-changing routine. He wore only conservative blue suits and for fifteen years drove a green Packard. He left the office at Savage Arms every day at five in the afternoon and demanded that dinner be ready a half hour later. He always got his way.

Eugene was afflicted with long bouts of depression that often lasted for weeks. During those times, no conversation was permitted at the table. There would only be the sound of the clinking and scraping of knives and forks. Then Eugene would get up and go to his study. He spent most of his time away from the office smoking his pipe in solitude, listening to the political commentary of Lowell Thomas on the radio and reading the dispatches from Europe by Vincent Sheehan of the *Chicago Daily News.* When he spoke to his children, it was usually in self-help clichés: "A stitch in time saves nine," or "You get out of a thing just what you put into it."

The only respite from this gloomy life was Christmas. "When we were little," Doris wrote in a paper for an English class at Radcliffe, "he dressed as Santa Claus and created great excitement, especially the time when, pretending to be climbing out of the chimney, he touched the draft and got covered with soot. The fact that his children have grown up doesn't lessen his Christmas paradise at all. He does his shopping after office hours, carefully hides all the packages in a back room and spends hours wrapping them. Attached to each gift is a poem, and the jokes of the entire year appear in that poetry. The family sits around the dining room table on Christmas Eve. Each one is requested to read his poem aloud and then celebration is always a howling success—not to mention that father's voice usually leads the chorus."

Doris wrote that her father "appears gruff . . . a typical hard-hearted businessman." She believed a careful appraisal of Eugene would show a twinkle in his eye. Maybe she saw it, but his son never did. Years later, thinking about his father, John D. MacDonald would curse the similarity between the two of them. "He appears most often when I catch a glimpse of myself in the bathroom mirror at such an angle that the look of my mouth and jaw reminds me of him," he wrote in a 1967 journal. "And it always makes me despise myself instantaneously, then tell myself what else can you expect from genetics, for God's sake, and was he so bad of a man? What kind of a man was he? I am afraid I shall never be able to determine that, but I will be able to accept the fact that I cannot appraise him truly. I cannot root him out of me in certain physical ways, nor in certain habits of mind and emotion, I expect. It seems wasteful to have to keep trying, or wanting to try."

After completing the eighth grade, Jack MacDonald entered Utica Free Academy. Usually, he was a good student—he had trouble with Latin because, according to his sister, "he read Galsworthy instead of Virgil"—and took mostly college preparatory work. In his final year he made a B in Spanish, a C in Latin, a B in English, and an A in Geometry. He had an 81 average. He also excelled at touch typing; he was one of only two boys in the class. He wanted to be a writer, but he thought he never would. His idea of who could be a writer and who couldn't smacks of the predestination of Calvinism. "I always had the secret wish that I had been born a writer," he said years later. "But it was on the order of wishing I had been born a seal, or an otter. I thought writers were a separate race, so marked at birth and totally aware of their gift from the beginning. I thought they were marked in some way. I worshipped writers but knew I could never be one."

Jack MacDonald graduated from high school in June 1932, one

month before his sixteenth birthday. Eugene decided he was too young to go to college. He gave his son a choice—a summer in Europe or a year at preparatory school. Jack chose to travel. In June he left for the continent with Harold Howell, a friend who was a few years older. They traveled through England, Holland, Switzerland, Germany, Italy, France, Belgium, and Austria. This was in 1932, as the Nazi Party was on the verge of taking over the government. When Eugene asked his son what he remembered most about Europe, the boy told his father, "The sound of marching feet from the cradle to the grave." He did not mention his audience with the Pope. Jack and Harold met two girls when they were in Rome who were scheduled to meet Pope Pius XII, but they couldn't go unless they were escorted by a male. The two boys agreed and went to the Vatican.

Jack kept a notebook during his travels. It's filled with drawings of Dutch windmills, the canals of Venice, and what appear to be either carnival masks or sketches of masked superheroes. Years later Mac-Donald would remember his world travels with pleasure, but as a teenager, he wasn't impressed, judging from this entry in his notebook:

Have you ever been abroad traveling—It's hellish.
Have you ever been in filthy railroads—It's hellish.
Have you ever been with Mr. Bieler—He walks like a duck,
talks like a duck and he looks like a duck.
Have you ever gone abroad traveling—the hell with it.
Have you ever been in trains and buses—the hell with it.
Have you ever been in Germany, England, France
gypping the way that they do.
Then to hell with the Germans and to Hell with the Belgians
And to hell with the whole damn crowd.

After his summer in Europe, Jack returned for a postgraduate year at Utica Free Academy before going to college. Although he believed writers were born, and he wasn't one of them, he still tried. During that year he wrote three essays for high school publications, and this poem, which was published in *The Academic Observer* in 1933:

DESTINY

His is a bookshelf musty with age,
And the deeds of men gone by;
Not the roar of motors, screams of wires
Nor the tales of men that fly.
He never skims the murmuring tide
On a cruiser bleak and gray,

For his small life is centered on
Some books, which all repay
His quiet road upon this sphere;
For from these tattered volumes here
He gathers all he's missed,
All that's passed from year to year.

The din of battle, clash of wind
And waves upon the shores
All come to him in glad array,
As o'er his books he pores.
We wonder now, as we look on him,
If his end defeats his means;
For during all those years gone by
He could have fulfilled his dreams.

Jack MacDonald might have been writing about himself—a boy immersed in books who believed his dreams would never become a reality. "I felt self-conscious about the writing I did in school," MacDonald said later. "As if I were faking it, pretending to be something far above my station." During his five years at Utica Free Academy he was on the debate team, the staff of *The Academician,* and a member of the science club, the Spanish club, the classics club, and the thrift council. "*This is that popular fellow called Jack / Who finds no task too hard to attack*" was the verse that appeared alongside his postgraduate picture. The picture shows a solemn young man with full lips and a shock of dark hair. Jack's eyes seem a little quizzical, but that might be because he wasn't wearing his glasses. He had grown into a gangly young man—he was six foot two—but far from athletic. Books, not sports, were his passion.

Eugene decided Jack should become a lawyer. Jack disagreed. They argued. "Once his mind is made up, he will stick to his point regardless," Eugene wrote about his son a few years later. "I can see myself in him in so many different ways. Perhaps it is due to the fact that I was born a Connecticut Yankee, with a Scotch background which produces stubbornness." This time, Jack won. No law school. But Eugene had other plans. If not law, then business. "I listened to my father's urging to go to the Wharton School. . . . As long as I couldn't be a writer, the second choices all seemed of equal merit," he wrote. In the summer before he started college, Jack worked as a manual laborer at the Stevens Arms Corporation plant at Chicopee Falls, Massachusetts. Eugene got him the job "so that he could appreciate the hard work required to earn his daily bread."

In the fall of 1933, Jack MacDonald traveled to Philadelphia to begin his studies at the Wharton School of Finance of the University of Pennsylvania. He studied business, just as his father wanted him to, and he lasted for a year and a half. In January 1935, in a sophomore English class, he experimented with stream-of-consciousness writing:

Damn the snow . . . this collar will never live through another winter like the last . . . especially if it decomposes as rapidly as it did then . . . people look as if the old Christmas humbug as got them again . . . I would like a new coat for Christmas, dear Santa Claus . . . you look as if you could use a coat yourself, Santa Claus, to keep the snow from drifting down your wrinkled neck while you shake a bell over that brass pot . . . brass pot full of nickels . . . a nickel will buy a cup of coffee or two doughnuts or an overcoat or a Rolls

Royce . . . please give me a nickel, Santa Claus . . . I bet he would look like that hulk yesterday when I asked him for a job . . . keeping this limp collar up to my ears is a harder job than he could give me. . . . at least it won't get colder tonight than it is now . . . no warehouse tonight . . . I'd wake up a corpse. . . . Excelsior! . . . the shades of night are practically collapsing . . . why did I let that overfed, overdressed bum shoulder his way by me . . . I am a worm . . . maybe that's why they won't give me a job . . . well, well, the street lights . . . I hope they warm it up a bit . . . I feel frozen in the stomach. . . . do you freeze in the stomach first . . . I think your feet do first. . . . that is, if you're not walking . . . I have been walking since the dawn of existence, or at least, let me see, ten hours. . . . right back at Forty Third Street . . . ten blocks from where I started . . . ten blocks in ten hours . . . ten blocks in ten hours . . . ten cups of coffee and two million dollars I haven't got . . . ten million streets and ten million snow flakes that are mine alone . . . no nickel, no job, no horse, no wife, no mustache . . . Ah! is it possible I am seeing a man as cold as I am . . . no, alas, no . . . he has gloves . . . methinks he is a blasted aristocrat . . . I am an atom of the proletariat mass . . . should I envy these people . . . should I want to take their food and homes and women . . . I don't . . . they just got the breaks, or they would be as much of a subject for the pound as I am . . . pound . . . pound of feet . . . pound of coffee . . . pound of sterling . . . pound of fat to keep me warm . . . warm is a fine word . . . it sounds thick and comfortable . . . can it be association or desire . . . that snow is lovely under the street lights . . . each is a star for an ardent lad to find on his lady's coat collar . . . each is a moist and melting star on my collar . . . Dear Santa Claus, bring me a new collar, you old dope.

His professor said it was "a very good piece of work, especially the way it is put together." He got an A. It wasn't enough. In the spring of 1935, his sophomore year, Jack MacDonald dropped out. He had the feeling of "not knowing where the hell you are or where you're going or why."

Once he left school, Jack caught a train and traveled the 116 miles to New York City. It was as if he were setting out on his own to experience the Horatio Alger life his father had lived. He abandoned the life of privilege—for that's what college was in those days—and took menial odd jobs. His father had been a lamplighter and a newsboy. Jack found work dusting books in a bookshop, waiting tables, busing dirty dishes, selling magazine and book subscriptions for the P. F. Collier Company.

It was terrible. Of course, 1935, in the midst of the Depression, was hardly a good year to find a job. After three months on the lam, Jack was back in school, this time at Syracuse University. He entered summer school and took enough courses to be accepted in the fall with two years of credits. Most of his courses were in the business school, and most of his grades were C's. Apparently Eugene was infuriated at his son for leaving school and stopped all financial support. Jack worked at odd jobs to stay in school. He was a janitor at a bookstore, a chauffeur for an elderly couple who liked to ride around town in their black Packard, a salesman at a fruit stand on the truck route leading into town, an all-night telephone operator at a doctors' building.

He stayed in school. But he was doing a different kind of writing now. It was all business:

> Dear Mr. Jackson:
> In this business they call me a tough credit man. The people who are out to get something for nothing from this store usually get a letter which curls their hair. Then, of course, there are the people who cheerfully let a bill slide for quite a while. These people usually pay up after a few reminders and a nice letter or so.
> Mr. Jackson, allow me to congratulate you. I know that you are not trying to get something for nothing. Yet I haven't gotten any word from you about a little matter of

seventeen twenty-five, after sending you six letters. Frankly, I don't know what to do. If I send a tough letter, we lose your trade, if I send a nice letter, nothing happens.

I decided to lay the case before you. I am asking you to be so kind as to write me, and tell me what kind of letter I should send you. Remember now, I don't wish to offend you, and yet I want to collect that bill, because that is why they are hiring me here. You are really the only person who can help me out of this dilemma.

Yours truly,
John D. MacDonald

He got an A on that one, too. His business professor said it was "splendid." Jack persisted. By the spring of 1937, he was less than a year from graduation.

Every morning, before classes, Jack MacDonald worked as a waiter at Fisher's Restaurant. One morning in March a tall, willowy blonde walked into Fisher's and sat down. Jack waited on her. Her name was Dordo. After he met her his life and his name would never be the same again.

CHAPTER 3

D ordo was Dorothy Mary Prentiss. She was born on February 18, 1911, in Poland, New York. Her parents were S. Roy Prentiss and Rita (pronounced Right-a) Van Woert Prentiss. Roy and Rita had met at Cazenovia Seminary on the outskirts of Syracuse, where both were members of the 1904 class. After graduation, Roy Prentiss went to work for Weed and Willoughby Co., a department store in Gloversville, New York. Roy Prentiss proposed to Rita by telegram on August 8, 1908. She wired back a one-word answer from her home in Poland to the store in Gloversville—"Yes." She sent her telegram collect.

Within the next few years, Roy Prentiss established his own department stores in Poland and Weedsport. Dorothy was the second Prentiss child—she had an older brother, Samuel Gilbert Prentiss. By her eighth birthday, Dorothy—or Dordo, as her family and friends called her—was already interested in the arts. In a letter to "Santy Claus," written in 1919, Dordo was asking for "some good paints" and "Huckleberry Finn and other books."

In the 1920s, Roy Prentiss sold his stores and moved his family west to California, where he was involved in aviation and oil specu-lation. He made money for a while, but when he died in 1926 the family was left without enough to live on. Rita and her two children returned to New York. Dordo, who was eighteen, enrolled in the College of Fine Arts at Syracuse University. In February 1931, five months before she graduated, she applied for a job teaching art at Cazenovia Seminary. There was only one problem. The art teacher at Cazenovia also had to teach French, and Dordo didn't know any. She suggested to Charles E. Hamilton, the president of the school, that she take a French course during her last semester at Syracuse and spend the summer studying the language at McGill University in Montreal. "It seems to us that your plan for taking the one course now and the summer courses would be sufficient to meet our needs," Hamilton wrote in a letter to Dordo. "I have placed your name in nomination. . . . In a few days, I shall hope to be able to notify you of your election."

She got the job. But Dordo had more on her mind than employment. She was falling in love.

Willard Golding Teed of White Plains, New York, the son of Leonard E. Teed, the Westchester County deputy treasurer, and Dordo were an item at Syracuse. Dordo called him Bill. He was a member of Delta Kappa Epsilon, she was a Tri-Delt.

In September 1931, Dordo started her job at Cazenovia. In April, she was rushed to the Hospital of the Good Shepherd in Syracuse for an appendectomy. It was performed by Dr. Howard G. Case, the president of the hospital's board of trustees. While she was still in the hospital, Dorothy got a letter from the president of Cazenovia. "My dear Miss Prentiss," he wrote. "It may aid your convalescence for me to tell you . . . that you have been reelected for the next scholastic year and . . . your salary will be raised $100, although in general all teachers have their salaries cut." But something else was happening in her life that was far more important than either an appendectomy or a raise.

In June 1932, Dorothy Mary Prentiss married Willard Golding Teed, at the home of her aunt and uncle, Mr. and Mrs. E. H. Prentiss of Geer Avenue in Utica. The ceremony was performed by Dean William H. Powers of Syracuse University. Her uncle gave Dorothy away. Her brother, Sam, was Willard's best man. There were five bridesmaids and a flower girl. Mrs. Ralph Read played the piano, Mrs. Leon Ellis sang. The bride wore white satin. She carried white roses.

It was in all the papers.

"Following a honeymoon at Lake Pesico, Mr. and Mrs. Teed will make their home at Utica," the wedding notice said. Only they didn't.

The marriage dissolved. In the fall, Dordo was back at Cazenovia Seminary, still teaching art and French. Willard was living with his parents in their modest stone-and-shingle house at 46 Park Avenue in White Plains. On May 10, Dordo got a letter at Cazenovia addressed to Mrs. Willard Teed. Inside the envelope was a

----

front-page clipping from the *New York Herald Tribune* of the day before:

Retired Deputy
in Westchester
$250,000 Short

Teed, Pensioned April 29
for 35 Years "Faithful
Service," Admits Tangle

WHITE PLAINS, N.Y., May 8—A shortage, believed to be about $250,000, has been discovered, it was learned today, in the accounts of Leonard E. Teed, who retired as Deputy County Treasurer April 29 after almost thirty-five years service, receiving, besides his $2,400 pension, his salary up to June 15 in recognition of "Faithful public service."

There was a note scrawled on the top of the paper:

"God only knows what will happen but it looks as tho it is prison for him unless he slips out. I was never so disgusted in my life. I will fix it up with you later." The note was not signed. A few years later, Dordo referred to Willard Teed as "just negative. . . . and you wonder how [he] gets in your story anyway. . . . If [people] were negative, they were never part of you and they never aroused any great emotion—except maybe relief from something." In 1951, John D.

MacDonald would write a book about an upstate New York attorney named Teed. At the end of the novel, *Judge Me Not*, Teed says, "In that other life, we were two different people, neither of them as sound as you and I. The old life didn't happen to us." He might have been writing about Dorothy and her Teed.

Dordo and Jack MacDonald began dating soon after they met at Fisher's Restaurant in March 1937. She liked him, but was dissatisfied with his name. Jack seemed too childish for a man so serious and determined. Also, her mother's dog was named Jack. So she began calling her new boyfriend John. He would never be Jack again—John was his name from then on. Dordo owned a cowardly cocker spaniel whose registered name was Shadowfall Chloe and who "was utterly convinced of imminent disaster from almost any direction," MacDonald wrote later. "On leash, when the horrors got too much for her, she would scrunch onto her belly and have to be either picked up and carried or dragged along with an ugly grating of toenails. If I reached slowly to pat her during our early acquaintanceship, she would run, screaming, and hide in the most remote corner she could find. Her eyes rolled white amid that black hair and she would pant with terror. Asleep she whined constantly, legs twitching as she fled the demons."

As Dordo and John spent more time together, Chloe began to accept him. In late summer, John proposed to Dordo in a poem:

I come to you with no gestures . . .
I come to you with abasement and pride . . .
I come to you with a million bright mornings, and heap them shining
    in your hands.
I give to you my margin of safety, my heart valve that has kept me
    from hurt, my permanent soul.
You are like the meadow-land beyond the small wood—
I will set a table of food in your season and call you sweet names,
    saying,
"I have rest for you: I will quiet the cymbals in you, the
    torment in you. I will drain you of your woe."
I ask of you the hope of years.

I ask of you your hands, and the golden talisman of your beauty.
I ask of you your warm life through years.
I bring many things and I ask many things.
It is of you my spirit swells, and the billion atoms of my being burst
*   with soul-lust for your warm glowing.*
I bring you the two-perused, my pledged margin.
Is it not enough for a million days?
The woods-smell and the ripe colors are ours now.

Is it not enough for all the dawns?
I am proud, and I feel that you are of the very fibre of my soul.
Yet I fear . . .
And I await you.

On August 15, John and Dordo got in her new black Ford Tudor and drove the 107 miles to Troy, Pennsylvania (pop. 1200), where they were married. They kept the marriage a secret. In the 1930s, a student at Syracuse University had to have parental permission to marry. Apparently, John felt he could not get permission from his father. Dordo, of course, who was five years older and no longer a student, didn't need permission. There is also the possibility that she was still embarrassed about her big wedding and the failure of her marriage to Willard Teed.

They lived together in Dordo's apartment. On August 28, John wrote his clandestine bride:

Finding that tomorrow is our anniversary, in fact two complete weeks since we have been married, I sort of figured that a lady at least ought to have a sort of letter from her husband, even if she does get it when yesterday was her anniversary. You see, I am not rolling in vile little green dollars at the present moment, and the sweat of my brow transferred to keys and paper is the only present I could possibly give you, and egotistically consider it worthy of you, my darling.

I thought you might like to know that I find myself completely in favor of marriage advantages, and as an institution I find myself viewing with favor the probability and possibility that I will spend all my days in it. You might like to know also that I love you, and in spending every day and every night with you, that love keeps agrowin', so that nothing in this world or life will ever do it harm.

We are two similar individuals. We spin around in a life full of comparative colour and retain our inviolacy in spite of people pushing buttons all around us, then when we first settle into what, in our fine youth, we would have considered a stodgy situation, it is strikingly imbued with all the emotional beauty that was lacking before. I believe that I have passed the point of question concerning existence, and should for some strange reason I die tomorrow, I would depart with the fervid conviction that life is worth living, a conviction that I had in no appreciable extent before. We are making a life for each other and cloaking it in a myriad of beautiful things. I am foolish enough to want you to keep this letter around, for only one reason. To amend my new-found incoherence when I want to tell you what I feel about all of this. Maybe what I am trying to say with all this mass of words is this: You have made me very happy, happier than I have ever been before, and I know this is going to last for life.

John graduated from Syracuse in January 1938—six months before he would have finished the Wharton School of Finance if he had stayed there. Although he was a C student, he was accepted in the M.B.A. program at Harvard. His classes began immediately. John was in an intensive short-course program that would allow him to graduate after a year and a half rather than the customary two years.

On July 3, John and Dorothy were officially married at the Prentiss home in Poland, New York. Apparently there was a rift between John and his grandfather, Hugh MacDonald, at the wedding. Dordo's mother, Rita, writes in a letter that she hopes John's grandfather "won't have to feel that he was 'cut' at the wedding. There is enough hatred and meanness in the world without continuing any or starting any more. I hope he does send John a nice present as long as he is able. It will do him good and John too. Maybe he is sorry now for some of the things he's done and if so, there's no use in rubbing it in." Rita also made oblique references to Dordo's earlier marriage. "I had an idea that you would find it different now than it has been," she wrote. "I am glad it is this way [rather] than a sorry one. I shall enjoy writing Mrs. J. D. MacDonald, too. Mother said this afternoon, 'It seems queer there isn't any Dorothy Prentiss anymore.' Well, I'm glad in many ways that there isn't. I'm glad she is Mrs. MacDonald."

John and Dordo and their dog, Chloe, moved to Cambridge, Massachusetts, living in a fourth-floor walk-up apartment in what had once been a Harvard dormitory. There was a touch of notoriety associated with the building—while it was still a dorm, Lucius Beebe, the journalist who reported on café society in Boston and New York, along with some of his friends, dropped a piano down the stairwell to hear what the crash would sound like. John spent all his time either in class or studying. The accelerated pace of his graduate school program didn't leave enough time for him to hold a job. Dordo was the breadwinner. She worked a sales route for the Kelling Nut Company, calling on urban and suburban drugstores.

Then Dordo found out she was pregnant. Her obstetrician was worried about her health and urged the MacDonalds to move from the fourth-floor apartment. But they couldn't. "We were trying to either break our lease or get permission to sublet from the brothers who then owned the building," MacDonald wrote. "In presenting the problem to one of the brothers at his office I had been somewhat disheartened to have him say to me, 'Listen, you, if you're both dead we collect from your estate. You got a lease.' "

So they stayed. And Dordo continued making her rounds for the Kelling Nut Company. Then, on March 21, she collapsed with convulsions and was rushed to Cambridge Hospital, where she was diagnosed with eclampsia, a kidney disease that affects some pregnant women. It causes severe swelling throughout the body, but it is worse when the nerves are swollen. That's what happened to Dordo. In

1939, immediate treatment was to put the patient in a dark, quiet room, which would relieve the convulsions, though any noise could set them off again. Then, with any luck, the child would be born. But the MacDonald baby was not due for another six weeks.

John got on the phone and called his parents and then Rita. He told them Dorothy had been hospitalized and it looked as if she would lose the baby. Margie and Rita took the next train to Boston. By the time they arrived on March 23, a premature baby weighing three pounds two ounces had been born and was being kept alive in an incubator. But now it looked like Dordo might die. She was listed in serious condition. She survived, but she and the baby were in the hospital for three weeks. At least a week passed before she was allowed to see her baby, John Prentiss MacDonald. "I feel so badly that you had to wait so long to see your own baby," Margie wrote on April 17, a few days after Dordo and the baby came home. "We are so anxious for everything to go along now in a satisfactory way as you both have been through enough for a while."

Dordo's hospital bills were $150 a week, and the doctor had to be paid as well. There was no money coming in, and Eugene was no help. He offered only to cosign a bank loan. They were helped out by Tad and Dedi Reid, some friends in Cambridge. Dedi was a secretary for the physician who attended Dorothy and her son. The Reids paid the MacDonald doctor bill and John gave them an IOU. To pay it off, of course, he'd have to find a job.

John graduated from the Harvard Business School in June 1939, and a month later he, Dordo, and the baby—who was variously called Johnny, Pen, Penny, and occasionally the Pencil—moved to Fayetteville, New York. He became a salesman for the Guardian Insurance Company. Eugene MacDonald told his son he thought selling insurance was a poor way to use a college education. John told his father he had taken the job to learn how to meet people and how to sell himself. He was a flop. He got fired. Then the family moved to Messena, New York, where John worked as a repo man for the Commercial Investment Trust Company. He got fired again in May 1940. The official reason was "curtailment of expense." The truth was simpler—he was a loudmouth who wouldn't follow orders.

The MacDonalds' living standards declined. "Such a remarkable life as you're leading," their friends, the Reids, wrote them in February. But it was apparent that all was not well. The MacDonalds didn't even have electricity. "I don't envy you the various kerosene contraptions you're surrounded with, and the plan of the apartment doesn't sound exactly perfect," they wrote. "But we are glad John likes the job. . . ." The letter also nudged the MacDonalds to pay off their debt. "We received your very impressive IOU. To avoid future complications, I might mention that altho you said there might be, there was no check in the last letter. Not that we care, but the accounts ought to start out with the same understanding at both ends of the correspondence."

There was still no help from John's father. "During the last year he has supported himself, his wife and baby not at the scale of living to which he has been accustomed, but none the less they have not suffered for something to eat or a place to sleep. In my contacts with him I have tried to make him independent, and I think he is succeeding," Eugene wrote.

Eugene MacDonald was a self-made man who didn't remember the goals he set for himself, but only the pain of being poor. It wasn't the value of work that seems to have made an impression on him, but the suffering. And so, like veterans who gleefully watch young recruits at basic training or fraternity members who love hazing pledges, he wanted to see his son suffer. He favored some sort of handed-down martyrdom. And so he refused to help John, believing that suffering and starvation would make him a better person.

So a year after he finished graduate school, John was the sole support of his wife and son, and he was living in a dump over a hardware store with kerosene heat. And he didn't have a job anymore.

There was one last chance.

"Because I had taken Army procurement courses at Harvard Business School, I was approached about accepting a commission as a First Lieutenant in the Ordnance Department. I accepted and reported to a Major Roy Bowlin at the Rochester Ordnance District," MacDonald wrote in an unpublished family history.

The Army. Eugene probably said it would make a man out of him.

CHAPTER 4

In June 1940, eighteen months before Pearl Harbor, John D. Mac-Donald enlisted in the Army. His son was fifteen months old, and, after running through three jobs like Sherman through Georgia, John needed some stability and security. So he became First Lieutenant John Dann MacDonald, 0-397110. Even with the fall of Poland to the Nazis the year before, the fall of Holland and Belgium in May, and the invasion and conquest of France in the month he enlisted, America was ostensibly at peace. President Franklin Roosevelt had declared the country "neutral" in 1939. So it was in this army of neutrality that John began his active duty at the Rochester Ordnance District in Rochester, New York, on August 26.

It was hardly a glamorous assignment. There were thirteen ordnance districts in the United States, and the one in Rochester was responsible for all of the state except the New York City metropolitan area. Its offices, located downtown in the Sibley Lindsay and Curr Building, were responsible for all purchasing, packaging, inspection, and storage of guns, tanks, and ammunition in the area. At first, John worked as a weapons inspector and then as the officer in charge of a statistics and reports section. He was a bureaucrat in a khaki suit who prepared reports, designed file systems, installed IBM accounting systems, and refurbished organizational charts. His job seemed so unmilitary.

"I remember . . . sitting in the little library of our rented house . . . with the Sunday afternoon symphony on the radio, reading, and having the program interrupted to tell us the Japanese had bombed Pearl Harbor. That was such an abrupt shock that it took me about five minutes to realize I was already *in* the Army, and had been for well over a year."

In February 1942, two months after the United States declared war on Germany, Italy, and Japan, John was promoted to captain. In July 1942, he was made executive officer of the Industrial Division. In October he was selected as district liaison officer for the Industry Integrating Committee. It was dull. John asked to be assigned to field duty. He was turned down. In November he was made an assistant to the officer in charge of the Schenectady suboffice. Dull, dull, dull. The MacDonalds moved first to Rochester and then to the Stonehenge Apartments in Albany, about an hour's drive from his office in the American Locomotive Company plant, where tanks were manufactured. They were in Albany for only seven months. On May 10, 1943, Captain John D. MacDonald was ordered overseas to be an ordnance officer in the India-China-Burma Theater.

In the fall, John sailed from Long Beach, California, on the USS *Hermitage* to Bombay. It was an Italian ship, originally the SS *Comte de Biancamno,* that had been appropriated by the United States as it tried to go through the Panama Canal. The trip was uneventful, but John remembered the voyage for "the best breakfasts I ever had."

> There were four of us and we would get up before dawn . . . and go roam the lower weather decks looking for the flying fish which had come aboard during the night. The genius in the group had fashioned a nice little stove out of tin cans. It burned that canned heat jelly they stocked in the life boats. We had a secluded spot aft on B deck, and by dawn's early light we were frying up flying fish filets, with filched butter and salt. Splendid indeed.

In Bombay, John met Roy Bowlin, an old friend from New York, now a colonel, who was his commanding officer. Bowlin and John flew to New Delhi, where he would be stationed. After outfitting himself in bush jacket and khaki shorts, John settled into his daily routine. His bearer, Endar, would come to his hotel room and wake him up every morning at seven-thirty and leave a breakfast of tea, bread, and fruit. He would report to work at eight-thirty. At twelve-thirty he left work and was driven back to the hotel, where his private waiter, Ali, served a heavy lunch. After eating, he went to his room for a nap and then returned to work at two. He left work at five, played a game of volleyball, showered, and had dinner at nine. On the surface, it sounds like a good life, right out of British wartime

movies—stiff upper lip, gin and tonic, and all that. But once the new-
ness wore off, John hated it. In letters home he wrote about an India
that had lost its charm:

> . . . I was quartered in a pretty good hotel. We had
> received our notice that we were going to have to move, and
> all the Indian bearers who were working for American offi-
> cers in the hotel also knew it. They are a sly lot, and not to be
> trusted. About the third night before we were to move they
> cleaned out about three rooms. I was sleeping without the
> door to the room locked, but my trousers were over a chair
> beside my bed. . . . Some Indian sneaked in during the night
> and removed my billfold and my cigarette case. . . . The cli-
> mate here is absolutely dreadful. No white people used to
> live here during peace time . . . but we are stuck on the plains
> of India and have been getting prickly heat and all sorts of
> discomfort from a temperature that for weeks on end stayed
> right between 110 and 120—with a pretty good degree of
> humidity. . . . I suppose that I shouldn't complain too much
> about this place though. At least it is a city, with restaurants
> and movies and such. I have [seen] just enough jungle coun-
> try to know how lucky I am. I am billeted in an apartment
> with three other officers, and we have our own cook, bearers,
> sweeper, etc. The worst part of this place is the monotony.
> There is only so much to do outside of duty, and when you
> have been to all the places once, there isn't much point in
> further visits.

Nor was John impressed by General Joseph "Vinegar Joe" Stilwell,
who headed the India-China-Burma Theater. He hated the man.

> Of all the mysteries surrounding the Orient, one of the
> most unfathomable is an imported product—"Uncle Joe."
> He isn't a hell of a lot to look at. He is a lean, well-kept

little man who looks in his sixties. His face is worn, with weather wrinkles around the eyes. He combines an outdoor look with the look of an ascetic. There is something of the falcon about him, the bird of prey. So here is his three parts, the scholar, the guide, and the hunting hawk.

One of the qualities which most of us carry around, usually a product of conscience, is mercy. Stilwell is startlingly and completely devoid of any such civilized quality. He is hard and ruthless, with the selfish intensity of purpose usually reserved for early Christian martyrs and political demagogues.

If this quality of ruthlessness were combined with sterling administrative ability, then Stilwell would merit the stars he has received. Unfortunately, however, his administration is befuddled. His various headquarters are wound around with endless coils of red tape. He holds the shears and doesn't know how to use them. He is one very good platoon leader, but a theater seems to be beyond him. However, rather than worry about it, he goes ahead at his own pace, loping through the jungle, completely ignoring the morass of official confusion reigning in the rearward areas. When he wants something he shouts, and he gets it, and more confusion exists. Half of the time of his subordinates is spent trying to guess and catch up with his latest unspoken policies. His word is law but his intermediate decisions hop around the wide field of military exigency like a flock of demented kangaroos. His ultimate aim, to get back into Burma, is clear and definite. For that aim he would sacrifice everything else in this world. It is left for his subordinates to wonder—when we get back into Burma, where the hell are we? North Burma is perhaps the least desirable place in the world. It's too bad Stilwell wasn't chased out of Shanghai or Singapore. . . .

His written and spoken word has that quality of ruthlessness, disguised by a fine dry humor, oftentimes so oblique that it leaves a sour taste in the mouth, like the bitter squash of the Chinese. . . . I read in the papers that someone has asked for a Congressional Investigation of the use this theater made of the long range penetration unit called Galahad, or Merrill's Marauders. They had better hurry and have the investigation because there aren't so many of those boys left. They were thrown in again and again and again long after any sane field commander would have removed them for a rest. They were decimated by the Japanese and by disease. They performed unbelievable feats of marching and fighting long after they were thoroughly "browned off" by a commander that apparently had no regard whatsoever for their welfare. . . . The true story of the blood, sweat, tears, madness, dysentery and cruelty of [these troops] will never be written. They were abandoned in the face of the enemy and left to fight over their destiny. There are damn few of them left.

To escape the war, John occasionally took trips to the countryside. He was repulsed. The Indians did not live up to his American standards of cleanliness. He was particularly disgusted by the use of cow dung for fuel.

A woman and a group of little girls, each with a round, shallow wicker basket on her head, go wandering off across the pasture land. The woman maintains a straight dignified course while the little girls dart off in odd directions, grabbing dried feces and placing them in the basket. It is odd to watch a little five or six year old girl go clambering over rough ground, stooping and picking things up and looking on all sides without disturbing the balance of a well-filled basket. They are gay and picnicky about such an excursion, and remind me of nothing more than school children with their teachers out collecting wild flowers. . . . There are religious uses [for cow dung] among the Hindus. Their reasoning is that if the cow is sacred, then any bovine excretion is also sacred. This leads to a practice among certain highly religious Hindu families of keeping a small utensil like a salt shaker at the eating place. This container is filled with dried and powdered excrement which is sprinkled very lightly over certain dishes. I have the word of men who were guests at dinner with such families, that it is only the first dish so treated that is likely to bother you, and then not too much.

John never got over his hatred for India. More than forty years later, in 1985, he wrote in a letter to a friend, "I have resisted all temptation as far as going back to Calcutta or Karachi or Delhi is concerned. To me that was a sorry country full of sorry people."

At home, Dordo coped. She and Johnny/Pen left Albany for Poland, New York, and moved in with her mother, Rita. But the quarters were too close for three generations. Within a few months, Dordo was in Utica in an upstairs apartment at 9 Beverly Place. Life, she wrote to him, went on:

Cold, rainy Sunday, warm house and Beethoven's First Symphony. Same ole pattern, but good for relaxing. . . . The wedding month was an expensive one, and I hoped for a respite after that, but $41 to the doctor, car insurance, and car repairs, Pen's tuition and such haven't changed the situation much. . . . Everyone's complaining about the liquor problem here. Scotch must be as rare or more so than it is where you are, but not quite so expensive. They actually refuse to serve it to women in the hotels and clubs now! That's chivalry for you. . . . I've been told that I will be offered a job, teaching part time at the Art Institute here. It all happened quite accidentally, when I took the kids to see an exhibit of marionettes last week, and the secretary found out that I had made them. They have been looking for someone desperately, and were alarmingly enthusiastic about my possibilities. It would be interesting, no doubt.

Dordo wrote every day. John was a lousy correspondent. By April 1944, he suggested that they write to each other only twice a week. "I am one of those selfish people who likes to get mail but hates to write it," he wrote in a letter home.

A year after John started work in India, he was transferred to the Office of Strategic Services, the Army's espionage wing, which later became the Central Intelligence Agency. On October 21, 1944, he was assigned to Colombo in Ceylon (now Sri Lanka) as the commander of the Branch Establishment of Detachment 404. He was promoted to major. He may have been in the spy business, but for John there was no cloak, no dagger. There was only another desk. Occasionally he was assigned to Burma and sometimes to China, where he fell in love with the countryside. His work was mindless. Years later, he recounted the bureaucratic tangles he saw:

A high level decision was made to supply U.S. combat equipment to Generalissimo Chiang Kai-shek sufficient to equip 30 Chinese divisions in order to drive the Japanese from mainland China. Because the Burma Road . . . was not finished at the time, it was decided that the equipment to be given to the Chinese divisions would have to be based upon U.S. Tables of Organization and Equipment prior to vehicular mechanization. . . . The Quartermaster General . . . gave a lieutenant I knew the responsibility of preparing the requisition. . . . My friend went back to [the quartermaster general] and started to raise questions . . . but he was unable to complete the question before the Colonel was roaring truisms about simple orders and following them and not bothering him with pointless questions. So my friend performed his chore in mechanical fashion. The [headquarters] staff commanders signed their portion of the requisition. It was . . . stamped secret on every page and relayed to . . . Washington. Back in Washington, a West Point officer eventually examined the requisitions. . . . A coded eyes-only message came from Washington . . . with the indication that it was top secret. I am quite sure that it has never been declassified. My recall is not perfect, but I believe that it is close enough. REF-ERENCE QUARTERMASTER PORTION OF YOUR REQUISITION. STATISTICAL SECTION COMPLETED PRELIMINARY STUDY OF EQUINE REQUIREMENTS OF 30 CHINESE DIVISIONS. NOT ONLY WILL ALL PRESENT TROOP SHIPS REQUIRE CONVERSION FROM TROOP CARRIERS TO HORSE CARRIERS, BUT WHEN DELIVERY TO CHINA OF ALL ITEMS COMPLETE, BURMA ROAD WILL BE PAVED TO A DEPTH OF 11 FEET 4 INCHES WITH HORSESHIT.

He also saw American jeeps and trucks used as landfill by engineers who were building a bridge across India. Too many jeeps and trucks had arrived, and they sat rusting in the fields. So they were pushed down a ravine and a road built over them. For an ordnance officer just recruited to be an administrator of spies, it seemed like a wasteful war.

When he was with Vinegar Joe Stilwell, the military objective was to get back to Burma by building a highway. The OSS saw things differently. Although MacDonald has never talked about what the unit's goals were, it's now documented that they wanted to regain the territory by starting a Thai underground. Information from this underground operation went from Bangkok to China and then to Ceylon and the OSS. Eventually, radio communication was established between Bangkok and Ceylon, but until it was, John had to take occasional trips to China.

John MacDonald was not feeling well, and Dordo sensed it from his letters. Because he was in espionage, all of his letters home were censored. He couldn't tell anyone where he was, he couldn't say anything about his condition or his work. Years later he would say that if you wrote about anything more than a postnasal drip it would get blacked out of the letters. Still, he managed to convey to Dordo the great depression he felt. And it worried her. In a letter to him, she told John how she felt and made suggestions about how to overcome his problems:

Your unfinished letter . . . just came and I feel so frustrated. I can't call you up [and] a cable is as slow as a letter. Nothing on earth concerns me as much as wanting to help you, and there doesn't seem to be a thing I can do. . . . You must have had sort of a famine of letters, too, of late. I'm sorry I got the impression you didn't want to hear from us, but your letters sounded so snooty for a little while that I just thought you were fed up with the likes of us, and had gone all-out for the British end of Army social life that India seems to offer. In fact I'm afraid one letter from me may sound a little snooty, too, or harsh, when you get it, but it's because I had only a vague indication of what was wrong when it was written, and it hurt my pride to have you ask me not to write, after you had so recently begged for mail. As a matter of fact, I thought perhaps you had filled the gap with personalities that had made us seem a little dim and remote. But it seems to be [yourself] that you've lost.

Naturally, darling, it makes me sad to have anything wrong with you, but sensing it, and not knowing is the awful thing. So let me urge you again to tell me anything and everything you want to or can. Above everything else we're friends, dear, and it seems as if anything can help you now, it's that. To know there's someone who cares terribly about you and your happiness, and who wants to understand, and will if you have enough confidence to get it on paper and out of your system. You may feel assured that if there's anything tangible, I wouldn't make an issue of it. When it will be a matter of years before you can come home, I hope I have enough intelligence (and experience) to know that only a few things last, and that what might be today's troubles and problems will probably be changed or left by the wayside by the time we are together.

You've got to work this out of you somehow. It's just my opinion, but I think the greatest two releases one can find are love and creative work. Under the circumstances, love might bring you more trouble than joy if you try to find an outlet for it there. (There aren't many loves one can live with, and I think we've both already found the satisfying kind.) In fact, so much are love and creativeness akin that it seems seldom possible to completely fulfill oneself in both ways at once. But writing is such a complete outlet, in its way that it might be well to try to overcome the natural lassitude that climate and the malaise have brought, and sit down and beat it out until some of that burden is off your mind, and the tension out of your spirit.

It's like trying consciously to be your own psychiatrist, to work out a way of action that will bring you back to your normal life. Your life isn't normal—but that's too, too common— our generation is just taking a beating they didn't ask for there. But some of us are more sensitive, less integrated, and some need to make a greater effort to maintain their balance. It seems as if to write is the best way you can control your situation; the Army controls so much of your life now. A dilettante sort of adjustment would give you little satisfaction, while to get started on what had been burning in you for years would be a growing way that would make your life richer.

Possibly writing for publication sets up an unnatural constraint between you and your self-expression. If you just wrote it down and sent it home, it might release some of it, and I could save it for you, because it might be useful to you later.

John thought about that letter, and he thought about writing. Years later he would say it was his idea to write short stories home to Dordo. But it was her letter that spurred him into action. He never mentioned that. He always said he chose to write fiction because censorship wouldn't allow him to communicate anything else.

A few months after Dordo's letter, John sat down and wrote in longhand:

Miller tilted his chair back cautiously, with the gentle regard for chair legs that all large men develop. . . .

That was the first sentence of a two-thousand-word story called "Interlude in India," and when it was finished, he sent it home to Dordo. When she got the manuscript, she typed it and sent it off to *Esquire*. That magazine was undergoing an editorial upheaval in 1945. Arnold Gingrich, the magazine's first editor, had left because of disagreements with his publisher, David Smart. In Gingrich's place, Smart hired Frederick Birmingham, who lacked Gingrich's literary skills. Birmingham wrote Dordo and told her the story was too short. If MacDonald ever wrote something longer, Birmingham said, they'd be happy to consider it. When she got the manuscript back, Dordo sent it out again, this time to Whit and Hallie Burnett of *Story* magazine. *Story* was an outgrowth of the little-magazine movement in America that began just before World War I. Burnett, who was editor of the anthologies *This Is My Best* and *The Seas of God*, started the magazine with Martha Foley in 1931 to promote new short story writers. *Story*'s circulation was probably never more than a few thousand, but its reputation and its influence were enormous. Burnett liked "Interlude in India" and agreed to publish it. He sent Dordo a check for $25. So John Dann MacDonald was a professional writer now. But Dordo decided to wait until he got home and surprise him with the news.

Meanwhile, back at the war, John's mental malaise was accompanied by physical ailments. On a trip to China he had contracted dengue fever, a tropical disease that causes severe pains in the joints and muscles. The fever caused rapid weight loss, and the treatment for it, Atabrine, a form of quinine, gave his skin a yellowish cast. In May 1945, he found out he would be going home soon, and he wrote Dordo:

> I get so tired of writing my few letters so full of excuses and apologies. I feel helpless in the grip of circumstances and plead constantly for your continued understanding. You have no idea how proud of you I have been and how much I cherish your stalwart backing up in the face of things which are

explicable, but not to you. However, the time is coming sooner and sooner when we can talk all this out. I feel, just as you have expressed, that our love will be refined and strengthened by this absurd and unbelievable separation. . . . Hold your breath, but when I get home in August I will probably be *out of the G.D. army*. It will mean I will be a hell of a long time in route and security will forbid my talking to you when I leave. I am sending you some money tomorrow . . . and when you don't hear from me for a long time and nobody does, get yourself set for the homecoming. I am mentally, physically, and emotionally exhausted. I am so tired and run-down that my old bones feel like aching lead. I am thin and nervous and in no mood to go into a long line of bull in this letter regarding the significance of the peace. Just love me and trust me and wait for me. . . . Be prepared in August to take off on the basis of a phone call.

On August 6, when the United States dropped the atomic bomb on Japan, John was aboard a troopship with six thousand other men on their way to Okinawa and from there to Los Angeles. He had a chance to fly home but turned it down. He was afraid that he looked so bad he would scare his wife and son. Maybe the thirty days it took him to get home by boat would let him relax and gain some weight.

When his ship dropped anchor at Naha Bay, the war was still going on. On Okinawa there were one million men, preparing for the invasion of Japan. Thirty-five years later, he remembered those days:

Each morning at first light, the kamikazes would come over from the Japanese mainland, very high, beyond detection, and drop straight down over the center of the island, and then come streaking out over the bay trying to dive into one of the naval vessels anchored further out. . . . Several nights later everything started to pop at once, a continuous roar of explosions. I was aboard the ship and a friend and I went out on the open deck. We heard there had been a cease fire. All the ships . . . were firing everything possible straight up. I stood there like an idiot and then heard something go hiss-tink on the deck nearby. We ducked below and watched the fireworks out of a porthole. We heard later from reasonably accurate sources that seventeen men had been killed outright during that celebration. At that time I was glad it [dropping the atomic bomb] had been done, and glad it was over. I was concerned with pragmatics, not moralities. I did not "hate" the Japanese, though he had fired at me in an impersonal effort to kill me. In general they were so tough and stubborn and so willing to die we thought them some sort of demented, beyond reason. We were glad that something had finally attracted their attention, loudly and specifically. Otherwise, it would have been a very long, difficult invasion.

John MacDonald arrived at Fort Dix, New Jersey, on September 8, 1945, and was discharged as a lieutenant colonel. Dorothy met him there and told him about *Story* magazine's buying his manuscript. "I can't describe what it was like when I found out my words had actually sold. I thought it was . . . I felt as if I were a fraud, as if I were masquerading [as a writer], as if I were trying to be something I wasn't," he remembered years later. "Then I thought, 'My goodness, maybe I could actually be one.'"

To celebrate, John bought some civilian clothes and he and Dordo went to New York for a night on the town. They went to the Three Deuces, a jazz joint on Fifty-second Street. Billie Holiday was singing, backed by the drummer Big Syd Catlett's combo. Billie and Big Syd were feuding, and every time she stepped close to the drums he would whack her on the ass. She would give a little jump and hit what sounded to MacDonald like a strange note.

At intermission, John and Dorothy went to the rest rooms, which were located backstage, up a flight of stairs, next to Billie Holiday's dressing room. As John started down the stairs, three enlisted men in uniform started a fight. Billie heard the fuss, stepped out of her dressing room, and grabbed Dordo. "Best you wait right here, dear," she said as she pulled Dordo inside, "until they get through with that thing. Gets rough here. That's why I got these two big dogs." Two boxers waited in the dressing room as her protection.

Outside, John tried to break up the fight. He forgot he wasn't in uniform. He grabbed the shoulders of two of the three men who were fighting, pulled them apart, and said, "Break it up, soldiers, knock it off, give me your—"

Then one of the soldiers knocked him about five steps back up the staircase. He was shocked, and he realized for the first time he wasn't in uniform. He had no gold insignia on his shoulder to protect him. "I got hit alongside the head, so there was no damage to speak of," MacDonald remembered later. "But I never will forget my shock at looking down at my clothes and finding out I was a civilian any damn soldier could clobber at will."

Welcome home, Colonel.

CHAPTER 5

In the summer of 1948, John D. MacDonald was driving south in
a green 1947 Ford convertible on the two-lane blacktop that led out
of upstate New York. His wife, Dorothy, was beside him, his son,
Johnny, was in the backseat, and his typewriter was packed in the
trunk. As they drove, they were all trying to learn Spanish with flash
cards. After two years working to make a living as a writer, he'd
decided to move somewhere warmer and cheaper than upper New
York State. Writing, he'd discovered, wasn't easy. And making a living from it was tougher still.

MacDonald had been trying to earn a living as a writer since
his Army discharge in 1946. He and Dorothy and Johnny lived in a
second-floor apartment on State Street in Utica. He wrote in a seven-
by-nine-foot office connected to the living room, formally a sort of a
storage area with one window looking out over the front yard. During his first four months as a writer he turned out more than 800,000
words and got a thousand rejection slips. He spent eighty hours a
week at the typewriter and made sure twenty to thirty stories were
always in the mail. "We had an evil-tempered mailman," MacDonald
remembered, "who'd bring a fistful of rejected manuscripts every
now and then, hammer on the side wall with his fist and yell, 'Mac-
Donald! MacDonald!' until I would come running down to take that
particular load of disappointment from him."

Initially, MacDonald tried writing for the slick magazines. "I was
writing wonderful beautiful things about dying blind musicians," he
wrote later, "but they didn't sell. And then Mike Tilden at *Detective
Tales* bought the second story for forty dollars in 1946 and then I
thought, well, maybe if I lower my sights a little and work a little bit
harder—by then I was a readjustment case—maybe it'll work."

John D. MacDonald had discovered the world of the pulps. Or, more
accurately, the pulps had discovered John D. MacDonald.

America's pulp magazines were the other side of the coin that had created Horatio Alger's novels for boys in 1868. At first there were the Buffalo Bill novels, published by Street & Smith in the 1870s. Buffalo Bill Cody was a real character from America's Wild West, of course, but the exploits in the books about him were fiction, written by Ned Buntline, a pen name of Edward Zane Carroll Judson. Soon after, in 1886, the first of hundreds of stories about Nick Carter, boy detective, appeared in the *New York Weekly*. His adventures continued in dime novels and pulp magazines for the next fifty years. In 1896, Frank Munsey, the prominent New York publisher of newspapers and cheap magazines, changed one of his titles, *The Golden Argosy*, from a boy's magazine to an all-fiction magazine for adults. It measured seven by ten inches, was a half inch thick, and was printed on untrimmed rough wood-pulp pages. It became the prototype for an industry. Before the metamorphoses of *The Argosy*, of course, there were dime novels. This new magazine cost half that—only a nickel. Munsey started an industry that would supply America with its entertainment for the next fifty years.

By the 1920s, there were hundreds of pulp magazines. There were adventure magazines, romance magazines, war magazines, detective magazines, spy magazines, sex magazines, mystery magazines, science fiction magazines, and even subcategories like Oriental mystery magazines and jungle adventure magazines. They carried titles like *All Story, Adventure, Railroad Stories, Sea Stories, Magic Carpet, Pirate Stories, Oriental Stories, Jungle Stories, Football Action, Fight Stories, Baseball Stories, Dare-Devil Aces, Sky Birds, Over the Top, War Birds, War Stories, Navy Stories, RAF Aces, Wings, Wild West Weekly, Western Story, West, Nickel Western, Western Roundup, Fifteen Western Tales, Detective Story, Black Mask, New York Stories, Clues Detective Stories, Mystery Stories, Racketeer Stories, Spy Novels Magazine, Detective Fiction Weekly, The Parisienne, Parisian Life, Saucy Stories, Pep Stories, Breezy Stories, Love Stories, Ranch Romance, Popular Love, Husbands, Horror Stories, Spicy Adventure Stories, Spicy Detective Stories, Spicy Western Stories, Spicy Mystery Stories, Dime Mystery Magazine, Dime Detective Magazine, Terror Tales, Horror Stories, Weird Tales, The Thrill Book, Strange Tales, My Self, Ghost Stories, Amazing Stories, Astounding Stories, Startling Stories, Thrilling Wonder Stories, Planet Stories, Marvel, Operator #5, The Shadow, Doc Savage, The Phantom Detec-*

tive, *Secret Agent X*, *The Wizard*, *The Avenger*, *The Spider*, *Nick Carter*, *Terence X. O'Leary's War Birds*, *Bill Barnes' Air Adventures*, *G-8 and His Battle Aces*, *The Mysterious Wu Fang*, and *Doctor Death*. To name a few.

It took 200 million words a year to fill these magazines. Writers like Walter B. Gibson, a magician's assistant to Houdini, Thurston, and Blackstone, was annually turning out twenty-four stories of sixty thousand words each about the Shadow. He maintained that pace for two decades. Arthur J. Burkes, known in the 1930s as the King of the Pulps, wrote a million and a half words a year. "Of course," Burkes told an interviewer for *The New Yorker*, "a million and a half is so *usual*. Lots of pulp writers do more than that." The pulps were a land of quantity over quality, but some good writing managed to appear in them. Ray Bradbury, Dashiell Hammett, Raymond Chandler, MacKinlay Kantor, Edgar Rice Burroughs, Max Brand, Luke Short, Tennessee Williams, H. P. Lovecraft, Paul Gallico, Erle Stanley Gardner, Raoul Whitfield, Cornell Woolrich, Arthur C. Clarke, and Isaac Asimov all had stories published in pulp magazines.

For the most part, however, pulp stories were written by about three hundred writers in New York City. Most of them lived in Greenwich Village. Another thousand regular contributors were scattered around the country. The writers sold stories to editors at Street & Smith, the Frank Munsey Company, Popular Publications, Standard Magazines, Dell Magazines, and Magazine Publishers, Inc. Their usual pay was a penny a word.

To get by, the writers lived in cheap hotels and ate at even cheaper cafeterias. In his memoir, *The Pulp Jungle*, Frank Gruber, a prolific writer of more than forty-eight novels and a pulp contributor, remembers those pulp days of the thirties: "I was already having my meals at MacFadden's Penny Restaurants. . . . In those days you could dine sumptuously for around nine cents per meal. A hamburger steak made of meat–flavored sawdust cost four cents, a good hard roll was a penny, coffee two cents (made from dishwater with a dash of chicory) and dessert, two cents. You ate the meal standing up, which was good for your digestion. The food was very filling."

Even a pulp writer's social life never interfered with his writing. Gruber remembers a party thrown by a writer in his small Brooklyn apartment. "It was a rather small apartment and the . . . guests who were there were jammed into the place so you could hardly move around. About ten o'clock in the evening [the host] announced that he had a deadline for a twelve thousand word story the following morning and had to get at it. I assumed that it was a hint for the guests to leave, but such was not the case at all. [He] merely went to his desk in one corner of the room and began to bang his electric typewriter. [He] sat at that typewriter for four solid hours, completely oblivious to the brawl going on around him. At two o'clock in the morning he finished his twelve thousand words and had a drink of gin."

This was the world John D. MacDonald entered when he sold his 4,500-word story "Female of the Species" to *Dime Detective* for forty dollars.

"I was dealing with a marketplace there, the pulps, that peaked and were beginning to sag a bit," MacDonald remembered later, "but they hadn't really gone out yet. So that in the American magazine market . . . there was room for about eight hundred pieces of fiction a month, as compared with American magazines now—I think a fair estimate is about ten a month. . . . It was very helpful to me because it was an 'Earn While You Learn' sort of thing. Also, their editors gave me hints on things I later would have found about by myself, but it would have taken much longer and would have been much more laborious."

But MacDonald was not immune to the charms of the pulp life. He particularly remembered one visit to New York City where he drank the afternoon away with Mike Tilden, an editor at Popular Publications, at a bar called Tim Costello's. "Tim Costello himself was tending bar," MacDonald remembered. "We stood at the bar and I had twelve straight-up Martinis between three and six o'clock. Mike was so impressed he wrote out a confirmation, saying that I did not suffer slurred speech or the blind staggers, and had Costello sign it. He sent me a photostat of the signed statement but it disappeared a few years ago. . . . The writer as jackass."

MacDonald's pulp writing paid from half a cent to two cents a word, with infrequent bonuses that raised the rate to three cents a word. In the beginning, that wasn't enough to keep a family of three going. "Along in April and May of 1946, though I had begun to sell some stories here and there . . . I began to think we might not make it," MacDonald wrote later. "I found a job as Executive Director of the Tax Research Bureau in Utica. I made that jump a little too nervously and hastily. I spent every spare minute writing. Through the summer the stories began to sell at a greater rate, and to better markets. We paid off our debts and began to build up a little surplus. By autumn I was still stuck with that job with an unwritten obligation to keep it for a year. I resigned on the basis of need to take Dorothy to a warmer climate. It was not entirely a pretext. She could have endured the winter, but she does not take cold well, and it was certain that she would spend a good portion of the winter in poor health."

They packed up and hit the road. Their first trip away from Utica had been a way to escape the ravages of winter, but it was also a trip away from the doubts his family had about his work as a writer. Everyone except Dorothy had worried about John's quitting his job with the Utica Tax Research Bureau and treated him as if he were a war casualty, as if he had to readjust from his years in Burma during World War II.

Of course there was some readjustment. Everyone who served in the military had to face a new world that was nothing like what people thought it would be. During the war, most people thought they would return home to a pre-Depression land of the 1920s. It wasn't like that. Soldiers came home to a nation where jobs were often scarce and available housing nonexistent. The suburbs began to grow, consumerism ran rampant, and veterans tried to make up for lost time by buying new cars, power lawn mowers, jewelry, dishwashers, washing machines, and marriage licenses. Couples married in record numbers, and the children from these marriages composed the biggest boom in births the country had ever known. Veterans everywhere were stunned by the changes in the United States. Many of them were dazed and confused. They had no idea what had become of the world they knew before the war and no idea of what they would do in this new postwar era. MacDonald was not among the hollow men who needed readjustment into this new world. At least he had ambitions and a goal.

John MacDonald knew he wanted to be a writer, and he knew he was working harder at the typewriter than he had ever worked before. Somehow, though, it was not the respectable occupation his family wanted for their only son. "Except for Dorothy, everyone thought I was a readjustment problem," MacDonald wrote years later. "Even today I do not know how much of her confidence in me was genuine and how much was a calculated effort devised for my morale. But I do know that her attitude was that it would be absurd to think of spending my life in any other way."

And so he and his family lit out for the territory—planning to make it to Taos, New Mexico. But they stopped instead in Ingram, Texas—"The Only All Rock Town in the U.S."—just north of San Antonio, where they lived in a small cabin on a hillside just outside of town. MacDonald cranked out fifteen stories for the pulps, selling them to *Dime Detective, Detective Tales, Astounding Science Fiction, Doc Savage, Liberty*, and *The Shadow* for about a penny a word. He wasn't getting rich, but he was paying his bills and there was no one looking over his shoulder telling him he should be back in an office wearing a suit and talking to people he couldn't stand.

A lot of MacDonald's early pulp fiction dealt with World War II subjects—the war in the Pacific, jungles, the Yellow Peril, secret agents in linen suits, rickshaws—and were ideal for adventure magazines like *Doc Savage*. But soon, as the war years faded from the public memory, editors began to tire of these Far Eastern tales. Babette Rosmand, an editor at *The Shadow* and *Doc Savage* magazines, realized that interest in these sagas of the Orient was failing, and she sent MacDonald a note: "John, it's time to take off your pith helmet." He took it off and never put it on again. But he continued to write. From his discharge in 1945 until his Mexico trip in 1949, more than a hundred of MacDonald's stories were published, most of them in the pulps. He was, by pulp standards, a success. "I don't know how long we're going to keep him in the pulp magazines," Harry Widmer, the editor at *Detective Fiction Weekly*, said, "but we're going to try to keep him as long as we can."

MacDonald and his family returned to Utica earlier than they had planned. In the spring of 1947, Dorothy's mother, who had planned to move from Poland, New York, to the MacDonalds' apartment in Utica, was diagnosed with cancer, and she wanted her daughter to be with her. In their old green prewar Ford convertible, John and Dorothy and Johnny made the long trip back to Utica, towing an Army-surplus jeep trailer. John was down to less than $100, and the car gobbled gas and oil. To save the little money they had, they traveled no faster than thirty-five miles an hour and drove for fourteen hours a day.

When they got back to New York State, the MacDonalds discovered their apartment was closed—Dorothy's mother had stayed in Poland after all—and a few big checks were waiting for him. Instead of settling again in Utica, John and Dorothy decided to move a few miles away to Clinton, the home of Hamilton College. "[We] believed in our innocence that a small college town might provide a pleasant atmosphere for the writer," MacDonald wrote later. "But to them I was some kind of freak, writing instead of doing real work." They bought a house on College Hill, surrounded by the campus. Later that winter, Dorothy's mother suffered a relapse. She was moved to Clinton, where Dorothy set up a hospital bed in the living room of their new house and acted as nurse, administering shots to her mother every four hours, turning her to make her comfortable, feeding her. She died in April.

After her death, upper New York State had little to offer the MacDonalds. Dorothy still suffered from the long, cold winters, and John was tired of being the odd duck—a writer in a small town. The MacDonalds rented their house on College Hill. The anticipated long evenings spent talking to intellectual professors about literature and history and politics and philosophy never materialized. Instead of literature, John's friends on the faculty wanted to talk about their department chairman; instead of philosophy they wanted to discuss tenure; instead of analyzing historical trends the professors deplored enrollment figures. The only politics he ever discussed was the strange Byzantine campus variety in which getting a window for your office was the equivalent of being elected to Congress.

During the war, John had won some money playing poker and Dorothy had invested it in land on Piseco Lake, a wilderness area sixty miles north of Utica. The MacDonalds planned to build a summer camp there, but they had no money. It made sense, they thought, to move to a place where it was cheaper to live. Mexico, they thought. Maybe Mexico was the answer.

The MacDonalds rented their house to a couple and their covey of pigeons, stored their furniture in an abandoned cargo trailer, and were on the road again. This time they were in a newer black Ford convertible, towing the same war-surplus trailer behind them. They drove through the wheat fields of the Midwest and across the flatlands of Texas, crossed the border to Mexico, sped down the Pan American highway to Mexico City, and headed up into the Ajusco Mountains and down to the valley beyond. Destination: Cuernavaca.

Nestled between two volcanos—Popocatepetl and Ixtaccihuatl—Cuernavaca has a violent and romantic history. The Spanish conquistador Hernán Cortez had defeated the Tlahuicas Indians there in a bloody massacre in the 1500s and had built a palace in the heart of town. Across from the palace is a cathedral built by the monks and priests who came with him on his conquests. Just beyond the cathedral are the Borda Gardens, an eighteenth-century Italian garden that seems less formal than its European models as the lush, tropical greenery spreads and makes a mockery of the plans and restraints of landscape architects.

Cuernavaca is also the city that Emiliano Zapata conquered during the Mexican Revolution. But most of all, Cuernavaca is home to the idle rich of Mexico City. These capitalist conquistadors came to what they call "the land of eternal Spring" and brought with them the sophistication and money to change what was once a sleepy, farming village into a sort of Central American version of the French Riviera. There is no ocean here, but there are magnificent palaces and European restaurants that can erase the world of business from the mind of even the most obsessed entrepreneur.

It was not Cuernavaca's physical charm or its millionaires or its history that attracted the MacDonalds. Early in 1947, both John and Dorothy had read *Under the Volcano*, a novel by Malcolm Lowry, an alcoholic British expatriate. Years later, MacDonald would say it was

----

one of five books he would take with him to a desert island. They were both fascinated by the Cuernavaca Lowry described in his story of depression and booze. In his novel, Lowry called Cuernavaca by a fictional name—Quauhnahuac.

The walls of the town, which is built on a hill, are high, the streets and lanes tortuous and broken, the roads winding. A fine American-style highway leads in from the north but is lost in its narrow streets and comes out a goat track. [Cuernavaca] possesses eighteen churches and fifty-seven cantinas. It also boasts a golf course and no less than four hundred swimming pools, public and private, filled with the water that ceaselessly pours down from the mountains, and many splendid hotels. . . . Far to his left, in the northeast, beyond the valley and the terraced foothills of the Sierra Madre Oriental, the two volcanos . . . rose clear and magnificent into the sunset. Nearer, perhaps ten miles distant, and on a lower level than the main valley, [was] the village of Tomalín, nestling behind the jungle, from which rose a thin blue scarf of illegal smoke, someone burning wood for carbon. Before him, on the other side of the American highway, spread fields and groves, through which meandered a river, and the Alcapancingo road. The watchtower of a prison rose over a wood between the river and the road which lost itself further where the purple hills of a Doré Paradise sloped away into the distance. Over in the town the lights of [the] one cinema, built on an incline and standing out sharply, suddenly came on, flickered off, came on again.

This was the Cuernavaca the MacDonalds were seeking, not the land of conquistadors and revolutionaries and millionaires. And it wouldn't cost much to live there—one requirement MacDonald had as he pounded out short stories for the pulps. But there was more to Cuernavaca than the history books or Lowry's novel told. When

Lowry arrived in 1936, he was attracted by the large American colony in the city.

Of course, the lure of Mexico for the literati was not limited to Cuernavaca. The late 1940s was when Jack Kerouac and Allen Ginsberg went on the road and found whores and drugs in Mexico City and some sort of nirvana in the country's small towns and villages. Mexico in those years was a paradise for nomadic American writers, just as it had been for D. H. Lawrence when he went there to write *The Plumed Serpent* in 1926 and for André Breton, the founder of the surrealist movement, when he visited the country in 1938.

The expatriate American bohemians gathered in Cuernavaca to talk about projects and dreams, discuss literature, and, occasionally, to write, and the city also glittered with once-popular Hollywood stars. The MacDonalds saw the fading movie actress Paulette Goddard at a bullfight in Mexico City on a trip they made from Cuernavaca. She had been a Ziegfeld girl in the 1920s, had starred in sexy roles in a lot of 1940s movies, and now was entering the twilight of obscurity.

"We came to the aisle going out of the arena just as Paulette Goddard got there. . . . She's down here getting a divorce from Burgess Meredith," Dorothy wrote to her family in Utica. "And we had been watching her. . . . John met her in India, so he spoke to her, and she was very friendly, so they walked out all the way, having a fine little chitchat."

The ambiance of Cuernavaca in the late 1940s shines from MacDonald's description of a party in the city in his novel *Please Write for Details:*

The new house . . . was a fraud. It had no artistic unity. It was part California modern, part half-ass Japanese and part Mexican exuberance. . . . The people seemed equally fraudulent. There was a badly faded screen star with an arrogant manner, a surly poodle and a handsome and stupid young consort. There was a current film star, vast and blond, who had apparently practiced the rather nasty habit of being able to laugh one peachbasket breast out of its skimpy hammock of fabric. The length of the delay before she noticed the unveiling was apparently in direct ratio to the possible unimportance of the onlooker to her career. She was accompanied by a small, bald man with exceptionally hairy hands. Then there were three self-important and rather surly young men from the field staff of one of the picture magazines, accompanied by three glossy young women from Mexico City who had no English. And there were two novelists, one reasonably notorious, and one tall female poet who looked like an Australian tennis star, male, and dressed the part. And several staggering, bellowing drunks of both sexes, and a score of the usual expatriates with the usual diversity of mates, legal and extralegal, rather more than half of them heterosexual, rather more than half of them from the U.S. Rick and Puss Daniels were both small, gnarled red-headed people who had inherited some sort of automotive concession in Mexico, and who busied themselves with making odd and rather ugly ornaments of enamel baked on copper. Concealed speakers played recorded music, flamenco, bullring, and *mariachi*. Prism lights imbedded in the paneled ceiling made drama of casual groupings.

The everyday life of the MacDonalds in Mexico was far from that of the glitterati that populated the palaces and cantinas. But some of the people they met were as bizarre as any of Lowry's or MacDonald's fictional characters. There were, for example, the Rigsbys, Lorraine and Hop. Dorothy wrote in a letter to her relatives:

Lorraine is a Unitarian minister's daughter. Originally from Rochester, and is pretty, has the best of character and interests, but a little dumb. Her former husband is a neurosurgeon, and she has two nice kids, six and nine. Hop is the very successful ex-editor and writer we told you about. His wife was apparently an alcoholic, and he has two girls, eleven and fifteen. . . . We were amazed to hear on Tuesday that

Hop had left Lorraine and moved into a hotel, leaving her with four kids in a strange country and not able to speak a word of Spanish. . . . Hop has fits of what is apparently real insanity and beats up Lorraine, throws everything he can get his hands [on], abuses the kids and becomes very violent. All week long we've been terrified he would kill one of them because he kept going back to the house and threatening to. . . . Then we found out he's been having them for years, and Lorraine was not very smart to come down here with him and the kids. . . . Friday he went back to the house, made one last horrible scene, and is now all straightened out again. This last [scene] was the worst one yet, probably brought on by his book, which he worked on exclusively for two years, being suddenly returned by the publishers. He's not used to disappointment.

And there was Adela McNair, a would-be seductress, who told the MacDonalds she planned to break up their family and take John away. "The truth is, she was not a Lady before she married a (rich) American," Dorothy wrote, "but she is not now going to endanger her [new] status as a lady by being seen in the kitchen. When they entertain [her husband] and the female guests get the food ready. . . . She's comparatively harmless and terribly colorful and amusing. . . . We like her about as much as you could like a terribly precocious child, which she is. . . . She told John New Year's Eve that she was going to break up our family. He spanked her. She still works at it every minute. . . . If she breaks up our home, something's wrong with John's head, which I doubt."

In Cuernavaca John and Dorothy rented a small brick house at 8 Jacaranda Street, three miles north of the central city. It was a mile east of the main highway, and from their front door they had a view of the two volcanos. Johnny was enrolled in a private English-speaking school, and a woman named Esperanza worked for them as a maid. Years later, MacDonald would use characters based on Esperanza in the novel *Please Write for Details* and the novella *Border Town Girl*. Dorothy described her to her family:

Esperanza has always lived in a mud hut with a dirt floor, and no doors and windows, on beans and tortilla three times a day, but she sure caught on fast, and we are a little sick of her being a Queen. She is fine and sings all day as long as things go her way, but too often her way is so completely unsanitary or so based on my activities . . . that it's hopeless, and rather than trying to learn or being grateful for all the concessions we make to her that the average Mexican servant never heard of she sulks and balks and goldbricks until you'd rather do the work than look at her. . . . She ran out on her first job because she wouldn't take orders, and this is her second. If she has to work again . . . she will find that no Mexican family will buy the same food for her that they eat, or take her riding, or give her clothes or teach her to make her own, or pay her one-third more than any family we know pays or give her the rest of the day off when they go to an afternoon movie. I have taken so much that bordered on insolence because I felt that having so much more ourselves merited a lot of humility, and she is proud—proud, but it is a relief to think that the next time perhaps we can find one a little dumber, with a better disposition, who might be a little happier in the kind of work for which she is being paid.

They also added the luxury of a part-time gardener named Joaqúin. "He is very pretty, looks like Bambi, and has been just as shy until recently. . . . John and Joaqúin had a wonderful conversation. . . . The MacNairs just moved to a house near us, and wanted Joaqúin to work in their garden part time, as he does here. He decided he has too many jobs (which he has), so we asked him if he would recommend one of his friends for the job. He said, '*No porque mis amigos son todos borrachos*'—No, because all my friends are drunks. John said, '*Si, todos mis amigos son borrachos, tambien.*'—Yes, all my friends are drunks, too."

Mexico, complete with servants, was even more affordable than the MacDonalds could have hoped. Total expenses: $115 a month, easily within the budget of a pulp writer on the lam from upper New

York State. John kept to his writing schedule that year in Cuernavaca—up early, a quick breakfast, and then four hours at the typewriter, time off for lunch, and four more hours of writing. MacDonald approached writing the way any Harvard M.B.A. would. "I thought you got up in the morning and went to work and worked until lunch and then went back to work until the day was over—with good business habits as in any other job," he wrote late. "It wasn't until my habit patterns were firmly embedded that I discovered that writers tended to work a couple of hours and then to brood about it the rest of the day."

John published more than sixty short stories for the pulps during his year in Mexico, mostly with lurid titles like "The Case of the Carved Model," "My Husband Dies Slowly," "Blonde Bail for the Master Murderer," and "I'll Drown You in My Dreams." So many of his stories were published that the magazines had to devise pseudonyms for him—Scott O'Hara, John Lane, Peter Reed, John Wane Farrell, Henry Riser, and Robert Henry—so no one would know he often wrote almost an entire issue. Although he was best known for his hard-boiled detective fiction, he also churned out science fiction and sports stories—anything for a penny a word. Occasionally he got lucky and sold a story to the slick magazines, like *Women's Day* or *Argosy,* which was no longer the early pulp magazine but now an adventure-oriented men's magazine. Those early years working for the pulps were an apprenticeship for MacDonald, and like any apprentice, he learned by imitation. His asylum in "You've Got to Be Cold," published in *Shadow Mystery Magazine,* bears an astonishing resemblance to the hospital run by Dr. Anthor in Raymond Chandler's *Farewell, My Lovely;* in "But Not to Dream," published in *Weird Tales* in 1949, a professor of entomology is changed into a giant moth much as Gregor Samsa becomes a cockroach in Kafka's *Metamorphosis.* His first stories also showed a heavy debt to the early tough-guy writers of the pulps. "There is a special debt we owe them," MacDonald wrote in a 1976 *New York Times* review of James M. Cain's *The Institute,* "a debt to Chandler, Hammett, and Cain. They excised pointless ornamentation, moved their stories forward with a spare, ruthless vigor, and so superimposed the realities we already knew with characters we could believe that they achieved a dreadful, and artistic, inevitability. They were the big guys, changing the definitions of suspense and readability, forcing all us smaller fry to cut more cleanly and deeply, to delete the windiness of tortuous explanation, to get on with it—showing instead of telling."

In August 1949, *Collier's* published "Louie Follows Me," a story about big-city gangsters. "We were living in Mexico when the money came for 'Louie Follows Me,'" MacDonald remembered later. "It was the first check I had ever received with four figures to the left of the decimal point. It seemed incredible to be paid so well for something I so enjoyed doing, and which gave me so much satisfaction when the words went especially well together."

What MacDonald did best was tell stories. But he often had trouble ending them, either because he lost interest in his characters or was in a hurry to start another story. "I tend to neaten things up too carefully at the end," he said later. "Many of my solutions are too glib." He also pushed for happy endings where the villain is punished and the hero and his girlfriend ride off into the sunset. It was not an unusual formula in the 1940s when Hollywood was still operating under the Hays Code, which demanded separate beds for married couples and the triumph of virtue. Popular writing simply followed the Hollywood rules—after all, a lot of the pulp writers were also writing screenplays—and softened the sex and muted the endings. Sometimes the sexiest thing about the pulps was the covers. The book publishing world wasn't much better. Lawrence's *Lady Chatterley's Lover* and Henry Miller's two *Tropic* novels were banned in the United States. Characters in Norman Mailer's *The Naked and the Dead* used "fug" as an expletive.

MacDonald sold his work to the pulps through his agent, Captain Joseph Thompson Shaw, a former editor of *Black Mask* magazine. Shaw was the midwife of American hard-boiled writing. He had nurtured Dashiell Hammett, discovered Raymond Chandler, and helped a score of other writers, including Erle Stanley Gardner, Carroll John Daly, Raoul Whitfield, Horace McCoy, and Paul Cain, develop a lean, spare style that was different from what was being written for other pulp magazines in the 1920s. "Cap" Shaw earned his nickname in World War I when he was a bayonet instructor. He was a national champion swordsman and was said to be the only man in New York City licensed to carry a sword cane as a concealed weapon. Six months after he took over as editor of *Black Mask*, Shaw published his manifesto in the June 1927 issue of the magazine. "Detective fiction, as we view it, has only commenced to be developed," he wrote. "However, to be convincing . . . [it] must be real in motive, character and action . . . must be plausible . . . clean and understandable. . . . Therefore word has gone out to writers of our requirements of plausibility, of truthfulness in details, of realism in . . . the portrayal of action and emotion. . . . Slowly, but surely, we are molding the contents of this magazine along the lines of this purpose." Shaw wanted to be a writer, but he was a terrible one; as an editor, however, he was a genius. Ten years later, in 1936, Shaw left *Black Mask* over a salary dispute and went to work as a literary agent for the Sid Sanders Agency. He struck out on his own after Sanders died, and on the recommendation of MacKinlay Kantor, MacDonald became his client. Now, at age seventy-eight, Shaw was handling a new generation of hard-boiled writers and MacDonald was his star. He sold more than fifty of the short stories MacDonald sent him from Cuernavaca.

Mexico agreed with John D. MacDonald. When he wasn't writing, he often went fishing in Lake Tequesquetengo or played with Pancha, the stray cat the family adopted to take the place of Roger and Geoffrey, the two they left behind in Utica. It seemed like a writer's paradise, but then that damned graduate student from Michigan had to interfere.

In 1948, Kenneth Millar, born in Los Gatos, California, in 1915, was a thirty-three-year-old graduate student at the University of Michigan. He had earned a B.A. from the University of Western Ontario in 1938 and a master's degree in English at the University of Michigan in 1942. During World War II he was a lieutenant in the Navy and served as a communications officer in the Pacific. After the war he returned to Ann Arbor to get his Ph.D. He was writing his dissertation on Coleridge. Millar was married to Margaret Sturm, and while he was away in the Navy, she began writing mystery novels. Her first, *The Invisible Worm*, was published in 1941. By the time the war ended, she had published five more. Not to be outdone by his wife, Millar, in what may have been an effort to escape Coleridge, wrote three detective novels on his own. But there was some confusion among mystery readers. People wanted a Margaret Millar mystery and they ended up with one by Kenneth. By the late 1940s, Millar was developing a new protagonist, a California detective named Lew Archer. So he decided to come up with a pseudonym for himself. He adapted his father's name—John Macdonald Millar—and became John Ross Macdonald. His first Archer novel, *The Moving Target*, was published in 1949. The author's name was listed as John Macdonald.

The real John MacDonald's mother happened on *The Moving Target* at a bookstore in Utica and bought twelve copies. That was the beginning of the confusion.

John D. MacDonald wrote his agent, who wrote Harold Ober, Millar's agent. There was a problem. "The publisher and the agent were in agreement that everybody had goofed," Macdonald remembered later. ". . . Everyone agreed that I could restrain them from using that name. I had that legal right. However, they suggested another way out of the dilemma. Mr. Millar was under contract to do a series of books. . . . It could be a very big handicap to have the second and subsequent books in the series come out under another name. What if they changed the name slowly? John R. Macdonald on the next one, then John Ross Macdonald, and then Ross Macdonald, with the idea that subsequent reprintings of the first three would be credited to Ross Macdonald. I thought it over. . . . By and large the writing trade is a class act. . . . It is only the hanky stompers who seek revenge for unintended slights. . . . I felt pleased with myself for being so amiable."

Nonetheless, six years after the compromise was reached, *Cosmopolitan* magazine promoted a Lew Archer novel on its cover as "A New John MacDonald novel." John D. MacDonald was furious.

I couldn't get mad at the magazine because they were just out there doing their magazine thing. . . . But I remembered how *very nice* I had been about not exercising my right to restrain the use of my name. . . . I finally . . . sent [Millar] a virulent and intemperate telegram. In due course I got a letter from him, handwritten on three sheets of yellow paper. It was just as intemperate as my wire, and the gist of it was that inasmuch as he was known and respected all over the world, who the hell was I to come along and tell him what he could and could not publish. . . . I let it cool for a few weeks, and then I wrote a reasonable letter to him, giving him the whole history, and explaining why I had felt done wrong. It wasn't a warm and friendly letter, but it was reasonable. I even told him about my mother. His response was cool and reasonable. He said that he was sorry about the whole thing, but that it was not his job to check magazine indexes and it was not his fault his father was named John Macdonald Millar.

The confusion continued. "Probably the worst confusion will become evident when one of us becomes what they call posthumous," the real John MacDonald said later.

Mexico may have agreed with John, but Dorothy was getting homesick.

It is warm and beautiful here, and we don't see how we can afford to live at home again, so in the back of our minds is that the house in Clinton will have to go. . . . All our debts are paid, every one, and we are about to start saving money. Stories are still selling well, we are out of Christmas without being in the red for months, as usual, and once we get our money put aside for the trip home . . . we can live terribly well and save dough. . . . Surely there's nothing bad about that, and there's more advantages here than disadvantages, in climate, expense, even people generally. Yet it's so darn far from home and the few people who mean the most that you don't *feel* right. . . . I've been doing a bit of private psychoanalysis, wondering why I haven't been happier day by day down here when everything is so sunny and warm and colorful here and so barren and cold in Clinton at this time. It's because I'm trapped, we're all trapped by the low cost of living. We've been explaining for years to people who wondered why, with our comparative freedom, we don't live in a more salubrious climate, that New York state is our home, where our people are, and Piseco [Lake], and our roots, and that we don't want to be outsiders the rest of our lives. All of which is still true, but after you find such an ideal place, where you can live like a king and not worry about money, the idea of returning to a spot where the climate keeps you sick, and you are always fighting the wolf at your doorstep, just doesn't make sense. . . . If I weren't going to be 38 tomorrow, maybe roots wouldn't matter so much. . . . John is much more sensible about it, but then his family looks better from a slight distance to him.

At the end of the summer of 1949, John gave in to Dorothy. He declared his Mexican days over, and they packed the Ford and headed north to Utica. There were problems with Dorothy's mother's estate that had to be settled, their two cats needed attention, and they decided to begin construction on a summer camp on their Piseco Lake property. MacDonald's Mexican fiction—*The Damned, Border Town Girl*, and *Please Write for Details*—would not come for a few more years.

The MacDonalds stayed in Utica only a few months. Dorothy's homesickness was cured, and, as she wrote to her family in her letter from Mexico, John's family looked better to him at a distance. When summer faded into fall and the weather got chilly, they were on the road again, following the sun. This time it led them in a different direction—to Florida. But this trip was more than a sojourn. Once they arrived on Florida's Gulf Coast, John and Dorothy looked at each other and said, "Why not here?" Except for vacations, they would never live anywhere else. Florida became their home.

CHAPTER 6

The MacDonalds came to Florida in early September 1949. They came down the East Coast, cut over near Orlando, drove through Tampa, crossed the Courtney Campbell Causeway, and stopped in Clearwater, about thirty miles west of Tampa on the Gulf of Mexico. After spending the night in a motel, John and Dordo rented a two-bedroom frame house two blocks from the Gulf. They settled in and enrolled Johnny in school. The next day the cops showed up. John was charged with having a child in school but having no Florida plates on his car. He bought the license plates and became an official Floridian. Just another goddam day in paradise.

Florida had been in the paradise business for almost a century when the MacDonalds arrived. In fact, it may have been dreamed of as a latter-day garden of Eden for even longer. In his fictional biography of Shakespeare, *Nothing but the Sun*, Anthony Burgess has the young bard dreaming of Florida. It had always been a sort of paradise that attracted tourists. Like heaven itself, there are more people coming every day, and there are a lot of old-timers, but no natives. Ponce de León came to paradise from Spain in 1513, and named it Florida, which means flowery land. De León was looking for perpetual youth. Instead he found a fountain of sulfuric water. A half-breed from Alabama named Billy Powell moved south to paradise in the 1830s and became Osceola, chief of the Seminoles. He was killed by the U.S. Army. Get-rich-quick artists in the same era moved to paradise with wagons full of silkworms and mulberry trees, the worm's favorite food, to start a silk industry to rival China. California had gold, Florida would have silk. Fifteen years later a blight killed off the silkworms and the mulberry trees. The farmers switched to oranges, and a freeze killed their crop in 1835 and again in 1895. Paradise? Some people still thought so. Doctors in the East advised patients with tuberculosis to go to Florida to recover. Another fountain of youth opened, this one owned by John Whitney, who also owned a nearby hotel. Hyperbole abounded. "Insects are neither numerous nor troublesome," one flack wrote about the American paradise while Florida state officials were telling the swarms of new residents that "roaches, like the poor, will always be with you."

And yet it was this unshakable belief that Florida could improve your health that gave the state its first wave of prosperity in the twentieth century. Henry Flagler, a robber baronet from New York who was a lesser partner in John D. Rockefeller's Standard Oil, brought his wife, Mary, to St. Augustine in the late 1870s to recover from a bronchial condition. She got better, but Flagler couldn't stand the place. To him, the stench of death was everywhere. People wandered the streets wheezing and coughing their consumptive lungs out. Henry Flagler couldn't take it. Even though Mary was getting better, they went back to New York. Every winter Mary's doctors advised her to go back to Florida. Every winter Henry said she could go alone. She never did. In 1881, she died. Flagler mourned for a while and then, a year after Mary's death, consoled himself with a fountain of youth more conventional than the spring Ponce de León found. He married a flaming redhead named Alicia who was eighteen years younger than he. She was a nurse who wanted to be an actress. A few months after the marriage, Flagler and the lovely Alicia went to St. Augustine—this time for his health. His doctor had found a disorderly liver and prescribed Florida. On this trip, Flagler fell in love with St. Augustine. If there was any consumptive hawking and spitting on the street, he didn't see it. He decided to build a hotel, and, more important, he decided to build a railroad. The hotel, the Ponce de León, was made of poured concrete in a gaudy Spanish style. The railroad was more conventional. It ran from Jacksonville to St. Augustine and later was extended to Palm Beach and then into Miami. At stops along the way, Flagler built more hotels.

On the West Coast of Florida another railroad man, Henry Plant, began laying track to get rich people to travel to the Gulf Coast. It was a race of sorts, but both Plant and Flagler forgot a couple of facts about rich people. They don't like to mix with anyone else. And they are fickle. Henry Ford had made Florida more democratic with his assembly-line production of the automobile. In the 1920s, Florida real estate was selling for prices rivaled only by gold and diamonds, or so the story went. You could buy land in the morning and sell it in the afternoon for an enormous profit, the agents said. But that land boom suffered the same fate as the silkworms and the orchards. It went bust. By then the rich had found another place to vacation and the temples of Mammon they called hotels had been replaced by small motels with pink neon trim. Even the rich had never been able to use Florida year-round, but a quirky inventor named Carrier found a way to cool a room and remove the humidity from the air at the same time. Finally, Florida was habitable year-round. So when MacDonald and his family rolled into Clearwater the rumble of air conditioners had become a rival for the waves of the Gulf of Mexico as the sound of Florida.

John enrolled his son in school and sent for his cats, Geoffrey and Roger, and they were mailed to him by Railway Express. Although they were in Florida and not Mexico, 1949 was not much different from the year before in Cuernavaca. John sat at the typewriter all day and knocked out story after story in the pulp writer tradition, drank some gin after work, and then started writing again the next day. He was not so much a writer as he was a writing machine. "Utican Writes 300 Stories in 20 Months," read a 1947 headline in the *Utica Observer-Dispatch*. By 1949 his pace had slowed. He wrote only seventy-two stories that year. At this point in his career, Mac-Donald took pride in his output. He saw himself as a businessman, not an author. In "Professionally Yours," an article published in the 1950 *Writer's Yearbook*, MacDonald wrote about his profession with a cold, academic dispassion: "Prior to free lancing, I was involved in systems and methods in the Industrial Engineering field, and secured a graduate degree from the Harvard Graduate School of Business Administration. Today, as a writer, I am a small businessman in a highly competitive field, fabricating a product for sale in a buyers' market, and required to establish my own merchandising and marketing procedures."

MacDonald outlined the best way for a writer to make money— where to live, what kind of paper to use, how to keep records, how to handle relationships with editors and agents, marketing, and finances. It was as dull as a dissertation and as sound as a sermon.

On where to live: "The ideal environment for the practicing free lance has been discovered by many. . . . It is a small resort town where the writer can live cheaply due to the fact of year round residence. Social rigidity is lacking. It is possible to achieve, if one so desires, the isolation of a large city. It is equally possible to find small social groups more stimulating than in a more normal codified settlement."

On tools of the trade: "Paper envelopes and type face must be considered as elements of packaging. Does an editor, faced with two alternately useable manuscripts, select the one with the most visual appeal? That question cannot be answered. Yet, if it happens to you only once in two years, the return will justify the use of top materials. Use twenty-pound bond of high rag content. Have an attractive cover-letter form printed. Have your own mailing labels printed."

On files and records: "A writer's file is supposed to: a. Give the current status of each completed work. b. Show what rights have been sold or retained. . . . You can keep data on three by five cards in a much handier way than in a box file. Victor, which I believe is owned by Remington-Rand, puts out expensive visible book files. . . ."

On business relationships: "The first relationship is, of course, with magazine editors. In order to keep this relationship on a healthy basis we must be able to analyze it from the editor's point of view. . . . Follow what [your agent] says to the letter. Give the relationship a chance to function. His monetary motives are aligned with yours and he has forgotten more about publishing than you will learn."

The article goes on for more than seven thousand words. Mac-Donald may have been seduced by what he called "the creative act itself . . . a confusing, emotionally exhausting, nerve frazzling process," but he never lost sight of his business education. That's why he wrote so little science fiction in his pulp days. "For a 3000 word pulp fantasy, there may be only two possible markets," he wrote. "A 4000 word detective short can appeal to twelve or fourteen markets." And, he said, never specialize. "The last two years show very nicely what *did* happen to specialized writers. A man selling exclusively to Street and Smith pulps had the floor kicked out from under him overnight. A man selling air-war saw a market buying forty yarns a month shrink down to a market that can buy six or eight a month.

Western writers are seeing a shrinkage. A spread over all types is your insurance."

In the summer, when the heat and redneck tourists engulfed Florida, the MacDonalds went to north to Piseco. They returned in the fall and moved into a larger house, and John resumed his routine. Only now there was a difference—he didn't notice it at first but it would change his life forever. The pulps were dying.

Actually, the death knell for the pulp magazines began during World War II. Paper was rationed during the war, and that drove publishers to kill the marginal or quirky publications. Fewer magazines meant fewer stories, and that meant not as many writers could make a living. By the end of the war almost all the titles featured science fiction, westerns, or detective stories. But it was more than the war that ended the era of the pulps. In June 1939 a publisher named Robert Fair de Graff started Pocket Books, America's first paperback imprint. It was the beginning of a revolution. Originally, paperback books were all reprints—the first Pocket Book was *Lost Horizons*, which had been a best-seller in 1935. Other titles included plays by Shakespeare, a mystery by Agatha Christie, and a children's book titled *Bambi*. In the beginning, the paperbacks were high-minded, with as much emphasis on education as on entertainment. All that changed, however, when other publishers got into the act—Avon in 1941, Popular Library in 1942, Dell in 1943, Bantam in 1945, Graphic in 1948, Pyramid, Lion, Checker, and New American Library in 1949. In 1945 there were 112 paperback titles in print; by 1951 there were 866. For the most part, it was still a reprint business. And then along came Wilford H. Fawcett and Gold Medal Books.

The paperback imprint grew out of a Minneapolis magazine empire created by dirty jokes. After World War I, Fawcett, who had been an Army captain in the war and a police reporter for the *Minneapolis Journal* before that, put out a mimeographed sheet of off-color jokes called *Captain Billy's Whiz Bang*. Originally, Captain Billy meant his magazine to be for a few ex-servicemen, but it caught on and by 1923 had a circulation of 425,000. Fawcett's smut magazine was so successful that in 1926 he brought out another, *Smokehouse Monthly*, to compete with it. Captain Billy's wife, Antoinette Fisher

Fawcett, was not to be outdone. When she and Captain Billy divorced in 1932, she started the *Calgary Eye Opener* to compete with him. Meanwhile, Captain Billy was branching out. He started *True Confessions* magazines in 1922, followed that with a handful of pulps (*Triple X, Battle Stories, Screen Secrets*), and began publishing so many magazines that in the years before World War II he had more than sixty titles. He also moved his business operations to Connecticut and his editorial offices to New York City. He designed his magazines for newsstand sales, not subscriptions.

Captain Billy died in 1940, but his sons kept the Fawcett empire profitable with new titles like *True* and *Family Circle*, although World War II paper shortages caused them to suspend forty-nine magazines and keep only fourteen.

In 1945, Ian Ballantine, the head of the British-owned Penguin Books in America, decided to set up his own company. When he did, he took the Curtiss Circulating Company contract with him. Curtiss, the owner of *The Saturday Evening Post* and *The Ladies' Home Journal*, had been distributing Penguins to newsstands all over America. Now they would be the distributor of Ballantine's new Bantam books. When that happened, Penguin arranged for the Fawcetts to become its distributor. Two years later, Fawcett began to distribute another paperback line, New American Library. And how the money rolled in. Fawcett wanted to start its own line of paperbacks, but was hamstrung by a contract with New American Library that said Fawcett could not compete for reprint rights. Fine, the Fawcett boys said. So they did something that was unheard of in those days—they commissioned paperback originals and marketed them under a new imprint, Gold Medal Books. At first, Fawcett published nonfiction books made up of material taken from its magazines. The books had titles like *The Best of True Magazine* and *What Today's Women Should Know About Marriage and Sex*.

The editorial Director of the new Fawcett Gold Medal line was Ralph Daigh, who had been with Fawcett almost continuously since he graduated from college in 1930. Gold Medal Books paid writers a $2,000 advance for each title. Initial printing was 200,000. When the print run was increased to 300,000, the author's advance became

$3,000. For the most part, Gold Medal Books were category titles—
westerns, thrillers, and mysteries. For the westerns, Daigh found
Louis L'Amour. For mysteries and thrillers, he discovered John D.
MacDonald.

MacDonald had written a detective novella, *The Brass Cupcake*, for
the pulps, but his agent, Joseph Shaw, saw a chance to make more
money if the story was lengthened and offered to Fawcett as a Gold
Medal original. MacDonald said years later that it was not just a matter of padding the manuscript to make it longer, but of recasting it in
another form. Still, he thought the form was determined by money.
"One of the clichés of the writing profession is to say that content
determines the length," MacDonald said years later in an interview
with University of South Florida professor Ed Hirshberg. "This is
only part true. The market *and* the content dictate the length. There
are many published novels which probably would have been more
successful as short stories, or if they had been kept to 25,000 to
30,000 words in length, although the novelette or novella is not really
marketable in this era."

MacDonald's first novel was about an insurance investigator, Cliff
Bartells, a former cop who has been thrown off the police force of
Florence City, the small west Florida town where he lived. Hammett's Sam Spade got bounced from the DA's office for insubordina-
tion; MacDonald's Bartells was more self-righteous—he quit because
of police corruption. It's not an exceptional novel. An old woman
comes to town for a vacation carrying $750,000 worth of jewelry.
She gets bumped off. Her niece comes to town, and Bartells hooks
up with the niece, solves the murder, and gets the girl. But while the
plot of *The Brass Cupcake* was not much, MacDonald established one
of his trademarks in this first book—he digressed. Bartells talks about
Florida:

> Before the war Florence City was a quiet, middle-class
> resort. But the war expanded the field of endeavor. Gambling
> houses, breast of guinea hen under glass, seagoing yachts from
> Havana, seventy dollar night-club tabs for a quiet dinner for

two—with the appropriate wines of course. The bakers from Dayton and the shoe clerks from Buffalo still came down, but the high rentals had shoved them inland off the beaches, in as far as the swamps and the mangroves and the orange juice factories.

A new group had taken over the beaches. Middle-aged ladies with puffy faces and granite eyes brought down whole stables of hundred-dollar call girls, giggling like a sorority on a social welfare trip. But the rate was bumped to two hundred to cover the higher cost of accommodations and the traveling expenses. Sleek little men with hand-blocked sports shirts strolled around and made the Bogart gestures.

Boom town, fun town, money town, rough town. Lay it on the line. You can't take it with you. Next year comes the H bomb. Put it on the entertainment account.

MacDonald's insurance investigator was tough, but he was no sadist. He left that to Mickey Spillane, the comic book writer and circus acrobat who dominated American crime writing in the 1950s. For the most part, Spillane's sadism was directed against women. But treating women badly was a convention of hard-boiled writing. Dashiell Hammett's Sam Spade used women as commodities, and Raymond Chandler's Philip Marlowe hated them so much that a room almost had to be fumigated after a woman left. But Spillane's sadism was deeper than either Hammett's or Chandler's. Part of it was the times. Sadism, particularly against women, was everywhere in the late 1940s and early 1950s. And nowhere was it more apparent than in the successor to the pulps, inexpensive men's magazines. Theodore Peterson, author of *Magazines in the Twentieth Century*, wrote:

Sadism, masochism, fetishism, perversions, all were implicit in the prose and pictures of a covey of magazines—*Night and Day, Wink, Brief, Paris Life, Keyhole, Eye, Pepper, Candid Whirl,*

Cover Girl Models, Scope, Picture Fun, Flirt, Eyeful, Beauty Parade. The female with an enlarged bosom was one of their staples . . . but when she posed in the nude or its approximation, it was not always with simple seductiveness. She wore stilt heels or let her long hair drape her body; she was enmeshed in chains or covered with gilt and powdered glass which, the caption pointed out, could "cut into the skin." She wrestled lion cubs and vicious dogs. She was shown being flogged, being frozen in a cake of ice, being shot from a cannon. Alongside such photographs were articles and picture spreads of men who had died in racing accidents or prison breaks, who earned their living surviving dynamite blasts or wrestling matches with alligators, who exposed vice or profited from it. Some of the magazines exploited sex and sadism in alternate features as their editorial pattern. They represented a world of morbid desires and dark, seething repressions.

The same readers who bought these magazines were the audience for Spillane's books. And it was a hell of an audience. His first book, *I, the Jury,* sold more than six million copies. Naturally, MacDonald the businessman knew hard-boiled would sell, and so there's a hint of Spillane imitation in *The Brass Cupcake.* But there's a big difference. Spillane's Mike Hammer kills his women. MacDonald's Cliff Bartells plans to marry his, at least after he convinces her he wants to be a cop even though she has all the money in the world.

After *The Brass Cupcake* was published in October 1951, MacDonald acknowledged his debt to Spillane in a parody of the former comic book writer's style that he sent to Dick Carroll, his editor at Gold Medal Books:

It was one of those afternoons when the greasy sunshine flooded Third Avenue like a men's room with a broken john.

She came out of the alley lapping at her juicy red lips with her pointed spicy tongue.

I shouldered her out of the way and blew the smoke off the end of the rod. He lay there in the alley and he was dead. I don't know why I did it but I aimed at him and blew off the other half of his greasy skull. It was a dirty world full of dirty people and I was sick of it. I felt the crazy anger welling up in me. He lay there in the alley and he was dead. She rubbed her thorax against me. I blasted his teeth out through the back of his neck.

Pat shouldered her out of the way. He was picking his greasy teeth with a broken match. A smart cop, that Pat.

"I knew you was going to go kill crazy again, Mike. This has got to stop."

I knew it couldn't stop. Not while there were people left in the world. Dirty people in a dirty world. I had to kill all that I could. Even if they lifted my license. He lay there in the greasy alley in the greasy Third Avenue sunshine and he was dead, and I was glad I'd shot his greasy skull apart.

"Mike, Mike," she gasped, stabbing her tongue unto my ear. It tickled.

I fingered her haunch, then shoved her away hard. She looked at me with those wide spicy hot eyes.

"You haven't fooled me a bit," I rasped. Then I laughed. My laugh sounded like two Buicks rubbing together.

She knew what I meant. She said, "Look what I can give you, Mike." She unlatched her Maidenform.

I looked at it. I felt the sadness, the regret. But the anger was there. Pat sucked on the greasy match. He turned his head. He was a good cop.

The first shot nailed her against the alley wall. While she was slipping, her eyes still pleading with me, I wrote my initials across her gut with hot lead. It was tricky shooting.

Pat sighed. He said, "Mike, the D.A.'ll have something to say about this."

"Screw the D.A.," I said. My voice sounded like a lead nickel in a stone juke box.

We walked out of the alley, down through the soggy sunshine. Somehow, I felt very tired.

MacDonald's total output for 1950 was fifty-four stories and one
novel. The next year it would be twenty-nine stories and four novels. The times were changing, and so was MacDonald. For five years
he had written pulp fiction. Now he was a paperback writer. But so
far, about the only difference in the two was length. There were no
reviews, no book signings. There was, however, an article about him
in the *Clearwater Sun*. "Beach Resident Proves All Writers Are Not
Screwballs," the headline proclaimed.

In late 1950, John met Richard Glendinning, another of Captain
Joseph Shaw's clients, who lived in Sarasota. Before World War II,
Glendinning has been on the advertising staff for *Vogue* and then
associate editor of *Country Life*. During the war he had been a lieutenant commander in the Navy. When the fighting ended he moved
to Sarasota and worked as a freelance writer. Like MacDonald, he
was a paperback writer, and like MacDonald he worked for Fawcett
Gold Medal Books. Glendinning convinced MacDonald to leave
Clearwater and move to Sarasota. It was quieter there, the town was
not overrun with tourists, and Johnny, who would be in the seventh
grade, would have the benefit of better schools.

It sounded good to John, and he and Dordo decided to move.
They put down a deposit on a house Glendinning found for them,
but before John could start putting things in boxes, he had to finish
Murder for the Bride, his second book. Just as he was not immune to
the early-fifties influence of Spillane, he was also not immune to the
anti-Communist mania that was sweeping the country, and it showed
in *Murder for the Bride*. The book is the story of a man who unknow-
ingly marries a Communist secret agent, who is killed only a week or
two after their honeymoon. When the bereaved husband searches for
her murderer, he finds a nest of Reds, the standard menace for a popular novel in the era of Senator Joseph McCarthy. Getting the Reds
was almost as sure a path to publication as the small-town sex of Pey-
ton Place would be five years later.

With *Murder for the Bride* finished, John, Dordo, and Johnny moved their possessions to Sarasota to store them before leaving for the summer at his cabin in Piseco, New York. But there was a surprise waiting. There was no house. The man who took the deposit he had paid had taken the money and run. MacDonald panicked. Then he got in touch with Randy Hagerman, an old New York newspaperman who lived in Sarasota. Hagerman had a house for rent on Casey Key. John took it sight unseen.

CHAPTER 7

The town John D. MacDonald moved to in 1951 was unlike any other in Florida. Like the rest of the state, Sarasota was created by big money during the Gilded Age. But there was a big difference. Tampa and Miami were built by railroads. Sarasota was built by elephants. In 1905, John Ringling, one of the Ringling Brothers of circus fame, decided to move to Florida. At first, Ringling thought he wanted to live in Tarpon Springs, a small fishing community north of Tampa. Tarpon Springs, as it turned out, didn't want anything to do with the Ringlings, no matter how many elephants they owned. "The rich sportsmen wintering there formed a small, closed community," writes David C. Weeks in *Ringling: The Florida Years.* "This exclusive company was cool to 'new money' and disinclined to accept circus people." In other words, they thought John and his wife, Mabel, were cheap carny trash.

The Ringlings moved away on their yacht, the *Louise II,* and sailed down the Gulf Coast to Sarasota, where Charles Thompson, one of the Ringling circus managers, lived. Thompson and Ralph Caples, a former railroad man and advertising agent, talked John Ringling and his brother, Charles, into moving to Sarasota. Nobody there would high-hat the circus kings. The two brothers moved to the small Florida fishing town in 1911. In 1927, Sarasota became the winter quarters for the circus. From then on, the city would never be the same. According to David Weeks:

The immediate effects of the circus move were expected; new jobs constructing buildings and rail lines at the old fairgrounds, the influx of a winter crew and the attraction of tourists. In the following decade as many as 100,000 visitors came each winter. The circus brought an alien culture for this Southern town. Sarasotans found themselves living among performers and families (many of them European) whose traditions and customs contrasted, sometimes vividly, with local life styles.

Sarasota, with its circus winter quarters and its collection of wild animals, became home to Florida's first theme park. Towns like Daytona and Miami and St. Petersburg had beaches. Sarasota had a show every day during the peak winter season. It was a feature not overlooked by Walt Disney four decades later.

Yet John Ringling was more than a showman. He was also becoming a major collector of European art. The same year he brought the circus to Sarasota he began plans for the Ringling Museum of Art. Much of the huge Italianate museum was built by circus employees when they were out of work during the winter. Three years later, in 1930, the museum was completed and Ringling's collection of paintings by Titian, Rubens, and other Renaissance and baroque artists were moved into the twenty-one galleries the building contained. Ringling did not stop with the museum. A year after the museum opened, the School of Fine and Applied Arts of the John and Mabel Ringling Museum of Arts opened. So this small, sleepy fishing village on the west coast of Florida was turned into an entertainment center and an artist colony by a circus magnate. No one would ever think of him as cheap carny trash again. And Sarasota's reputation would change over the years. It would become a subtropical fusion of high culture and low. Masterwork paintings coexisted comfortably with the rigging and nets of the Flying Concellos. Portraits by Velásquez hung in the museum while garish banners by Snap Wyatt advertising the Rubber Skin Man ruffled in the breeze only a few blocks away. There was also a strange democracy in Sarasota, missing in the Florida towns that has been reinvented by the robber barons. Flagler's Palm Beach and Plant's Tampa were mostly for their rich friends. In Sarasota, the Human Cannon Ball might live next door to an attorney, and Prince Paul, a dwarf who played the Mayor of Munchkin Town in *The Wizard of Oz*, might discuss the stock market with the doctor who lived up the street. When everybody is so different from everyone else it makes both conformity and hatred more difficult.

In any other small Florida city, a group of writers would be the town oddballs. A few years earlier, a small colony of pulp writers spooked the other residents of Anna Maria, Florida, when they walked up and down the beach plotting murder mysteries and spicy sex stories. But in Sarasota, it was different. A bunch of writers seemed as respectable as Rotarians in a town populated by clowns and sword swallowers and wild animal trainers.

The writers' colony at Sarasota was a post–World War II phenomenon. Like Sarasota itself, the mixture was both high culture and low. Budd Schulberg, the author of *What Makes Sammy Run?* and later of the screenplay for *On the Waterfront,* lived in Sarasota, and so did Leslie Charles McFarlane, who under the name Franklin W. Dixon wrote eighteen Hardy Boys mysteries and as Carolyn Keene wrote four books in the Dana Girls series. Eric Hodgins, the author of *Mr. Blandings Builds His Dream House*, was in Sarasota in the early fifties, and so was Joseph Hayes, a paperback writer who scored big with *The Desperate Hours.*

But the dean of the writers who lived in and around Sarasota in the 1950s was MacKinlay Kantor, an old tramp newspaper reporter who worked on papers in Iowa and Chicago, then moved west to Hollywood and wrote screenplays for MGM, Paramount, 20th Century Fox, and Samuel Goldwyn. When World War II came along he became a war correspondent covering the Royal Air Force. When the war ended, he joined the New York police force as a uniformed cop, worked there a couple of years, and then, reverting to his previous occupation, went to Korea as a war correspondent.

Along with these odd jobs, Kantor wrote novels. In 1934 he wrote *Long Remember*, about the Battle of Gettysburg; a year later he wrote *The Voice of Bugle Ann*, about a foxhound and her master; in 1936 he wrote *Arouse and Beware*, about Yankees escaping from a Confederate prison; then he wrote *The Romance of Rosey Ridge*, a love story of post–Civil War Missouri. Other Kantor novels included *The Noise of Their Wings*, about passenger pigeons; *Cuba Libre,* about a Cuban revolutionist; *Gentle Annie*, a novel of Oklahoma at the turn of the century; *Happy Land*, the life of a boy killed in World War II; *Wicked War*, a novel about Western cattle wars; and *Signal Thirty-two*, about a New York City policeman. In 1956 his novel *Andersonville* would win the Pulitzer Prize. Yet Kantor had no grand ideas about his prose.

"My stories have appeared in an appalling number of magazines, sublime, ridiculous, penny dreadful," Kantor once said. "I used to write a great deal of stuff for the pulp detective and crime story magazines, in the years when I had to make my living that way, and I don't think my rather complicated talents were harmed in the least. The severe routine of such endeavor stimulated my sense of plot and construction, which needed such stimulation very badly indeed. I was well aware that the stuff I wrote had little value except that in most cases it made entertaining narrative."

For better or worse, Kantor would become John D. MacDonald's mentor. The old man could be maddening. He was the most right-wing of conservatives. Hemingway once said his career would go better if he would resign from the Confederate Air Force. According to his son, Tim, he constantly referred to Martin Luther King as Martin Luther Coon. "Working with the New York cops in the later forties, when he was writing *Signal Thirty-two*, he not only adopted the prejudice they owned, he bathed in it," Tim Kantor wrote in his memoir, *My Father's Voice*. "He smelt as much of prejudice as he did of the cigars he loved to smoke. . . . *Nigger, Jig, Black Bastard* or *Bitch. Goddamn PRs* (for Puerto Ricans). *Spick.* I heard all those terms—he *used* all those terms—to the point of sickness." But still, Sarasota was his turf, and if you were a writer and lived there, you had to deal with him. Besides, there were times when he could be charming. He was tall and lean and had a pencil-thin mustache like Ronald Colman, and some said he knew the words to all the popular songs written since the turn of the century.

The MacDonalds moved into their first Sarasota home, on Casey Key, in September 1951. They enrolled Johnny in the Out of Door School, an exclusive elementary school with an exotic reputation. It was considered strange because most of its classes were held outside, and because when the school was started in 1924, the founders encouraged nude bathing. Five months later the MacDonalds bought a house on Siesta Key, where they would live for the next seventeen years. In August, MacDonald's science fiction novel *Wine of the Dreamers* was published. According to MacDonald, it was "a symbolic novel of how when original purposes are forgotten, the uses of ritual can be destructive." The copywriters for Fawcett described the book as "pale laboratory creatures living in a remote sealed off world. Their game, their religion, their release, is to dream and their dreams carry across a galaxy." It was MacDonald's first science fiction novel, and his first book to attract critics. Specifically, it attracted William Anthony Parker White.

White, writing under the pseudonym H. H. Holmes, was the science fiction critic for the *New York Herald Tribune*. Using the name Anthony Boucher he was the mystery critic for *The New York Times* and *Ellery Queen's Mystery Magazine*. He was also the editor of the anthology *Great American Detective Stories* and the author of a handful of mystery and science fiction novels. But it was as H. H. Holmes, writing for the *Herald Tribune*, that he first mentioned MacDonald. In his column for October 14, 1951, Holmes wrote, "The story is smoothly and readably told despite a number of implausibilities in detail and in basic content which kept this reviewer . . . from maintaining any suspension of disbelief." In fact, if it hadn't been for White's column, MacDonald might have gone through those early paperback years with no national reviews at all.

MacDonald's next two books, *Judge Me Not* and *Weep for Me*, came and went in critical silence. He should have been grateful. *Judge Me Not* is memorable only because MacDonald used the name of Dordo's first husband, Teed, for the protagonist. The book ends with a sort of Armageddon in a whorehouse, a vision of the apocalypse matched only in the Bible or first novels by writers from the Iowa Writers' Workshop. *Weep For Me* was so bad that years later Mac-Donald asked Fawcett to take it out of print. "It should die quietly in the back of used paperback book nooks," MacDonald said years later. "It's really quite a bad book . . . imitation James M. Cain . . . with some gratuitous and unmotivated scenes."

Day-to-day life for MacDonald was about the same during these early days in Sarasota as it had been in Clearwater. He was up every morning, ate some breakfast, and then wrote until noon, took a break for lunch, and returned to the typewriter until five. Then he had a few martinis and dinner, and went to bed about ten. It was the monotonous life of a man who fancied himself a writing machine. But there was one exception. Every Friday at noon, MacDonald got up from his typewriter, got in his car, and drove to the Plaza Restaurant for the weekly luncheon meeting of an informal group of Sarasota writers.

The meetings began in downtown Sarasota in December 1952 with a small luncheon at the Plaza Restaurant in the Orange Blossom Hotel. MacKinlay Kantor was the host, and the guests included Richard Glendinning, the Gold Medal mystery writer, and Joe Millard, another Gold Medal author who novelized the Clint Eastwood spaghetti westerns—*A Fistful of Dollars, For a Few Dollars More*, and *The Good, the Bad, and the Ugly*. Kantor was leaving for Spain in a few weeks, but he told Glendinning he thought the meetings should continue. In late December, after Kantor was on his way to Europe, Glendinning circulated a memo:

> Certain dubious characters, who thinly disguise laziness under a fierce, false beard of authorship, met a few weeks ago at the Plaza Restaurant to inflict fearful ear-bangings upon each other. It was later unanimously agreed that such tedium should not be allowed to die, and that further sessions, dedicated to no useful purpose, be held on a regular schedule.

It was to be a dutch-treat luncheon, and the meeting would be every other Friday at one P.M. It was an informal gathering—there were to be no bylaws, constitutions, or charitable contributions. No papers were to be presented, no book reviews discussed, and no writers workshops. During the first meeting the frequency of meeting was changed to every Friday.

It was MacDonald who suggested the group meet every week. "They wanted to meet once a month at first," he said in an interview in 1983. "But I told them that was lousy, that I could never remember which week to come. Once a week, I could remember." MacDonald attended the first meeting and, except when he was out of town, went to the luncheons every week until he died.

In later years, this nameless writers' group was often compared to the Algonquin Round Table—the group of writers who met every week during the 1920s for wit and whiskey. But there was one big difference: Dorothy Parker was a member of the Algonquin group. She wouldn't have been allowed at the table in Sarasota. It was a boys' club—no girls allowed. Lillian Hellman was once in Sarasota with S. J. Perelman. He was invited, and he asked if he could bring Hellman. He was told no, and he said that if that was the way things were, he wouldn't come either.

The group returned to the Plaza after a few weeks and stayed there until the place went out of business. The meetings of the group were filled with equal parts serious drinking, loud storytelling, and liar's poker, a game played with the serial numbers on dollar bills. "Three rounds are played each week," an article in the *Sarasota Herald-Tribune* said. "To the uninitiated onlooker the game seems hopelessly complicated, and more than a few of the diners at nearby tables cast bewildered looks as they watch [the writers] pull dollar bills from their wallets and holler out bids of 'six eights' or 'seven twos.' The real skill involves bluffing about the digits of your own bill and discerning who among your opponents might be lying as well." Losers buy the drinks, and at the end of the year a plaque is given to the worst liar—the man forced to buy the most rounds of drinks. The game always began with a toast to the memory of Leslie McFarlane, the man who wrote the Hardy Boys books. In his will McFarlane left money to buy the first round of drinks whenever the group met.

In September, Kantor returned and the club became his. Years later, Larry L. King, who had lived in Sarasota while he was working on his novel *The One-Eyed Man*, wrote that Kantor was "the dean of a sizable Sarasota writing colony. He headed up a club that lunched each Friday." MacDonald never challenged him, but they were not always on the best of terms. "I knew MacKinlay Kantor during the final 30 years of his life," MacDonald wrote Robert Gottlieb, who was head of Alfred Knopf in 1985.

We were friends, but not what you'd call real warm friends. We were always a little stiff legged circling each other. I think that was my fault. I have a tendency to get a little more smart-ass than the amenities require. In maybe the fourth year of our friendship—he too lived on Siesta Key—he kept asking me to join a little group which would convene at his house so he could read to them from the book he was working on at the time. I kept making excuses which grew ever more lame, and I think he should have put a wet finger in the wind and stopped asking. I guess he thought he was bestowing a gift and could not understand why I kept rejecting it. Finally I lost patience and said—to paraphrase—"Mack, dammit, I write prose to be read to oneself, not aloud. I have been trapped into a couple of readings by other writers. Never again. It becomes the smirking creator dragging the humble barefoot half dressed concubine through the streets of the cheering village, and I find it an embarrassment. Thank you, but no." This created a monstrous huff, or snit, or whatever, which he continued for a few years by now and then coming to me at the weekly writers' lunch table with an imitation of friendly fatherly interest, saying, "John, why don't you get off this mystery crap and write a real novel with some depth and some substance." This was an almost feminine way of getting back at me for a fancied insult.

In the meantime, MacDonald kept writing. In 1952, Fawcett published *The Damned*. Nobody reviewed it, even though it carried a cover blurb that said, "I wish I had written this book—Mickey Spillane." At that time MacDonald had never even met Spillane. "Ralph Daigh, who was editorial director at Fawcett . . . loaned Spillane a set of galleys," MacDonald remembered later in an interview, "and Mickey brought them back in and he said casually, "That's a good book. I wish I had written it.' Ralph wrote it out on a card and said, 'Here, Mick, sign it.' Mick said, 'Yes, I'll sign it.' . . . When the book came out, Spillane's editors and lawyers and agents descended like a cloud of locusts on Ralph saying, 'You can't do this. Spillane never gives a blurb.' He said, 'Gentlemen, I have it in writing and signed by Mr. Spillane and I have it dated. Now what do you want to do?'"

The Damned sold two million copies. MacDonald was beginning to find his fictional voice. Geoffrey O'Brien wrote in *Hardboiled America*:

> Gold Medal's greatest find was John D. MacDonald . . . [who] proved himself from the start the kind of perfect story-teller who makes all other aesthetic considerations meaning-less. To read him is to hear a spoken voice—pausing, digressing, joking, all the while drawing you into the yarn. It's not that the story is so remarkable; you've heard some-thing like it before, you may even recognize chunks of it from another of his books, and after a while, it will blend into all the others. The anecdote may be utterly banal. It's the *voice* that grabs you, the sure rhythms with which it measures out its story. And it can be any kind of story. . . .

The Damned is a novel as hard-boiled as a nineteen-minute egg. The story take place at a ferry crossing across the Rio Conchos from Matamoros in Mexico to Brownsville, Texas. The ferry breaks down, and the novel is the story of the people who wait in line to cross from one country to another. Here's how MacDonald describes the death of a bullfighter's girlfriend and then the bullfighter:

> And she had to have a light on, because she was one of those who had to have a light on, and when she sud-denly gasped and stiffened under him, Del turned his head and saw the bullfighter standing there, face twisted, eyes gone

dead, aiming one of the guns they had used underwater. The short spear with the harpoon on the end fitted into a slotted tube, and fat rubber bands slammed it out of the tube. As the rubber bands made their vicious whacking sound, Del threw himself up and back, and the thing made a quick gleam in the lamplight and chomped into Amparo with a sound that was both hard and wet. It hit right under her left breast and she half turned toward the bullfighter. She made the smallest of gasps and put both hands on the shaft and pulled at it very delicately, but the barbed head had turned inside her, precisely as it was designed to do. She coughed in a most delicate and ladylike way, and shivered just a bit, and died very quietly, as though to make up by discreetness during her last moments for twenty years of bounding lustiness.

As Del came off the bed, the bullfighter hurled the gun itself and Del eeled away from it and came in fast, thinking only of putting the character out of action long enough to give him time to think. He caught the face with stone fists, and with all the precision he wanted, but with too much manic behind the blows and too much force, and the kiss-off punch lifted the bullfighter's feet from the floor and the first part of him to hit the floor had been the back of his head, and the floor, unhappily, had been tile. When Del rolled him over and fingered the back of his head, he felt the sickening looseness. Some piece of the bone must have cut into the brain in a strange way, because during the time of dying the lean bullfighter legs made the same hesitant running motions as a sleeping dog chasing rabbits up the dream hills. The bulls come out of the tunnel into the sun so black that they look like a hole cut from the night. And the running legs could not carry Larra away from the horns of this last bull.

So he had turned out the light and locked the door and later tossed the key into some roadside cactus. . . .

In New York, and in literary Sarasota, for that matter, MacDonald's literary and sales triumph didn't go unnoticed, but they were hardly the main topic of conversation. Paperback books were being declared as big a menace to the American people as Communism, and publishers and authors were holding their breath, waiting to see what would happen next.

In May 1952, one month before *The Damned* was published, the Speaker of the U.S. House of Representatives appointed the Select Committee on Current Pornographic Materials. The committee's first hearing was six months later, but it was apparent that the "pornography" Congress was investigating was paperback books. John B. Keenan, the director of public safety for the state of New Jersey, had already labeled paperback books and their publishers tools of the Red Menace. "If the Communists are not behind this drive to flood the nation with obscenity, to weaken the moral fiber of our youth and debauch our adults, then it is only because the greedy businessmen are carrying the ball for them," Keenan said. E. C. Gathings, a Democrat from Kansas, was the chairman of the Congressional committee, and before even one witness was called, he was already calling paperbacks "the kind of filthy sex books sold at the corner store which are affecting the youth of our country." Paperback publishers were accused of "the dissemination of artful appeals to sensuality, immorality, filth, perversion and degeneracy." The first witness before the committee was the Reverend Thomas Fitzgerald, a Catholic priest who was director of the National Organization for Decent Literature. He said paperback books caused "moral damage" and the "loss of ideals" that led to juvenile delinquency.

Then Ralph Daigh, John D. MacDonald's editor at Fawcett Gold Medal Books, took the stand. The Gold Medal book that outraged the committee was *Women's Barracks* by Toreska Torres. Daigh told the committee that *Women's Barracks* had sold more than a million copies and that "good books" sold millions of copies. "Good books," he said. "No particular type."

"You think it compares favorably with Shakespeare's books?" a congressman asked.

"I don't think that is the question," Daigh answered, "I think both are eminently entitled to publication, exposure to the public."

"And the book sells for a quarter," the congressman sneered.

"Yes sir," Daigh answered. "And Shakespeare sells for a quarter in some editions, too."

But it wasn't just tales of lesbian love like *Women's Barracks* that bothered the congressmen. MacKinlay Kantor was also labeled a pornographer for his novel *Don't Touch Me*. Representative Edward Rees, a Kansas Republican, was particularly hard on Kantor and his book when he questioned John O'Connor, the chairman of the board of Bantam Books. The question was whether children should read *Don't Touch Me*.

REES: I am not talking about MacKinlay Kantor; I am talking about the material in this book. Do you think it is good for folks to read?

O'CONNOR: If they wish to read it.

REES: Do you think it is good for children?

O'CONNOR: I think the only question is whether it is pornographic

REES: That is not the only question. I am just asking you, do you think children ought to read this book?

O'CONNOR: I don't think I would give it to my daughter to read, for example, if that is the answer you want from me.

REES: Well, that is one answer, yes.

O'CONNOR: I don't think this particular book is one that is good for adolescents to read, no I don't.

REES: Do you think it is good for anybody to read? Do you think it is something that does a fellow good?

O'CONNOR: If a man wished to read it, why not, or a woman, an adult person.

REES: So you think it's all right to put that out?

O'CONNOR: I think so. Why not?

REES: Well, if you had read the thing you would know why not.

O'CONNOR: I have read it and I don't think . . .

REES: Do you like it?

O'CONNOR: No, I don't say I like it. I read a great many books. I read them professionally, so perhaps my opinion of a book would be different from your opinion as far as its . . .

REES: I am afraid it would be under these conditions. I am asking you now, do you think the book you have mentioned, *Don't Touch Me*, do you think that it is a good book to put out on the newsstands?
O'CONNOR: Would you let me make a statement of my opinion with respect to this book?
REES: Answer whether it is a good thing to put out on the newsstands for sale to the public.
O'CONNOR: For adults, why not?
REES: Because of the stuff that is in it.

The hearing lasted for five days. The congressmen railed against literature, they railed against the artists—many of whom came to the paperbacks when the pulp magazines closed—who painted the lurid covers for the paperbacks. And then it was over. And then it was forgotten. Except, really, it wasn't. Whatever respect paperbacks originally had was tarnished by the hearings. And although the alleged obscenity of paperback books slipped out of the columns of the newspapers, it never left some people's minds. Seventeen years later, it still plagued MacDonald. He wrote to his friend John Binns in 1969:

The other night I *did* blow up like a broken rocket. A man I have always thought rather pretentious and silly, and who sells mutual funds, greeted me when I walked into a party with the friendly question, "When is your next smutty book coming out?" Then he turned to the man next to him, a fellow I did not know, and said, "John makes a nice living writing dirty books." Maybe he was trying to be cute. I don't know and didn't care then and don't now. So I shook my head sadly and said, "You are sick. You must have sexual hangups that need professional attention. Incidentally, how many widows and orphans have you screwed lately, churning their accounts, rousting them from one fund into another at that nice eight percent in front?" While he got white as a sheet, I told his buddy that my acquaintance made a good living off innocent and unsuspecting investors. The stranger walked hastily away. I was threatened with suit. I told him to go right ahead and sue, but stay out of dark parking lots or I wouldn't leave him with enough teeth to pronounce "smutty."

If MacDonald's books were ever thought to be smutty, it must have been either because all paperback books were considered smutty or because of the paintings of half-dressed pneumatic women by Barrye Phillips that appeared on the first editions of his books. Because there is a secret about John D. MacDonald that is as amazing as the fact that Walt Disney could never draw Mickey Mouse. John D. MacDonald couldn't write a sex scene. "I am personally offended by books in which the author dabs in a bit of raw sexuality here and there to attract the pimpled trade," MacDonald said years later. "Nor do I think explicit or specific sex acts need be described. Everyone knows what they are. A friend of mind says it is like trying to write about Christmas. You bore the reader." For MacDonald, though, it was more than being unable to write erotic description. He couldn't even write dialogue between a man and a woman that wasn't stilted. Most of his man-woman scenes sound like something out of a 1947 Loretta Young movie—meaningless natterings filled with "darling," and "dear." It was even apparent to Minnesota high school student Dawn Parsell when she wrote him in 1980. "Did you ever notice how many times the men and women in your books call each other 'darling'?" she asked. "Yes," MacDonald answered, "and how often people throw up. A Chicago newsman called this to my attention and I gave him a bit part in *Copper,* darling. Darling is a useful form of address because it can carry a whole range of feeling from intense personal warmth to icy cynicism."

Still, his dialogue sounds as if it's out of *The Stranger, The Farmer's Daughter, The Bishop's Wife,* or other Hollywood pap Loretta Young had to struggle through.

The paperback hearings in 1952 might also explain why Mac-Donald always winced when he was referred to as a paperback writer. Perhaps "paperback" and its association by the congressmen with smut made him queasy. "I did a sufficient number of books for

Gold Medal to become classified as a paperback writer," MacDonald mused years later. "That always seemed to me to indicate some kind of fragility in the area of the spine. It did not matter at all that of my first twenty-five published books, thirteen were in hard cover before they were in paperbacks. I had become typecast."

In fact, MacDonald's next book, *Ballroom of the Skies*, was first published in hardback. The novel is set sometime after World War III, when the three most powerful nations on earth are Iran, Brazil, and India. As it turns out, the leaders of the Galactic Empire have always come from earth. In order to be a leader, it seems, a person must come from a strenuous background. And so earth is kept constantly at war to provide the stress necessary for leadership. Years later MacDonald said that his two science fiction novels, *Wine of the Dreamers* and *Ballroom of the Skies*, were companion pieces:

> The two novels . . . provide two congruent methods of accounting for all the random madness and unmotivated violence in our known world and two quite different answers as to why, with all our technology, we seem unable to move a fraction of an inch toward bettering the human condition and making of life a universally more rewarding experience. . . . Herein there are no bug-eyed monsters. . . . There are no lovelies being rescued by space explorers from giant insects who talk in clicks and carry disintegrators. No methane atmospheres. Nothing emerging from the evil swamps. Not even a single dutiful robot, harboring either electronic love or the cross-wired circuitry of rebellion. . . . These are more about people than things.

The truth is, John D. MacDonald was tired of writing science fiction. Although he still considered himself a generalist and prided himself that more than twenty of his novels were not suspense or crime books, *Ballroom of the Skies* was his last science fiction. He explained:

I think [science fiction] is a marvelous exercise of the imagination, as you can say things behind the scenes in science fiction that you wouldn't dare say in straight fiction. Don't tell this to any science fiction writer, for God's sake, but I got the feeling that it was a little too easy. You are cheating on reality. I remember I had an argument with MacKinlay Kantor . . . and I said to him, "You know, I have a problem when I want to define character. If I want to make a guy really stupid and excitable I have to *build* that," I said. "But you and those historical things—you can have him run into a room and say, 'They just fired on Fort Sumter and the whole thing will be over in two weeks!' and okay, you've lined your guy out as a stupid fellow.' It's almost the same kind of thing in science fiction. You can cheat, you can do a pretend history. . . . Contemporary reality is the most difficult thing to write about because we're all in the midst of a big cloud of dust and you hear the horses running by but you don't know who's winning."

For the most part, MacDonald's life wasn't much different from that of a middle-management executive at Kodak in Rochester. On Friday the Kodak executive went to the Rotary Club; MacDonald went to his writers' group. For a rebel who left home to pursue the bohemian and solitary craft of writing, he led a surprisingly middle-class life. Every summer he went back to New York State and stayed in his cabin at Piseco. Occasionally at Christmas he went north to see his parents. But mostly he worked. He went into his office at home and he sat at his desk and he wrote. And wrote. And wrote. Larry King, the author of *The Best Little Whorehouse in Texas* and *The One-Eyed Man*, remembers a sojourn in Sarasota while he was waiting to see the galley proofs for his first novel:

During the week those writers or artists who wished company flew outside their homes large "drinking flags." In the absence of such a banner, each homesteader was left to work

in peace until the Friday luncheon. By mid-week I usually
went cruising in the hope of spotting one or more welcom-
ing flags; only a couple of the older fellows, and John D. Mac-
Donald, failed to occasionally fly their flags during the week.
I later concluded this perhaps had something to do with
MacDonald and Kantor having published fifty-odd novels to
that point.

Other people might fly drinking flags; MacDonald sat at his desk
and he wrote. Johnny had appendicitis, and he and Dordo took him
to the hospital and suffered through the operation and brought him
home. And John sat at his desk and wrote. He hired an architect to
build a guesthouse at his home, and while it was being built he sat at
his desk and he wrote. He sat at his desk and he wrote *Dead Low Tide*
and *The Neon Jungle* and *Cancel All Our Vows* and *Contrary Pleasure*.
He enrolled Johnny in Oakwood School and then he came home
and sat at his desk and wrote *Area of Suspicion* and *A Bullet for Cinderella* and *Cry Hard, Cry Fast* and *Border Town Girl* and *Murder in the
Wind* and *Death Trap*. He had an operation for a hernia and a fibroid
tumor and he came home from the hospital and he sat at his desk and
he wrote *The Price of Murder* and *The Empty Trap*. He took some time
off and went to Cuernavaca with Dordo while Johnny went to
another part of Mexico and got typhoid fever and had to be taken to
the hospital in Mexico City. When he got well, John and Dordo
took him home and he entered Rollins College and John D. came
back to Sarasota and sat at his desk and wrote *A Man of Affairs* and
The Deceivers. He took a trip to New York, went on a cruise to the
Bahamas, and saw Johnny enrolled at the University of New Mexico
for a summer field course in archaeology and he came home and
then Dordo had an operation for a cyst and polyps in her breast. And
he took her to the hospital and brought her home and he sat at his
desk and wrote *The Soft Touch*.

Then on a 1957 Friday afternoon at the writers' group, after the
games of liar's poker ended and the drinking got serious, MacKinlay
Kantor made MacDonald a bet. And everything changed.

CHAPTER 8

MacKinlay Kantor was needling John D. again about the quality of his writing—about how all he wrote was mysteries and other paperback trash. When are you going to write a *real* book, John? he wanted to know.

It made MacDonald mad.

He looked at Kantor and guaranteed him that within thirty days he'd write a book that would be serialized in the magazines, be a book club selection, and be turned into a movie. But he made it more than just a guarantee. He bet Kantor $50 he could do it. Kantor took the bet. And John D. MacDonald went home and wrote *The Executioners*.

Kantor was wrong about the quality of MacDonald's writing, of course, but in a way he was right. Most of MacDonald's books in the first half of the 1950s were great industrial products. They established a franchise for him. People bought a John D. MacDonald novel off the spinner racks at a drugstore or from a newsstand in a bus station because of the author. The novel itself didn't matter. It could be a romance, a mystery, a thriller, some science fiction. As long as it was John D. MacDonald and had that narrative voice that can hook you after five minutes, it never disappointed. Readers bought John D. MacDonald books the way they buy Whitman's Samplers. People don't buy that famous yellow box of candy just for the Cherry Cordial or the Vermont Fudge. They hardly notice when the Malted Milk Caramel or the Peanut Butter Puff disappears from the collection. After all, it's the box, all the pieces in their variety, not each individual confection, that they like. It was the same with a John D. MacDonald novel—guaranteed to give you hours of pleasure, no dirty or embarrassing parts, and a good story with a satisfying ending. And you could finish the whole thing on a bus ride from Chicago to St. Louis. It would be a decade before Fawcett turned MacDonald's name into a logo, but that's what he was becoming. Buy a Mustang or a Fairlane, it's still a Ford. Read an attempt at the naturalist novel like *The Neon Jungle*, a romance like *Cancel All Our Vows*, or a thriller like *A Bullet for Cinderella*. All of them are different, and yet they are all the same, just as one MGM movie is like another but unlike a product from Warner Brothers. The British crime novelist and critic Julian Symons called them "production-line efficient fast-moving American thrillers." And yet Symons thought MacDonald stood out from the other industrialists of storytelling. "Behind the machined efficiency of the plotting . . . there are interesting ideas about the nature of corruption and the increasingly mechanical form of life in America," he wrote in *Mortal Consequences*, his history of detective stories and crime novels.

It was this machinelike efficiency that Kantor was trying to get MacDonald to overcome. He was trying to goad him into writing a good novel that would stand alone, not as just another product of the John D. MacDonald writing machine. Of course, MacDonald *was* writing fast-moving American thrillers, not mysteries. Even though Mickey Spillane's Mike Hammer still had his imitators—Richard Prather's Shell Scott, for example, or Michael Shayne, the detective created by Davis Dresser writing as Brett Halliday—the hard-boiled dick had become a parody of himself. Fred Astaire danced as a private eye in front of a backdrop of pulp magazines in *The Band Wagon* in 1953. Al Capp, the cartoonist who drew the comic strip Li'l Abner, created the comic bullet-riddled detective Fearless Fosdick at about the same time. The French film director Claude Chabrol wrote in 1955 in an article about detective stories on film:

Success creates the fashion, which in turn shapes the genre. What corresponded to the vogue for the detective story . . . was the creation of a genre which rapidly gave way, predictably, to mediocrity and slovenly formulae. . . . Misfortune willed that [it] should carry within it the seeds of its own destruction. Built as it was on the element of shock and surprise, it could only offer even the most imaginative of scriptwriters and the most conscientious of directors a very limited number of dramatic situations which, by force of repetition, ended up no longer producing either shock or surprise.

Enter the American thriller. A thriller is usually about an ordinary guy who gets caught up in a bad or evil situation by circumstances. He turns down the wrong street, hails the wrong cab, decides to try a new bar for an after-dinner drink, meets a new girl, or is mistaken for someone else. And things are never the same again.

The master of these thrillers was Cornell Woolrich, a New York novelist who went to Hollywood for a while, wrote for the movies and crafted the thriller form, then went back to New York to live with his mother and drink himself to death. Woolrich wrote a series of novels with "black" in the title—*The Bride Wore Black, The Black Curtain, Black Alibi, The Black Angel, The Black Path of Fear,* and *Rendezvous in Black*—that may have been one of the factors that gave film noir and the French novels called *série noire* their name, but also were the framework for the thriller. Set in seedy hotel rooms, cheap dance halls, run-down movie theaters and police station back rooms, Woolrich's novels are able to evoke "with awesome power the desperation of those who walk the city's darkened streets and the terror that lurks at noonday in commonplace settings," wrote crime novelist Francis Nevins, Jr. "Woolrich has no peers when it comes to describing a frightened little guy in a tiny apartment with no money, no job, a hungry wife and children and anxiety eating him like a cancer." Twenty-one of Woolrich's novels and short stories, including *Rear Window, The Bride Wore Black, Deadline at Dawn,* and *The Night Has a Thousand Eyes,* were made into movies.

There were others who wrote thrillers—writers like Dorothy B. Hughes, David Goodis, and Patricia Highsmith—but it was Woolrich who perfected the form. Most of the authors who wrote thrillers set their novels in the city, where dark streets and giant shadows added to the feeling of paranoia and doom. It took John D. MacDonald to bring that fear out into the sunlight, past the city-limit signs, and into the suburbs.

The Executioners was the first time MacDonald had written about the suburbs. It was only natural he would set the novel there. America was becoming a suburban nation. Ever since the development of Levittown on Long Island in the postwar 1940s, Americans turned their dreams to suburbia. City life was frightening and dark, filled with bad people. The suburbs were clean and white and bright. You could have a lawn, just like the rich people at Newport. You could buy a station wagon, you could join a country club and become an Episcopalian. You could buy a grill and cook steaks and drink martinis in the quiet of your own backyard. So Americans moved by droves into the new subdivisions. They wanted to start over again, away from the dirty pavement and cheap apartments of the city. But John D. MacDonald showed these new suburbanites the truth of heavyweight champion Joe Louis's words: you can run but you can't hide.

Two things make *The Executioners* work—the villain and his crime. The villain is Max Cady and his crime is stalking. The novel's protagonist, Sam Bowden, is a successful lawyer with a wife and two children who live in a fine suburban house, own a station wagon and a boat, and enjoy the respect of the community. Cady is an ex-con who got sent up for thirteen years for beating and raping a fourteen-year-old girl. In his trial, Bowden was the chief witness against Cady. It was his testimony that sent Cady to the pen. And now Cady was out of jail and he was in Harper, where Sam Bowden lived. Cady was going to make up for those thirteen years by stalking Bowden and his family. According to MacDonald's description of Cady, the man is barely human: "[Sam] remembered how he had looked in court. Like an animal. Sullen, vicious and dangerous. And physically powerful. . . . Dark hair grew low on his forehead. Heavy mouth and jaw. Small brown eyes set in deep and simian sockets. . . ."

This is the creep who starts hanging around the Bowden family, day and night. Sam tells his wife, Carol, what it was like when he first saw him in downtown Harper:

I had a lot of chances to observe him. And the more I listened, the more a warning bell rang, louder and louder. You don't have to be a trained psychoanalyst. Somehow, when a person is different, you know it. I suppose we all run in a pack, in a sense. And there are always little clues to the rogue beast. I don't think Cady is sane. . . . I don't know what word the doctors have for it. Paranoid. I wouldn't know. But he can't blame himself. I tried to tell him it was his own fault. He said if they're big enough they're old enough, and she was just another Aussie bitch.

The novel eventually becomes a conflict between the forces of law and vigilante justice. The law is unable to respond to evil because of civilization, while the more brutal answer to the problem of stalking is abhorrent to most people.

The Executioners was published in hardback by Simon & Schuster. And those cloth covers made a difference in critical coverage. With this novel, MacDonald's writing got coverage far beyond Anthony Boucher's column in *The New York Times.* Boucher, incidentally, quibbled about the novel. "His ending does avoid some of the questions he has raised," he wrote. Anne Ross also raised doubts in her review for the *New York Herald Tribune:* "Mr. MacDonald, who is an old hand at all sorts of fiction, tells an exciting story which keeps you reading from start to finish. He is no practitioner of the distinguished style, or the sensitive detail, but he can spin an expert yarn." *The New Yorker,* in its "Briefly Noted" column, said the book was a "competently written ingenious story. . . . The various characters have their rather sticky domestic moments, and they are a good deal less interesting than the monster dedicated to exterminating them, but altogether the effect is unusually chilly." A critic for *The Saturday Review* said the book was a "fine situation piece involving [an] ordinary guy faced with a potentially explosive crisis."

MacDonald was beginning to break into literary circles. He was also picked up by a book club. *The Executioners* was an alternate selection with the Dollar Book Club and went through three printings. And yet all those readers were not as important as one man on the West Coast who got a copy of the book, read it and liked it, and decided to make a movie of it. His name was Gregory Peck.

Peck was one of the country's great movie stars. In the late 1950s, he was best known for his performances in *Roman Holiday, The Man in the Gray Flannel Suit, Moby Dick, Beloved Infidel, On the Beach*, and *Designing Woman*. By 1958, when *The Executioners* was published, the Hollywood studio system was on its last legs. Stars like John Wayne established their own production companies and acted as producers. Peck decided to do the same thing with *The Executioners*. He would star in it as Sam Bowden, of course, but he would also produce it. Initially, Peck wanted his friend Telly Savalas to play Cady, the villain. But Savalas wasn't box office in the late 1950s. Robert Mitchum was, and he got the part. The movie got a new title, *Cape Fear*, and was a success, but it didn't impress MacDonald. Five years later he was calling it a "dreary moving, I mean unmoving, picture." But MacDonald shrugged it off. He never expected much from Hollywood in the first place, and Hollywood didn't disappoint him. He explained his philosophy in a 1965 letter:

> I made the decision to avoid the responsibility of any artistic control of anything in any other medium, figuring that perhaps I could achieve the same result by dealing only with people I think might be tasty, and then sticking them severely enough so that they have to go to top talent to get their bait back. . . . Artistic control on any continuing basis would mean accepting the responsibility, and doing some of the work, and making decisions, and I would rather channel all such efforts into whatever book or books are on the fire at the time. And I cannot for the life of me adjust to sitting down and talking to people about what should be done about this and that. It gives me an itch I can't reach.

He told the novelist Elmore Leonard some years later, "I decided in the beginning they didn't know diddly about writing books . . . and I don't want to know how they make movies."

Nonetheless, he attended the Florida premiere:

> When it opened in Miami, Mitchum, Peck and [Polly] Bergen were otherwise occupied. So they toted the author over there to help Barry Chase promote it on opening night at six or seven theaters. We were sirened around in limos like Mexican generals, and upon rounding one fast corner I read on the marquee ahead, "Welcome Barry Chase and James McDonald." I had tasted fame. . . . Artistically the movie warped the concept of the novel—which was that no matter how threatened you might feel, you don't get police protection until you have been hurt. But I stood on those stages and said it was a fine movie. When they asked if I had someone like Barry Chase in mind, I said, "Sure." But she wasn't in my book. She had been written into the script.

So with *The Executioners* MacDonald won his bet with MacKinlay Kantor—he wrote a book that was published in hardback, was sold to the book clubs, and was made into a movie. But Kantor was reluctant to pay MacDonald the $50. He said that since MacDonald's book was only an alternate book club selection, he hadn't lost the bet. But he changed his mind and paid off anyway.

It was about the this time, in 1958, that MacDonald began worrying about his drinking. Maybe he was knocking back too many martinis at night. Maybe those long Friday sessions at the writers' club that often lasted late into the evening were giving him circles under his eyes and a slight tremor in the morning. Maybe he remembered that time in New York when he reached across the desk and grabbed an editor by his clothes and pulled him out of his chair and said that if the title of his novel was changed to *Teased to Death* he would find the editor and beat him like a gong. Whatever it was, he felt he was too close to the edge. For a young major in India during the war, there couldn't be too much booze. For a pulp writer feeling his oats in New York in the late 1940s, there wasn't enough gin in all of Christendom to quench his thirst. But he was in his forties now, and worried that the habits of his youth were not healthy for a middle-aged man. So he quit drinking for a while and set up a two-year schedule. First, he decided, he would have no booze at all. That lasted for a few months, and then he changed the rules. Now it was no booze within fifty miles of home. He passed that test and then changed the rules again: no booze at home, but okay elsewhere. Finally, he decided he could have booze anywhere. "Had I decided I still couldn't handle it after the two years schedule was over, I would have quit forever," he wrote later.

The late fifties were probably a good time for MacDonald to practice abstinence, because that's when Johnny first started to have problems. Or at least that's when Johnny started acting like his father. In June 1957, Johnny graduated from Oakwood Academy, a prep school in Poughkeepsie, New York, run by Quakers from the American Friends Service Committee. During the summer he traveled with the Quakers in Mexico, got typhoid, and was taken to Mexico City to recover. In September he entered Rollins College in Orlando. These, of course, were the pre-Disney years, when Orlando was a sleepy citrus town. Rollins College was an expensive private school with a bit of a reputation as a progressive institution. It was a Rollins professor who, in 1933, left the school to establish Black Mountain College, one of the most important communities of artists and intellectuals in the country. But that was 1933. This was 1957, and Johnny lasted only a year and a half. He completed his freshman year, took the summer off to study archaeology at the University of New Mexico, returned for the first semester of his sophomore year, and then dropped out.

When John D. left the Wharton School at the University of Pennsylvania, he ran away to New York. Johnny did the same thing in 1959. Within a few months he was living in an apartment with his cousin Baird Prentiss. He set himself up as an apprentice to a sculptor until September, when he entered New York University to take fine arts courses. That didn't last long either. He spent the summer in Sarasota, returned to New York as an apprentice to Calgagno, the sculptor, and stayed there until January 1960. Four months later, he was off on a trip to Europe with an art teacher from Rollins and his family.

Once he was in Paris, Johnny studied painting for a while, then split with his teacher and his family and walked across France to the eastern shore of Italy. From there he went to Greece. In September, he wrote home and told John D. and Dordo he was coming home to continue his education, "if it is OK with you." It was, and Johnny hopped a ship, the *Santa Maria,* and returned to Sarasota via Paris, Spain, Lisbon, the Madeira Islands, and Venezuela. He got home a week before Thanksgiving. In February 1961, he was off again, this time to Cranbrook Academy of Art in Bloomfield Hills, Michigan. At Cranbrook, Johnny fell in love. The girl was Anne Guthrie Colfelt of Wayne, Pennsylvania. She was a graduate of Baldwin School and Mount Holyoke.

After he met Anne, Johnny made up for lost time. He passed all his courses, went to the Utica campus of the University of Syracuse to make up courses he had missed by dropping out of school and traveling, and went back to Cranbrook, and on February 3, 1962, Johnny and Anne were married at Old St. David's Church in Wayne, Pennsylvania. The society columnist for the *Sarasota Herald-Tribune* said the Colfelts were "an old Main Line family."

Johnny may have been like his father in dropping out of school to seek independence. He may have taken a cue from John D. about travel in Europe. He may have inherited the industriousness that saw him grind out courses at both the Utica campus of Syracuse University and at Cranbrook Academy and eventually get a Master of Fine Arts degree. But there was never the menial work that Eugene MacDonald forced John D. to do in order to get money for college. There was not the constant harping about money. Johnny wanted to be an artist in much the same way John D. wanted to be a writer. Eugene MacDonald insisted on a business career for his son, a career in which money was the only important thing. John D. gave his son the chance to study art, the chance to explore new possibilities, the chance to fail. And he never complained to Johnny about money.

Meanwhile, Dordo was having the first of the many bouts with cancer that would plague her the rest of her life. In 1958 she had an operation for polyps and cysts in her uterus. Two years later, in December 1960, she was back in the hospital for a D and C and for surgery. A month later, in January 1961, she had a hysterectomy.

But that was not the end of the bad days. Six months later, on June 7, John D. MacDonald's father, Eugene, died. After the funeral, John D. gradually acquired the symptoms of acute anxiety. In 1981 he wrote about those days and his near-breakdown to a psychologist: "He had copped out on me. [He] died before I could prove to him what a great kid I was (at 44!). I never seemed to be able to live up to what he expected of me." He was worried about himself, and so he went to the Mayo Clinic to undergo analysis.

Mayo's told me I was too old for analysis to be effective, that I should come back to Sarasota and set up some conversations with a psychiatrist. There were three in town at that time and I knew all three socially and considered them all a bit dreary and not too bright. So I got some texts on the problem, and started a diary of my totally horrid dreams, and in time, bit by bit, all the symptoms cleared up. It took over a year.

And yet his career continued. After he wrote *The Executioners* in 1957 he continued to crank out novels—eight more by the end of the decade. And as the 1950s came to a close, he decided to try his hand at journalism. On Friday the 13th of November in 1959, MacDonald wrote to Guy Paschal, the editor of *The Lookout*, a small monthly magazine in Sarasota, and offered to write a column. "I noticed your brave solicitation of anonymous editorials that past summer," he wrote. "If anonymous editorials are possible, surely an anonymous column might strike your fancy." He asked for complete protection of his privacy, and a top right location on one of the first five pages, in a box, with a border around it. No editing would be allowed. "If any column does not suit you for any reason, just scrap the whole thing, and it will bother me not at all. I have been rejected by *Playboy* as being too rough for their readership. It shall be your concern to discard anything you think actionable."

He was indifferent to the column's name. "I am wide open for suggestions on what to call the column. The only one I have been able to come up with is *Off the Beat.* I should like to have it signed by T. Carrington Burns. I see him as a snide and fussy fellow with violent opinions, a wide range of interests, a sense of justice, a furled umbrella, and a nervous twitch in the left corner of his mouth."

Paschal agreed to run the column. And although it covered a lot of topics from art to politics, its main focus, from the beginning, was the environment. This is from his first column:

We drove out Bird Key way the other day in a sad ceremonial mood to look at where the big pines had been. After driving between the pines for so many years, it was disconcerting to have them on only one side. It gave somewhat the same feeling as walking with a pronounced limp. We parked for a bit. Lovely morning. The big dredges were contentedly masticating, while opportunistic birds awaited the goodies spewed onto the brand new land.

The felled trees were disappearing with a haste we might have labeled as guilty had we not known it was merely a demonstration of Corporate Efficiency. During the days of the old bridges when Sunday traffic in season would often congeal for twenty irritating minutes, the shade of those tall pines kept many a stalled tourist from frying like a mullet in his own grease and suntan lotion.

We gazed at the astonishing emptiness where the pines had been, and wondered what sort of entrance gate would be erected there by Mr. T. T. Watson at a reputed cost of $10,000. One would not care to hide that much entrance gate behind a row of solemn middle-aged pine trees which the State Road Department was glad to have done with. And it would have been most difficult to take effective photographs of the gate for promotional brochures with those pines standing in the way. And one never has to saw a rotten limb off a gate. It is only living growing things which require tender and expensive care. Doubtless that $10,000 gate will be built for the ages, whereas one hundred years is about the most you can demand from even the most cooperative pine tree.

He wrote about art, defending abstract expressionism; he wrote about politics, decrying the redneckery of the political establishment in Sarasota; and, of course, he continued to rant about people spoiling the environment. He wrote this in May 1960:

We believe true progress can only be measured by the preservation, protection, strengthening and glorification of the two factors which made us unique—the cultural strength and ferment, and the special beauties of the beach, bay and approach. Every zoning-buster, anti-planner, and bay-filler is degrading us for the sake of his own pocketbook, be he individual or huge corporation, citing the holy name of progress on *his* terms. Every businessman who fails to support cultural endeavors—yet opens his foolish pockets for those things *every* community sponsors—such as pageants, ball clubs, band uniforms, parades and conventions—is being a commercial donkey. His boosterism is vintage Sinclair Lewis. One day he will find out he has nothing left to sell but the climate. In a world so implacably conformist it seems sinful for us to lay waste to both aspects of our uniqueness, and go baying and hallooing down the cheap road to the ordinariness of most other resort areas. . . . If this is conservatism and snobbery, we confess guilt. . . . There is *no valid justification* for filling one more foot of bay. Profit is not progress.

He wrote the column through July 1961, when Paschal folded the magazine. "Now that you have collapsed your fearless journal," MacDonald wrote to Paschal in December 1961, "I find myself without an outlet for my periodic crochets, complaints and irritabilities. I find it difficult to retain an audience for verbal expression of my woes, because friends with broken legs are rare, and the hale ones are prone to walk away in the middle of my more heated diatribes."

A year later he began writing a series of six guest columns for the *Sarasota Herald-Tribune.* They were occasional columns, published only when MacDonald felt like writing, never on any regular basis. He wrote about boating, art, cats, and, of course, the environment.

MacDonald would become known for writing novels about Florida as a sort of paradise lost, but that would come later. In the 1950s and the early 1960s, he wrote mostly about Northeast industrial towns. Between 1950 and 1963 he wrote only eleven novels about Florida. A total of twenty-seven novels were set somewhere else. And even the ones set in Florida did not have that edge of doom, the feel of a destroyed Eden. There was one exception—*A Flash of Green,* published in hardback in 1962 by Simon & Schuster. It is a not so thinly disguised account of the attempt to fill in Sarasota Bay and the tale of a corrupt newspaper reporter who helps the evil developers. The reporter is properly cynical when he explains how the developers will get their way:

The new syndicate will petition for a change in the bulk-head line along the bay shore of Sandy Key, to swing the line out to enclose eight hundred acres of so-called unsightly mud flats, and request county permission to buy the bay bottom from the State Internal Improvement Fund. The commissioners will set a date for a public hearing, at which time prominent local businessmen will go to the microphone, one after another, and say what a great boon this will be to the community, a shot in the arm for the construction business and the retail stores. Captive experts will get up and say the fill with have no effect on fish breeding grounds or bird life, and will not change the tide pattern so as to cause beach erosion. It will be nicely timed, because a lot of the militant bird watchers and dogooders will be north for the summer, and they won't give the ones who are left here much time to organize the opposition. The commissioners will change the bulkhead line and approve the syndicate application to purchase. The trustees of the IIF will sell the bay bottom at an estimated three hundred and fifty dollars an acre, and then the drag lines and dredges will move it. It's going to be a steamroller operation . . . and it's going to run right over anybody who stands in the way.

A Flash of Green was the beginning of much of the environmental musing that filled MacDonald's mysteries of the 1960s and 1970s, just as another 1962 book, *A Key to the Suite*, was a sort of blueprint for *Condominium*. It was a book about the inner workings of a Miami Beach hotel, and it was a beginning of the MacDonald method of teaching readers details about things—hotels, stamp collecting, the weather—as he tells a story. *A Key to the Suite* is about intrigue at a major industrial convention in Florida, but MacDonald is quick to instruct readers:

The Sultana had been planned and constructed as a resort-convention hotel, and the huge convention hall was a separate structure, joined to it by an umbilical cord eighty feet wide and over two hundred feet long. This corridor was adjacent to the Arabian Room, the main dining room of the hotel. When no convention was in progress, or when the convention hall was being used as a sports arena, the corridor could be blocked off by an intricate accordion-door system.

When a convention was in progress, the corridor formed an ideal place for exhibits. The lighting, electric outlets, floor covering had all been planned with this in mind.

With these books of environmental concerns and the details of American life at midcentury, MacDonald seemed to be making a turn away from the assembly-line thriller. And he probably would have continued in that direction if he hadn't gotten a call from Knox Burger, the editor in chief at Fawcett Gold Medal Books. Burger told MacDonald that people were avoiding him in the halls, they were turning their backs on him at the drinking fountain, and he felt there was a dotted line around his throat. Only one man could help him, Burger said, and that was John D. MacDonald. And with that telephone call from New York, MacDonald's life changed once again.

CHAPTER 9

People were avoiding Knox Burger because he had let one of Fawcett's most prominent authors go to Pocket Books, a rival publisher and the creator of paperbacks. The author was Richard Prather, creator of the bumbling hard-boiled detective Shell Scott, who was the hero of twenty-three novels. Prather was not much of a writer—*Twentieth-Century Crime and Mystery Writers* says his books are filled with "uneven plots and dialogue, wordy exposition, mixed similes, sexual hyperbole, off-color puns and one-liners." But, the encyclopedia adds, you can also see the comic vitality that carried him through decades of writing. Prather was a blue-collar writer. There was no Ivy League, no Harvard Business School in his background. He attended Riverside Junior College, then enlisted in the Merchant Marine and worked as an oiler, fireman, and engineer. Since 1949 he had been churning out the Shell Scott books.

Richard Prather lived by the hard-boiled cliché. Here's how one of Shell Scott's clients is introduced in the 1950 novel *Case of the Vanishing Beauty*:

I saw her when she pulled up and parked across the street but I didn't pay much attention. I noticed her because she was driving a brand new Cadillac convertible with the top down. Just like my buggy except hers was a lot younger. She had on a fur coat that looked like money and she left the top down on the convertible, even though it looked as if rain would start pouring any minute. My office is between Third and Fourth Streets, about midway down the block, and she headed right across the street, jaywalking. She could have been headed for Arthur's liquor store. She wasn't. I was still looking out the window when she came in the door behind me. I turned around and got my first good look at her. I'd had the steam heat on most of the day, and it was warm. She peeled off the fur coat and draped it carelessly over the chair in the front of my desk. That was O.K. with me. She was a long-haired and long-limbed blonde on the pleasant side of thirty—rather pleasantly on the pleasant side—and she was built to wear sweaters. She *was* wearing a sweater, practically wearing it out, and the things she could do for a French bathing suit were worth mentioning.

Prather was a right-winger who liked to demonize liberal politicians. He named a villain Humphrey Huberts, a reference to the Democratic senator from Minnesota who became vice president in 1964. Knox Burger didn't think it was funny, and he took the name out. That sent Prather into a snit. About that time Herb Alexander, the president of Pocket Books, offered Prather $100,000 a year if he'd change publishers. Prather took the money and ran.

Knox Burger was getting the blame for losing him. It was a major financial loss to Fawcett. Shell Scott sold a lot of books. That's when Burger called John D. MacDonald, his friend since the late 1940s. MacDonald had first come in contact with Burger in 1949, when he was living in Mexico. He had been knocking out short stories for the pulp magazines at $50 or $60 each. Then he got a letter from *Collier's* magazine—from Knox Burger, who was then fiction editor at the magazine. *Collier's* wanted to publish MacDonald's story, Burger wrote, and they were enclosing a check. It was for $1,000 and it was the first check in four figures MacDonald ever got. Six years later, in 1955, MacDonald came across Burger again. Burger had left *Collier's* and was now editor of Dell First Editions, a paperback rival to Fawcett Gold Medal. MacDonald had a personality conflict with Dick Carroll, his editor at Fawcett, and switched to Dell, where Burger was his editor. Nine of his books were published by Dell. Then, in 1958, Burger moved to Fawcett. MacDonald went with him. Now he wanted John D. to start a detective series to make up for Prather's loss.

MacDonald thought about it. He had turned down a series once before. Back in 1952, Ralph Daigh had suggested that MacDonald do a series for Fawcett, but John D. said no. "I had the uneasy feeling that were I to come up with a successful series, I might be stuck with it," MacDonald said later, and be "unable to sell work of any other kind. I think my hunch was valid." But this time it was different. At first he joked about writing under a pseudonym—Dick Panther. Nobody laughed, and he was talked out of it. Even though Mac-Donald wrote his magazine column in Sarasota under the pseudonym T. Carrington Burns, he later said he opposed pen names. "The writer is in the business of dropping his trousers in the town square and it is unfair to wear a mask while doing so," he said.

MacDonald began working on the series in 1962. First he had to come up with a character and give him a name. MacDonald called his detective Dallas McGee. He explained why in an interview with Edgar Hirshberg, his biographer: "I have a friend here that I've had for a hundred years named Dallas and the name intrigues me because it has a nice flavor about it. I think lots of times geographical names are fun, and easy to remember, like Tennessee Williams or Vermont Royster. . . ."

Once he had a character, he had to decide how to distinguish one McGee book from another. He didn't want to number them, because then a reader might feel compelled to read them in order. MacDonald discussed this problem with friends on a trip to New York. He and Ralph Daigh, Knox Burger, Max Wilkinson, his agent, and some other friends were sitting around a bar called the Red Devil, trying to figure out the titles for their new series. MacDonald talked about the problem in a speech he gave in 1983:

Our premise was that the titling should permit the reader to read the series in any order he wished and that the titles should be in some pattern easy to remember. Musical terminology, days of the week, months of the year, varieties of gemstones—all of these were discarded, and I believe it was Knox Burger, who edited all the early ones, who suggested colors. I approved, Max Wilkinson approved, and so we drank to Dallas McGee and wished him well.

MacDonald went back to his unpublished manuscripts and found places to insert the title phrase. Until then the titles were unrelated; now they were color-coded, and that made them marketable as part of the Dallas McGee series, not just as three unrelated novels. Then, on November 22, 1963, John Kennedy was assassinated in Dallas, Texas. And MacDonald changed his hero's name. The assassination "gave the name a resonance I did not want. I wrote out twenty names and did not like a one of them. MacKinlay Kantor suggested I look at a list of Air Force bases. He said they had pretty good names. And Travis was a good name in California."

And yet even with a good name for his hero, MacDonald wanted to make sure he could develop a character he could live with:

I did a book called *The Deep Blue Good-by*. The title was OK, but the hero was horrid. . . . He was very heavy-handed and somber and Germanic. He was very moody and very gloomy and he had a lot of drab observations about the world, and I didn't even send it in. I put it on the shelf as a failed attempt. I tried again, and he came out to be a real lightweight, full of quips and pranks and glib puns and cheery funny remarks, and I couldn't stand him. So then I wrote *The Deep Blue Good-By* for the third time, and I found somebody that would be kind of halfway between the two, and it seemed like I could live with him. To make sure I could live with him I sent him up to Fawcett and told them to hold onto him while I tried another couple of books. I did two more, and both Travis and I seemed to survive the experience. So we went ahead and published them. . . . In 1964 they were released one a month for three months and they did right well in the marketplace . . .

When Raymond Chandler converted some of his short stories into *The Big Sleep*, the first of the Philip Marlowe novels, he used a process he called cannibalization. He took characters and situations from his earlier short stories, combined them, and made them part of his novel. MacDonald did the same thing when he created Travis McGee. In the 1961 novel *Where Is Janice Gantry?* there is a character who is very much like McGee. His name is Sam Brice. Like McGee, he'd been a professional football player. "I'd been Sam Brice, full-back, the big ground-gainer in the West Coast Florida Conference, with offers from every semi-pro college team in the East. . . . I had let the wide world whip me and I had come home after three seasons with the National Football League with my tail tucked down and under."

His career also involved a college team and a few years as a pro. But there was a difference. Sam Brice got thrown out for gambling and McGee got his legs crushed. In *The Turquoise Lament,* McGee has a brief conversation with a football fan:

> "Say, dint you play some pro? I heard Dave here say McGee. First name?"
>
> "Travis."
>
> "Oh, sure. Tight end. Kind of way back. Like you were up there two years and you got racked up bad. Give me a couple of minutes and I can come up with the Detroit guy who clobbered you."
>
> I stared at him. "Nobody can remember *me*, much less who messed up my legs. . . ."

Travis McGee is a "salvage consultant" who says he is taking his retirement in chunks, and only works when he needs money. In *The Deep Blue Good-by*, Travis explains what he does in a conversation with a woman named Chookie McCall:

> "Were you kidding me that time we talked about . . . about what you do for a living?"
>
> "What did I say?"

"It sounded sort of strange, but I guess I believed you. You said that if X has something valuable and Y comes along and takes it away from him, and there is absolutely no way in the world X can ever get it back, then you come along and make a deal with X to get it back and keep half. Then you just . . . live on that until it starts to run out. Is that the way it is, really?"

"It's a simplification, Chook, but reasonably accurate. . . . Because I am sort of a last resort, the fee is fifty per cent. . . . I like to work on pretty good-sized [cases]. Expenses are heavy. And then I can take another piece of my retirement. Instead of retiring at sixty, I'm taking it in chunks as I go along."

Travis McGee fit in with the wave of antiheroes appearing in American pop culture in the 1960s. By 1960 it had been seven years since Mickey Spillane's last Mike Hammer novel. The new paperback hero was James Bond.

Who would have thought small-time gangsters like Bonnie Parker and Clyde Barrow could become American existential heroes thirty years after their death? What prophet would have predicted that America's children would briefly abandon consumerism and in the process make millionaires out of denim manufacturers? What soothsayer would have believed that a character vaguely like Robin Hood could be made from a beach bum and could become as popular as Bond? It was a different country after the Kennedy assassination. Americans were no longer being asked what they were going to do for their country. They were being urged to tune in, turn on, and drop out. MacDonald's McGee had already dropped out. He lived on a houseboat, an island of sorts, and he bitched about credit-card capitalism. But MacDonald wouldn't let him turn off. Here is McGee musing over his lot in life in *Nightmare in Pink:*

I thought of death and money and blue-eyed tears. And some other blue eyes gone blind. This emotional obligation did not fit me. I felt awkward in the uncomfortable role. I wished to be purely McGee, that pale-eyed, wire-haired girl-finder, that big brown shambling boat-bum who walks beaches, slays small fierce fish, busts minor icons, argues, smiles and disbelieves, that knuckly scar-tissued reject from a structured society, who waits until the money gets low, and then goes out and takes it from the taker, keeps half and gives the rest back to the innocent. These matters can best be handled by the uninvolved.

McGee might have been a more romantic and adventurous version of Sam Brice. And he might have the copper hair and huge bulk of the pulp hero Doc Savage. But there was a big difference. Brice lived in a quiet cabin by a lake, McGee on a spectacular houseboat at a marina. To come up with that setting, MacDonald cannibalized another one of his books, the 1959 novel *The Beach Girls*, which takes place at Stebbins' Marina at Elihu Beach on Florida's east coast. McGee, of course, lived aboard a houseboat named the *Busted Flush*, which was always anchored at Slip F-18, Bahia Mar Marina, in Fort Lauderdale.

In *The Beach Girls*, a character named Captain Orbie Derr describes life at Stebbins' Marina:

A bunch of us were on D Dock, as usual, lounging around on cushions and chairs taken off the boats. Tin washtub full of ice and beer. I'd set my charcoal grill up on the docks and loaded it. Later on we'd light it and cook up the 'burgs. . . . It was nice there, opening a beer once in a while, having a lazy argument about nothing at all, watching the night come on. The car lights were on over the other side of the Inland Waterway, going north and south on A-1-A, going back and forth across the hump-back bridge over Elihu Inlet. There wasn't much boat traffic up and down the waterway, and not much in the big Stebbins' Marina basin, just kids and old fellas running in to tie up their outboards over at A Dock where they keep the small stuff. On the other side of us, beyond the rickety old Marina buildings, traffic moved slick and fast, whispering by north and south on Broward Boulevard. It made D Dock like an island, a special quiet place, water licking gently at the hulls of the tied up boats.

It was not too different from life aboard the *Busted Flush,* created four years later, and certainly not different from the life led by the Alabama Tiger, who maintains a twenty-four-hour-a-day floating party on his boat anchored near the *Busted Flush.* In a sales kit designed to interest Hollywood in movie and television productions of his novels, MacDonald says Stebbins' Marina is "where a group of diehard individualists and eccentrics live aboard boats within sight and sound of the big tourist boom." And it is apparent why he chose this as McGee's home base. "It could make a strong serial anthology show because it is an encapsulated community, people trying to maintain a familiar way of life—with a constant flow of new arrivals creating new problems, new relationships, and, for some of the old-timers, solutions to old problems."

From the beginning, MacDonald had a feeling the McGee novels would be a hit. So he put McGee in Fort Lauderdale, not Sarasota, to protect his privacy. "I put McGee over on the other side of the state on a hunch," MacDonald said in an interview in *Motor Boating and Sailing.* "I thought there just might be a chance he would become popular, and if so, I certainly did not want my privacy compromised by having him live over here." Then he explained why McGee lived on a houseboat in a marina. It sounds like the publicity material for *The Beach Girls.* "I wanted him to be in a resort area because of the mix of people, and the constant change of personae. I put him in an apartment, then a beach shack, then a bachelor pad on a small private island, and suddenly had the sense to realize a live-aboard boat is a small private island with the additional advantage (for the writer) of mobility."

McGee was not the first fictional Florida private eye. Nor was he the first red-haired fictional private eye in Florida. Carroll John Daly's

Race Williams, a tough-guy detective who predates Hammett's Sam Spade, worked in Miami in the 1929 novel *The Hidden Hand*. And three authors, Wesley Price, Whitman Chambers, and Jack DeWitt, wrote hard-boiled novels about Florida in the 1930s and 1940s. But the best-known pre-MacDonald Florida detective was the redheaded Michael Shayne, the 1938 creation of Davis Dresser, writing under the name Brett Halliday. Most of the sixty-three Shayne novels are set in Miami. In addition to writing the novels, which regularly sold 100,000 copies each, he was the editor of *The Mike Shayne Mystery Magazine*, founded in 1956. But Shayne was never original. He, like detectives dating back to the turn of the century, was suave, well dressed, urbane. He lived in penthouses, not houseboats. And in the early 1960s, America abandoned the slick sophisticate for the rough boatsman.

Although MacDonald often went on rants against *Playboy* magazine and the philosophy of its publisher, Hugh Hefner, it was from the pages of that magazine that the *Busted Flush* was decorated. In the September and October 1956 issues of *Playboy* there was a twelve-page feature called "*Playboy's* Penthouse Apartment." It featured a bathroom with an oversized pale blue sunken tub and a huge shower stall, a bedroom with a giant bed, and a stainless-steel galley. All of that was part of the *Busted Flush*, although MacDonald did not use the "ultrasonic dishwasher" that cleaned with "incredible hi-fi sound" or the glass-domed oven that *Playboy* suggested. John D. also used the oversized bathtub and shower stall in his 1964 novel *The Drowner*. Miss Agnes, the electric-blue 1936 Rolls-Royce pickup truck McGee drives, is a parody of superhero vehicles—Batman's Batmobile or the Green Hornet's car, Black Beauty. Or maybe it's a spoof on James Bond's Aston-Martin. Whatever it is, it's a perfect Florida vehicle. It's a Rolls-Royce, and that's as glitzy as Miami. And it's a pickup, and the vehicle of choice for the redneckery in the rest of the state. Years later he talked about the truck and the boat as major ways he and McGee differed. "I wouldn't drive that damn car of his around the block," MacDonald said. "A bit of flamboyance in one's exterior like that car and the *Busted Flush* means that one becomes the observed rather than the observer. I prefer to watch and listen and observe. Therefore I have a minimum of flamboyance in my personal life because it would obscure—or make more difficult— my function of people watching. People watching is where stuff comes from for books."

But it was not the houseboat or the car that brought readers to McGee. It was usually the girls and the musings. The girls—there were always a lot of them—were important because they got better treatment than they had in novels by other detectives. It was easy to be the champion of women if you wrote hard-boiled detective stories. All you had to do was like them. Dashiell Hammett's Sam Spade used them and threw them away, Raymond Chandler's Philip Marlowe hated them; Mickey Spillane's Mike Hammer and Ian Fleming's James Bond killed them. But McGee paid attention to them, seemed to like them. And, completely against the way characters like James Bond or Shell Scott acted, he occasionally turned down their sexual overtures. MacDonald might not have been able to write dialogue between men and women without overusing the word "darling," but he could sure seduce readers with his interior monologue that spoke of caring and not just sex. Sex, he said in a way fictional private eyes had never said before, was not enough. In *The Deep Blue Good-by* he tiptoes out of a bedroom inhabited by a rather dim and drunken Corry:

> There are the little losers in the bunny derby, but they lose on a different route than . . . the ones you see in the supermarket on the nights when they double the green stamps, coming in junk cars, plodding the bright aisles, snarling at their cross sleepy kids. [They] save wistfulness for thoughts of the key clubs. They could be the center fold in anybody's sex book. You have to stay with the kicks. . . . The cats always show up. The phone always rings. Friends have friends. It isn't like anything was going to wear out, man. It isn't like they were going to stop having conventions. And you get a little tired or a little bored, so you throw a big fast busy fake and it is over in nothing at all. And learn the ways to work

them for the little gifts here and there. Like maybe a cruise. Or the rent. Or a couple of beach outfits by Cole. Friendship gifts. Not like you were really working at it. The ones work at it, there is always some character taking the money, and there can be police trouble and all that. You work waitress once in a while. The rest of it is dates, really. One date at a time. And some laughs, and if you're short, he can loan you. And other numbers to call when there are a whole bunch of guys.

It was a bad era for women, he felt, but just as bad for men. He thinks about it as he joins the Alabama Tiger's floating houseparty. Sometimes, as when he left Corry's bedroom, McGee is only an observer. MacDonald has described himself as a Calvinist, and sometimes he turns McGee into a stern Presbyterian preacher delivering a jeremiad:

These are the playmate years and they are demonstratively fraudulent. The scene is reputed to be acrawl with adorably amoral bunnies to whom sex is a pleasant social favor. The new culture. And they are indeed present and available, in exhausting quantities, but there is a curious tastelessness about them. A woman who does not guard and treasure herself cannot be of very much value to anyone else. They become a pretty little convenience, like a guest towel. And the cute little things they say, and their dainty little squeals of pleasure and release are as contrived as the embroidered initials on the guest towels. Only a woman of pride, complexity, and emotional tension is genuinely worth the act of love, and there are only two ways to get yourself one of them. Either you lie, and stain the relationship with your own sense of guilt or you accept the involvement, the emotional responsibility, the permanence she must by nature crave. I love you can be said only two ways.

McGee turns down five girls in *The Deep Blue Good-by*, but he's no saint. He also hops in the sack with three others in the same book. Usually when Travis McGee has sex with a woman, there's a whisper of all those psychology books MacDonald read when his father died. Travis, the beach bum, becomes Dr. Travis. Consider this from *A Purple Place for Dying*:

> It was her demon and her battle. It was a precipice and her knowledge that she could stop it at any time that gave her the boldness to approach even closer to the edge. On a sticky night in the X-Cell Motel on the east bank of Mobile Bay, the brink crumbled away under her hesitant footstep. With a soft, harsh, almost supersonic shriek, like a gaffed rabbit, she fell. . . . "Trav, darling, when I was a skinny brown kid racing around this little island, I had a sense of my own rightness. I had a feeling of access to life as if it would all open for me, in its own time. God knows how or why it soured, or why I slammed all the doors, why I had such a conviction of evil. Maybe a psychiatrist could track it down. But now it's like it used to be for me. I'm alive once more. And that is a gift from you, of course."

In the early 1960s, that passed for sensitivity. It was almost a feminist stance. Women professors wrote papers about Travis McGee and his enlightened attitude toward women. But the critic Robin Winks was more perceptive: "There no longer is a dependable heroic type. Travis McGee, John D. MacDonald's presumably lovable beach bum, is a male chauvinist who still thinks the best cure for a woman's blues is a good screw." Winks thinks Matt Helm, a "killing machine" of a spy created by Donald Hamilton, more truly believes in the equality of women. "Some have compared him to Travis McGee, though Matt Helm is a bit closer to Mickey Spillane, for he treats women as true equals, which means that he will shoot one in the back if he must, without that moment of hesitation (and paragraph of philosophy) that slows McGee's reaction time."

Winks may sneer at McGee's moment of philosophy, but those rants, musings, asides, and discourses are one of the elements that made the series a hit. The philosophical rumblings are an outgrowth of the magazine column MacDonald wrote as T. Carrington Burns. Of course, even Raymond Chandler occasionally waxed philosophical. In *The Little Sister*, Chandler has Philip Marlowe muse:

> Malibu. More movie stars. More pink and blue bathtubs. More tufted beds. More Chanel No. 5. More Lincoln Continentals and Cadillacs. More windblown hair and sunglasses and attitudes and pseudo-refined voices and waterfront morals. Now wait a minute. Lots of nice people work in pictures. You got the wrong attitude, Marlowe. You're not human tonight.

Chandler was cynical. So was MacDonald. But the philosophical asides were not what you remembered most from Chandler. Often they were the main feature of a Travis McGee novel. And, like his diatribe against promiscuous women, they more often than not had the tone of a preacher. Consider this environmental rant in *Nightmare in Pink*:

> New York is where it's going to begin, I think. You can see it coming. The insect experts have learned how it works with locusts. Until locust population reaches a certain density, they all act like any grasshoppers. When the critical point is reached, they turn savage and swarm, and try to eat the world. We're nearing a critical point. One day soon two strangers will bump into each other at high noon in the middle of New York. But this time they won't snarl and go on. They will stop and stare and then leap at each other's throats in a dreadful silence. The infection will spread outward from that point. Old ladies will crack skulls with their deadly handbags. Cars will plunge down the crowded sidewalks.

Drivers will be torn out of their cars and stomped. It will spread to all the huge cities of the world, and by dawn of the next day there will be a horrid silence of sprawled bodies and tumbled vehicles, gutted buildings and a few wisps of smoke. And through that silence will prowl a few, a very few of the most powerful ones, ragged and bloody, slowly tracking each other down.

You're not human tonight, McGee. Or should we say Mr. Burns? Mr. T. Carrington Burns?

McGee is "not a typical detective," MacDonald said.

He's a good vehicle for relieving my own frustrations and irritations about the current scene. . . . Travis is my mouthpiece, depending on what areas we're talking about. Every writer is going to put into the mouths of the people he wants you to respect opinions that he thinks are respectable. It's that simple. Suppose we're talking about a social, ecological ruin—the environment area. For example, in *The Turquoise Lament* he is flying into Sarasota and he remarks on the stacks of the mighty Borden Company up in Bradenton, and he says it's known locally as the place where Elsie the Cow coughed herself to death. Why not? That's my comment as well as his. As long as I'm making him a hero, it would be grotesque for me to give him an opinion at which I was at odds.

Anthony Boucher continued to champion McGee in *The New York Times*. "It is not at all startling to discover that Mr. MacDonald can create a series character just as well as he does everything else in the suspense field," he wrote in a combined review of *The Deep Blue Good-by* and *Nightmare in Pink*. "McGee is sort of a jackal of good will. . . . [He] gives MacDonald ample opportunity to picture and comment upon our society and mores, which he does probably better than anyone else in the crime field save Ross Macdonald."

But the strangest comment on the McGee series came from Richard Prather, the man who indirectly started it all. Prather apparently didn't like the McGee books, particularly the philosophical asides. In 1969 he wrote another Shell Scott mystery, *The Cheim Manuscript*. The villain is a criminal named Burper McGee who has a gas problem that causes one belch after another. Burper tries to ambush Shell Scott, but his stomach gives him away. Scott hears it and shoots Burper. Then there is no more rumbling.

There is no evidence showing what MacDonald thought of Prather's parody. He probably laughed all the way to the bank.

CHAPTER 10

I n 1966, John D. MacDonald turned fifty. By all conventional standards, he was a success. His novels sold well and got good reviews. He had a fine house in the tropics, a wife who loved him, and a son, Johnny, who was not much trouble. It was the sixties, though, and Johnny and his wife, Anne, changed their identities to Maynard and Lillian MacDonald in 1968 and moved to New Zealand with their new baby, Karsten. Some said the name change was a hippie thing; others believe it had to do with a bizarre religion. Nobody knows for sure, but the sixties had a strange effect on people. At this time, too, John D. MacDonald was touched by a malady that affects men of a certain age. Some call it male menopause. Others speak of a midlife crisis. But the rock-and-roll singer Jerry Lee Lewis named it best. He called it "middle-aged-crazy." And as he approached his sixth decade, John D. MacDonald was as middle-aged-crazy as they come.

It started in April the year before, a few months after *A Deadly Shade of Gold*, the fifth Travis McGee novel, was published. At a cocktail party, someone questioned the tactics of Elizabeth Lambie, a Sarasota real estate agent. John D. and Dordo had just decided to build a new house, and they wanted Liz Lambie to find them property on Siesta Key, a couple of miles from their home. Like a parody of McGee, John D. rushed to her defense. But he did not fight her detractors with muscle or gun. He chose the pen.

First, he told Liz Lambie what had been said about her. Liz Lambie shot back. "Perhaps you could point out to them that people who call themselves ladies and gentlemen do not make such statements about people, friend or foe, unless they are prepared to substantiate them. Failing that, apologies are customarily in order," Liz Lambie wrote to John D. Then he took up the gauntlet and wrote a four-page letter to the people who were talking about Liz at the cocktail party. He denounced the rumors and included a veiled threat:

I do not think I need to point out to you the extreme and immediate danger of making, at social gatherings, false statements which, if given credence could harm her professionally. It could be considered a legal and financial form of Russian roulette, because with her very existence at stake, she would be justified in any attempt to clear her name of slanderous statements. And so, in the best interests of all of us, and in the interest of undoing some of the damage done thus far, I would consider it a great personal favor to me and to Dordo if you would drop Liz a line of apology, saying you are sorry you did not check the facts more carefully before leaping to conclusions. Of course, if it would make you too uncomfortable to do so, a phone call would be a very gracious thing, and, I suspect, would make you feel better about the whole thing.

It was as if McGee's job of saving damsels in distress had been assumed by his creator. Maybe striking out to help a woman scorned doesn't seem crazy. But the defense of Liz Lambie was only the first incident.

In 1966, among members of what passed as the Alabama literary establishment, there were whispered conversations about one of the state's novelists who had moved to Florida. "Babs Deal," the Confederate literati whispered to each other, "Babs Deal is having an affair with John D. MacDonald." Maybe. Whether or not it was a full-fledged affair can't be proved. But something was certainly going on.

Babs Deal was thirteen years younger than MacDonald. She was born Babs Hodges in Scottsboro, Alabama, in 1929. For a while she worked in her hometown as a substitute schoolteacher, then joined the Army and was employed as a clerk-typist in the Judge Advocate General's office at the Pentagon. In 1951 she returned to Alabama and worked as a typist for the Anderson Brass Company in Birmingham. But typing and office work weren't enough, and so she quit her job, moved sixty miles west to Tuscaloosa, and entered the University of Alabama. She majored in creative writing and took courses from

----

Hudson Strode and one of his assistants, a lecturer named Borden Deal.

Before he enrolled in creative writing at the University of Alabama, Borden Deal had held several different jobs. Eventually he wound up at the University of Alabama. He graduated, but stuck around Tuscaloosa, writing fiction and working as a creative writing lecturer. Babs was one of his students, and she became the lecturer's pet. They were married in 1952. Both of them wanted to be novelists. Borden's first book, *Walk Through the Valley*, was published in 1956. Babs's first novel, *Acres of Afternoon*, was published in 1959. She also had to care for their three children, Ashley, Brett, and Shane. She had little time left for her passions for Alabama football and hillbilly music.

By the early 1960s, Tuscaloosa was no longer the, sleepy Southern university town it had been when the Deals married. In 1956 there was a riot when Autherine Lucy tried to integrate the University of Alabama; and in 1963 Bull Connor sent Martin Luther King to jail in Birmingham. It was the same year civil rights demonstrators were assaulted with fire hoses and attack dogs. The Ku Klux Klan was everywhere. The Grand Dragon, Bobby Shelton, lived in Tuscaloosa.

It was time for the Deals to leave. They moved to Sarasota and immediately became a part of the writers' colony. Borden, who was a loud, self-important kind of man, became a member of the Friday-afternoon writers' group. Babs, of course, was not allowed to join, even though she had written a lapful of novels. She didn't have a penis. Borden was a failure at liar's poker and was elected "Liar of the Year" because he could never bluff his way out of a bad hand.

At the time, the Deals and the MacDonalds were great friends. After the Friday writers' club meetings, Borden and John D. would pick up Babs and Dordo and go either to MacKinlay Kantor's house or over to the Deals for the evening. Deal and Kantor would play guitars. Everyone else would listen. And in the Deals' kitchen, in January 1965, MacDonald remembers later, Babs began giving him smoldering looks, or so John D. says in an eleven-page letter to Borden. Most of the details of the relationship between John D. and Babs come from that letter and Borden's four-page answer.

"She will catch your eye," MacDonald wrote. "She will widen her eyes, stare with curious intensity. She will wipe all expression out of her face, making her face quite slack, lips parted. . . . I think it might have been the second or third time we four were together that . . . I asked her just what the hell she was trying to do. 'You know,' she said. 'You *know*.'"

John D. tried to explain to Borden that there had never been any affair. But some members of the writers' group felt differently. They had seen them together, seen MacDonald admire Babs, who was a tall, willowy brunette with a deep Southern accent that could either annoy or amuse. After months of the eye contact, MacDonald said, Babs cornered him at a party at MacKinlay Kantor's house. "She stopped mumbling and turned directly to me . . . and said in utmost clarity in a tone which implied that I was being purposely stupid and thus exasperating her, dragging out every syllable, 'Ahhh love yew.' "

"And you love Dordo and you love Borden and I love Borden and I love you," MacDonald answered. "Now knock it off."

MacDonald said the affair, or whatever it was, ended. "It did not fatten my male ego, believe me," he wrote to Borden. "I do not feel 'loverly.' Approaching my fiftieth milepost, with one flat foot, hammertoes, varicose veins, dandruff, and apparently a receding gum condition which allows more morsels to be trapped between the the fangs than in the good old days of youth, I do not require that sort of focus to bolster esteem. I am very square insofar as the dalliance bit is concerned. I think that it is a trivial and degrading game."

And yet, it continued. The four of them, Babs and Borden and Dordo and John, went out together for dinner and dancing. Babs made a secret call to John D. and whispered, "Let's take off," and then hung up. And then, in another confrontation in the Deal kitchen, Babs said to John D., "What are we going to do about this?" Nothing, he answered, absolutely nothing. Later, at a restaurant called Whispering Sands, she asked John D., "Why don't we just go away together?" A minute later, John D. wrote, she answered her own question: "You don't want to go away with me, even if we could." And another time, she mused to John D., "I didn't know you could love two men at the same time."

The relationship continued. "The whole thing was, in some grotesque and saddening way, a kind of comedy," John D. wrote to Borden.

I also knew that I could fend off the hand-holding bit under the tabletop, and that when there came the meaningful pressure of her ankle against my leg under the table, I could damn well hitch my legs in the other direction too far for her to reach. Borden, at this point, if you can get your mind out of your groin for a moment, let me explain that physical contact is not necessarily sexual. It can be emotional, an affectionate romanticism, an affirmation of a totally different kind of closeness.

John D. dismissed Babs's feelings for him as a psychological problem brought on by Borden. And he told Borden so:

I realized I had long thought of her as sort of a wounded bird. She had been fouled up in a thousand ways by the circumstances of her childhood. Through her creative work, and with your understanding and help, she had worked herself up to a point of relative stability. I felt that the marriage was of utmost importance to her, and that she knew it, and so why this love for me, for God's sake. . . . So what the hell was Babs trying to do? Then I realized what it was. She is as deft at character insight as any of us. And so she knew, perhaps subconsciously right from the beginning of it, that I was as safe as a damned church, that I would not or could not betray Dordo or you. So I was a symbolic lover. On that basis she could continue her relationship with Dordo without appreciable guilt. But why did she need this kind of strange relationship in her life, a fixation never confirmed by me by kiss or caress? So it had to be a prop for her emotional stability. Why? Because she was leading an emotionally underprivi-

leged life. Not sexually underprivileged. But in those areas
of . . . excuse the expression . . . romance which a highly
evolved and very female woman like Babs needs. In all the
time I have been with you, in all the hours and all the places,
I have never seen, nor has Dordo, you make the smallest
slightest gesture of affection toward her. You are delighted at
her quickness of wit. You dance with her. But where are the
little tokens of affection, of approval of her appearance, which
she certainly must require?

The affair, or whatever it was, reached its dramatic conclusion in
September. John D. decided to tell Dordo about it, and he told Borden about that too.

I finally decided if I laid it all out to Dordo exactly what
happened and how it happened, and how I felt and what had
changed my mind, if I could make her understand, then she
could discuss it with Babs and find out this was not some oily
game *I* was playing. Dordo and I talked for hours. She was
incredulous at first. But I think that the truth, even in a
warped context, has its own ring and persuasion. It was emotionally exhausting for us. And it made a lousy week for both
of us. . . . I was afraid that Dordo did not buy my explanation
all the way. Few wives would. Yet, I suppose, were it not true,
why would I bring it up?

Dordo went to confront Babs. John D. was at home, waiting. He
was edgy. Then he heard Dordo's car.

As soon as Dordo turned into the drive I looked down and
knew from her face that she and I were all right. We sat in
the living room and she related the whole thing to me. She

said it had been grindingly difficult. When Babs began to huff and moan and bang her fist against the car door, Dordo had to haul her back swiftly from easy dramatics and get back to calm and reasoned talk. Finally Babs admitted the whole thing. But Dordo feels that Babs apparently believes that the tragic and unrequited love was reciprocated. One can see how it would be a necessary adjunct of the basic delusion, to believe it was returned. Otherwise one looks such a fool and a bother. . . . Babs said she had always loved Dordo more than she had ever loved me. Dordo said it was a curious way to show it. . . .

John D. was cruel to Borden in the letter. He called him rude, self-centered, inconsiderate, vulgar, coarse, and callous.

I do not know what you are going to do with your lives, and at this moment on this Sunday afternoon, I am too emotionally racked up to care a hell of a lot. You could have trusted me with your life, Borden. You should have known that. I was trying to keep your life intact, for God's sake. And Babs's. This is a small area. Should your marriage continue, as I hope you will make the effort to assure, we shall be running into one another. I assure you we shall never mention this to a single soul, either of us, as long as life continues. And there will be courtesy—nothing to clue anybody that we are not friendly. But can I trust you to respond in the same manner, Borden? Or do you think that for the sake of your pride or something that you have to nominate me as the villain of the piece? The curious innuendoes about some supposedly lurid local love life of mine leads me to suspect that you want to make me the villain. If you wish to do that within the bounds of your private relationship with each other, please feel free. But the very first time either one of us might happen to come across some ugly little distortion of this charade, which certainly became ugly enough in its own right . . . I shall certainly make it my business to correct any impression immediately and in detail.

Borden got the letter the next day. "What a weird little fantasy you are peddling this time," he wrote back.

I knew you thought you were God's gift to womankind, but this is utterly ridiculous. I do not know why you have felt it necessary to try to attack and destroy my wife. I do know that you have delivered the most profound insult that one man can give another. . . . Babs told me long ago that she was having a little difficulty with you, that at strategic moments you were indulging in idle romantic talk and that she didn't know how to handle it. I scoffed at the very idea. . . . Now you [are] trying to convince me that Babs is this terrible, sexually predatory female that you're having to beat off with a stick. . . . Here is this terribly evil woman who is forcing herself on you sexually. Here you are, a noble white knight. . . . I will not forgive you for slandering my wife in the service of your attempt to believe yourself Travis McGee. . . . I can only suggest, as strongly as possible, that you confine your sexual dreams of conquest to the fictional Travis McGee, where you do them much better. . . .

After that, silence.

Then, a little over two months later, on November 27, Babs Deal wrote a review of *Dark Places of the Heart* for the *Sarasota Herald-Tribune*.

Characters like Nellie and Tom abound in the world. . . . We have all known them, and most of us have come all too close to them at some point in our lives. They are emotional bandits. Neither is alive unless they have someone in their thrall. Nellie's method is the bludgeoning of kindness. She takes in prostitutes and invalids, divorcées and ladies recovering from unhappy love affairs. By the time they have consumed her cup of kindness they find they've swapped off a precious commodity—their souls.

Tom's method is simpler and one more readily recognized. He picks ladies of an uncertain age who also have their problems; divorce, widowhood, unhappy love affairs, poverty, loneliness, even cancer, and charms them with a sad smile and a mouthful of words. He truly isn't much interested in their bodies. Like Nellie, the soul will do for him, too.

Dordo clipped and saved the review. In the margin she wrote, "Am I imagining something or is there a message in this? Is someone trying to tell us something?"

Borden and Babs Deal were divorced nine years later.

Then there was the sermon to his sister in 1969. In it, John D. speaks in the voice of the most vitriolic Puritan preacher. Dorie had written her older brother a letter asking for his help in finding her husband, Bill, a job in Florida. John D. wrote back a letter that makes Cotton Mather seem gentle.

I *have* to hurt you. . . . You are an alcoholic. All the symptoms are so pathetically visible that I cannot kid myself about it. . . . First, your face. It is not any mask of tragedy or anxiety or any product of age. It is the all-too-typical potato-face, as it is commonly called, of the self-destructive drinker—lumpy, rivulated, out of shape and out of focus. . . . You know that I will do everything I can do to help. You remember that my first request to you was to stop drinking. You did not. I can see now why. I did not know how far down that sick road you had taken yourself. . . . You are so awful damned close to a booze farm right now, Dorie. I think you know that. I think it scares the hell out of you. . . . Do not write this off as dramatics. That would only be another sneaky, dirty little rationalization. The message is writ loud and clear on your face and figure and in your manner, and in the patterns of your conversation—contradictory, repetitive, semi-earnest, semi-sly. I *know* the disease, Dorie. I have good friends who have had it for untold years. Some have been off the booze for a decade. They are cheery, happy, energetic, optimistic—but one knock and they would go right from there to the alcoholic ward. . . . You need help. But I have to give you this letter, because it is what you have to have, or you will slip right out of life into some other kind of creature for whom there might be no hope at all. Pride, guts, love vanity and pure fright. You have them and you now have to put them to work. . . . .From then on you get every bit of help we can give. If you do not make the start, we will do all we can for your kids, but there will be nothing at all worth doing that we can do for you.

Of course, the middle-aged craziness was not all that happened during those years in the middle and late 1960s. Dordo used a bout of insomnia over the 1966 Thanksgiving holidays to design the new MacDonald home on Ocean Place.

"It became impossible for us to keep on living here on Point Crisp," MacDonald wrote in a family duplicated letter in 1966. "The road and right of way go right past the front of the house. People we do not know have an increasing lack of respect for the privacy we need in order to work. We found a piece of property about two and a half miles from here on Siesta Key. It has water on two sides. . . . It is at the end of a short unpaved road called Ocean Place. . . . But in order to properly prepare the property for the house we must put in thousands of yards of fill and build a breakwater across the front. This has been classified as a major project, and so we cannot expect permission to go ahead with it until mid April. The fill is to be trucked in, not dredged, but we have to buy a small hunk of bay bottom before we can put in the stone breakwater."

On a lesser scale, the preparation for the new MacDonald house sounds like the work of the fictional developers MacDonald had railed against in his 1962 novel *A Flash of Green*.

The mid-1960s were also the years it looked possible for John D. to get a chance to fulfill one of his long time ambitions and become a television comedy writer. In May of 1967, he got a letter from Virginia Caldwell, the wife of Erskine Caldwell, the prolific writer of the Southern gothic novels *Tobacco Road, God's Little Acre*, and scores of others. It seems the Caldwells were friends with a Hollywood comedian, Dan Rowan, of the comedy team of Rowan and Martin, and Martin was a Travis McGee fan. He wanted to start a correspondence. John D. leaped at the chance. He had been trying to write comedy routines since 1960, when he sent Jack Benny the plot line for three routines. "If I am on the wrong track, kindly file this in the nearest wastebasket," he wrote to Benny. "If not, I can come up with many more on the same basis if so requested, and would feel privileged to do so. . . ." Benny never wrote back. Then, a year later, he tried the same tactic with Bob Newhart. "I think I have a good ear for your sort of material," he told Newhart in a letter. "And have never tried to suggest any material to anybody because they—my few other favorites—have never been in the sort of spot you are in. Were you still doing things within your pattern, it would be effrontery to suggest anything. But now that you are devouring material like an ulcered hippo, perhaps you might grasp random straws, such as me. . . . At any rate, should you be so flooded with marvelous stuff this letter is an imposition, then just forget the whole thing. . . ." Newhart forgot it. John D. tried again with a couple of Fort Lauderdale comedians, Les Romer and Harry Howard, who worked at the Lauderdale Beach Hotel. At least he *knew* them. They had met when the comedians played a gig in Sarasota. "I enclose a draft of a routine which is probably just about as funny as a postnasal drip," he wrote. "I am an amateur truly. This is the first one I ever completed.

I am certain it will not fit your style, your timing, or your taste. Please let me know how horrible it truly is . . . be brutally frank with ol' John. . . . if it is hopeless stuff, for God's sake say so." They never wrote back, either. But now here was Dan Rowan, one of the stars of *Laugh-In,* a smash television comedy hit, and he wanted to correspond. John D. wrote Rowan immediately. "Next time you are in the area, please send a letter or wire to this address ahead of time and we will get out the good jelly glasses and ride around in my very small boat," he said. Finally, a comedian wrote back. Rowan was beside himself. "I haven't had a thrill like this . . . hell, there hasn't been another to compare. Now I can understand, faintly, some of the mail I have had in which fans have explained this is their first fan letter. . . . I consider the jelly glasses an invite and accept." It was the beginning of a friendship and correspondence that would last eight years.

But the change in his personal life was not the only new adventure for John D. He had decided to write nonfiction and to alter the pattern of the McGee books. It all began in 1966 when Dr. Carl A. Coppolino was indicted by the State of Florida for killing his wife, Carmela. He was also indicted in Freehold, New Jersey, for the death of Lieutenant Colonel William E. Farber. To a novelist who had been writing crime stories for over a decade, this sounded like a better plot than he could think up. And so he began to pursue the case, hoping to prove that old adage that truth is stranger than fiction.

CHAPTER 11

J ohn D. MacDonald was not alone in his decision to try non-fiction. In the mid-1960s a group of newspaper feature writers tested the limits of their form and invented what came to be called "New Journalism." According to Tom Wolfe, who named the genre and was its best-known advocate, writers in those days decided to try to write journalism that read like a novel. Wolfe, Gay Talese, George Plimpton, Rex Reed, and a handful of others began writing for *Esquire* magazine in a style that did, indeed, read like fiction. They were followed by Norman Mailer, whose book *The Armies of the Night* won the Pulitzer Prize for nonfiction in 1969. So it was natural for John D. to want to try his hand at factual writing. And, of course, it was natural for him to want to write about crime, because that's what he had been writing about for decades.

But before he wrote the Coppolino book, John D. tried his hand at a sort of autobiography. Actually, it was a biography of his cats, Roger and Geoffrey, and the other animals he grew up loving. It was quite a jump for a crime writer to attempt a book on house pets, but on the first page John D. made sure his readers knew this was no competition for Lassie. "This is not a luvums-duvums-itsy-boo book, about pooty-tats. . . . Someone said: Sentimentality is unearned emotion." MacDonald is true to his words. The book is never sentimental. It's also not much as autobiography, but then John D. always said he never wanted to write about himself. The facts about his life in the book are perfunctory—dates of graduation, trips to Mexico, and a lot of cat stories. It offers little insight into MacDonald, but then it was never meant to do that. "*The House Guests* was sort of a fragment of an autobiography," MacDonald told John Eastman in an interview in 1978. "And I feel sort of self-conscious about getting into [those] areas." It was supposed to be about cats. John D. summed up his feeling at the end of the book:

I owe a strange debt to both cats. We got them when I was trying to learn how to write. There were the fifteen years of Geoffrey, and . . . nineteen years of Roger. With no intention of seeming intolerant, I would like to say that I do not believe the dependent adorations of dogs could have formed the same necessary kind of emotional counterpoint. The elegant complexity of cats, the very formality of their codes of behavior, their unbribed response of sporadic demonstrations of affection in return for their demanded measure of household equality, their conservative insistence on order, habit and routine— these attributes seem more congruent with lengthy creative effort, more contributive to that frame of mind which makes such effort sustainable then could be any doggy devotion.

The House Guests was a labor of love. It only lasted through two paperback editions. Nonetheless, of all his books, it was one of John D.'s favorites. Near the end of his life he was preparing a new edition of it that he would publish himself.

The real work of nonfiction would come with *No Deadly Drug*. MacDonald was intrigued by the crime Coppolino was accused of, the murder of his wife, Carmela, in Sarasota and that of Lieutenant Colonel William E. Farber in Middletown, New Jersey. The two murders occurred within a month of each other, in 1965. By January 1967, MacDonald had written a magazine article for *Look*, "Lee Bailey versus New Jersey," which was a condensation of the eleven-day New Jersey trial. The article was five thousand words long. The book would eventually be 650,000 words. Initially, it was to be published by Fawcett, but John D. wanted this one, which he called *No Deadly Medicine*, to be published in hardback. "I have decided, with Pete Schmidt as my collaborator, that we shall do the Coppolino trials and hearings as a book or books for Doubleday," MacDonald wrote in a diary he kept briefly. "I believe that if I can take a few pages to New York showing how we will handle the problems of the book, Doubleday will advance us $10,000. We can then refund Fawcett's advance and go ahead with Doubleday."

John D. wanted his work to be a quality book, and that's why he wanted a hardcover publisher. "There will be too many quicky books on the newsstand and I am afraid paper covers would confuse our intent with the intent of others." The Coppolino affair was the 1966 trial of the century. Carl Coppolino was said to have killed his wife with a drug injection. He was also said to have injected the colonel, a neighbor near his former home in New Jersey, with a lethal drug. There were to be trials in two states. The New Jersey trial was first, and Coppolino was acquitted. All the papers covered it.

MacDonald's problem was that he wrote *No Deadly Drug*, as it was eventually called, as a long narrative that read more like an extended newspaper article than a novel. He may have wanted to try the Tom Wolfe method and chronicle truth with the aura of fiction, but it didn't work. John D. always said no one had ever written a book about a trial in the long, painstaking detail he used. Maybe, maybe not. Sensational trials have always been the fodder for crime journalists. Even crime writers who specialize in fiction get in on the act. Erle Stanley Gardner, the creator of Perry Mason and an early pulp writer, wrote *The Court of Last Resort*, a book that chronicled a number of true crime stories, and he covered famous real-life courtroom drama—the Sam Sheppard and Sir Harry Oakes trials, for example—for newspaper syndicates. While it's true that trials have moments of electricity and drama, it's also true that they are long, boring, and monotonous, like literary biography. Look at a reporter's notebook after a day in a courtroom and you are more likely to find doodles than quotes. That's why Perry Mason works best in a one-hour format. And that's why Gardner's television dramatization of *The Court of Last Resort* lasted only thirty minutes per episode.

John D.'s idea was to make the whole process—preliminary hearing, bail hearing, jury selection, and the trial itself—interesting. It's an impossible task. Even colorful lawyers like F. Lee Bailey, who defended Coppolino, get dull and dry as they wrestle with judges and precedence. And *No Deadly Drug* often reflects that.

"I think I finished off my yen to write about the real world with the Coppolino book," John D. wrote ten years after the book was published. "I could not move the characters around. They kept turning their backs on dramatic, obligatory scenes. Most uncooperative."

The book sold well—the John D. MacDonald name assured that. But the reviews were mixed. "The MacDonald name is magic in the suspense field, so one approached his first foray into true-crime narrative with anticipation. Soon, however, one wonders why he chose [this case]. . . . MacDonald writes with utter objectivity and great length [but] the true crime buff may wish that the writer had chosen a case of more interesting, less publicized character," *Publishers Weekly*'s reviewer wrote when the book came out. And Charles Willeford, a Florida crime novelist and great fan of MacDonald, was also disappointed. "This was a long and arduous job, a task so difficult one cannot understand why a novelist of MacDonald's stature would take the time to research and write it. At any rate, it is done, well done, and MacDonald fans can now hopefully look forward to the further adventures of Travis McGee," he wrote in the *Miami Herald*.

John D.'s problem with *No Deadly Drug* was his scrupulous attempts at objectivity. "[It] focuses upon the very human aspects of [the] people, attempts to use the novelist's insight to illuminate these aspects of a common humanity," MacDonald wrote in a discussion of the book, "and by *not* taking positions regarding guilt and innocence, truth and lies, refrains from turning these people into two dimensional symbols one is more accustomed to find in the usual book about trials where the writer has appointed himself an advocate." And yet it is taking sides, writing with an attitude and a chip on his shoulder, that accounts for the success of the Travis McGee books. MacDonald shows that without that attitude he can be as dull as any hack writer for any Gannett newspaper in America.

In a letter to his sister, Doris, written just before the book was completed, John D. washed his hands of future nonfiction. "If I had it to do over again, I do not think—knowing what I know now—that I would have ever gotten into the Coppolino trials. It is far too demanding, requiring too much concentrated effort over too long a time. It has cost me—or will cost me by the time it is all done—a minimum of three novels in time and effort spend."

And yet all of John D.'s effort was not in a vain. *No Deadly Drug* was his first taste of the big book, so when he tried *Condominium* a few years later he understood what he was getting into. After the Coppolino book, reviewers routinely praised John D.'s novels for their great attention to detail, a trait he has picked up during his stint as a court reporter. He also learned to deal with topicality—developers in *Condominium*, television preachers in *One More Sunday*, and real estate charlatans in *Barrier Island*. Not a bad education for a first-time journalist.

Meanwhile, back to Travis McGee.

By the time he wrote the tenth in the McGee series, *Pale Gray for Guilt*, MacDonald realized he had a problem. His main character didn't have anyone to talk to. He solved the problem by re-creating Meyer, a freelance economist who lives on a boat near McGee's *Busted Flush*. Meyer was mentioned in two early McGee novels, *The Quick Red Fox* and *A Purple Place for Dying*, but he didn't come alive as a character until *Guilt*, which was written in 1967.

"I just got bloody tired of having McGee go through those interior monologues to explain to the reader what was going on," John D. told an interviewer for *Criminal Intent* magazine. "I finally realized he was going to have to have somebody he could bounce conversation off, but I didn't want to have a clown, a Sancho Panza or a Doctor Watson. I wanted to have a second lead who would have some stature and I thought it wouldn't be too unlikely to have a freelance economist living aboard a boat in Florida. It would be a good life and he could go off lecturing and publishing papers and teaching seminars. He turned out well because he's a man who makes friends rather more readily than does McGee. . . . He's a bit more sensitive man than is McGee."

There had always been questions about whether or not Travis McGee was modeled after John D. MacDonald. The answer, of course, is only in a fanciful way. But with Meyer, it's different. McGee's sidekick is very much like MacDonald. You can see it in the results of a Multiphasic Personality Inventory Test that John D. took for a psychology professor at the University of Alabama. The test consists of hundreds of true-false questions. John D. took the test three times on three different days. He took it once as himself, once as McGee, and once as Meyer. "I tried to answer all those questions the way I thought that they would answer them," MacDonald said. "The three sets of answers went up for grading, and I turned out to have considerably more kinship to Meyer psychologically than to McGee, which was amusing."

John D. had a nagging problem with his McGee books. Even with Travis talking to Meyer, he could not find a way to talk about what he considered to be the issue of the day—race. The middle and late sixties were the time of the civil rights movement, and names like Montgomery and Birmingham and Selma were etched into the public consciousness in a way that would forever change America. Even Travis McGee in his offshore houseboat surrounded by willing women and pleasant afternoons drinking gin and listening to jazz could not ignore what was happening. The problem was, John D. was not sure what was happening, and he was not sure how to get it in his books.

MacDonald was a certifiable white liberal. He gave money to the American Civil Liberties Union; he supported Democratic candidates for governor of Florida and raised money for them; he spoke out in favor of John Kennedy and wept when he died. But still, there was this race thing. There were few blacks in upstate New York when he grew up, none in his unit of the segregated Army during World War II, and not many in the resort area of Sarasota. So he was confused. He expressed that confusion in 1969 letter to a young fan:

The gigantic (?) riots in Birmingham the last time Martin Luther King appeared there . . . involved 300 black youths out of a total black population of 18,000. Out of 18,000 people of any shape and color and location, certainly 300 would be delighted for any excuse to run through the streets shouting and throwing things. Life is quite dull for most people and any violent change eliminates boredom for a while . . . The liberal attitude toward the black in America has been silly and embarrassing. The liberal seems to want to think of the black as a kind of dusky white man who is "just like everybody else." Imagine two men trying to talk to each other, one nine feet tall and the other three feet tall, and they try to keep the conversation on that level and those subjects which will have *no* reference to height at all. Yet each of these men are aware all the time of height, and the difficulties their size has imposed on them. Constructive dialogue can take place when white men and black men accept their essential differences, include them in statements and opinions, and go on from there. Every living thing has a right to be what it is because genetically it has no choice. So don't feel nonplussed about being unable to judge the rights and wrongs of the racial bag. You are in good company. Most people are fumbling around in the murk looking for answers.

To try to find a way out of the murk, John D. wrote to Len and June Moffatt. Early in 1965 the Moffatts, who lived in Downey, California, started *The JDM Bibliophile*. The first issue was a one-page mimeographed sheet listing all of MacDonald's novels. They distributed about one hundred copies. The *Bibliophile* was only one of the Moffatt homemade publications. Most of the others—which included *Moonshine* for the Fantasy Amateur Press Association—were about science fiction and fantasy. The second issue of the *Bibliophile* was up to nine pages. In addition to lists of MacDonald's works it included articles from fans about MacDonald, news about the author, and letters to the editor. The Moffatts sent copies to John D., who was pleased by the fanzine and became a regular contributor. They also mailed a copy to Anthony Boucher, who mentioned it in his column in *The New York Times*. Circulation soared into the thousands, and the Moffatts found they were devoting more and more time to their publishing hobby. So it was the Moffatts to whom John D. wrote about his confusion over race. In his new McGee novel, *The Girl in the Plain Brown Wrapper*, MacDonald included a Negro maid. He wanted to know if she sounded real.

The Moffatts read the book and wondered what the problem was.

"We got the impression you wanted to bring the race problem into the novel, and that you were concerned about the way you (and McGee) handled it. . . . Would the maid respond to McGee in this way or would she respond some other way? . . . June suggested we show the pages to some friends of ours who were certain to have some reactions on the subject."

The friends were Lil and Kris Neville. She was a black woman from Watts. Her husband was a white man from Missouri. And indeed they did have opinions.

"Lil's . . . reaction was the impossibility of communicating the situation to Mr. MacDonald in a way that would be meaningful to him, and that any suggestions she would offer would just get him uptight with defense mechanisms and would serve no constructive purposes," a letter to the Moffatts from the Nevilles read. "I think we all agreed that the portrayal of McGee was of a well-meaning man with an inability to see past the stereotypes he carries."

MacDonald wrote back to the Nevilles. The speed typing he took in high school, coupled with his IBM Selectric typewriter, made it easier and faster for him to write than to talk. Their correspondence continued for more than a year. MacDonald tried to understand race, but it was no use. In his last letter to the Nevilles he wrote, "We want so badly to find the answer, but there isn't any answer but time itself. . . . At least I have fumbled my way through the thickets to the point where, at last, I can see why [Lil] was so skeptical of my certainty that I *could* empathize." MacDonald never tried to write about black people again.

Travis mused in *The Girl in the Plain Brown Wrapper* as he thought about the black maid named Lorette:

No solutions for me or thee, not from your leaders be they passive or militant, nor from the politicians or the liberals or the head knockers or the educators. No answer but time. And if the law and the courts can be induced to become color-blind, we'll have a good answer, after both of us are dead. And a bloody answer otherwise.

While MacDonald remained confused about race, his mind was clear on the war in Vietnam. "I think all wars—with the possible exception of fighting to repel an army invading one's own country—are rotten, cruel, wasteful, senseless and in violation of human dignity and purpose," he wrote in a 1970 letter to his niece, Susan Robinson, his sister's daughter. "I see no difference between this war and World Wars I and II and Korea, except possibly that this one has had worse public relations and publicity than most. I am amused by the people who call this war immoral and illegal. That statement supposes that there is such a thing as a legal and moral war. Nonsense!"

But he was not in agreement with his niece about the student antiwar movement in America:

Hey, aren't they teaching you any history in school? Ever hear of the Oxford movement? In 1934 when the world was beginning to get tense, *one third* of all the college students in this country signed a declaration that they would never go to war under *any* circumstances. Another third said they would fight only if America were invaded. This is a far more significant and consistent percentage than today. And many many stayed with their beliefs. Thousands served their time in prison. There were peace marches and demonstrations and riots. . . . In your generation there is the kind of arrogant belief that this is the *first* generation to ever make an organized protest against anything. Someday find out how many were killed in New York City during the draft riots during the Civil War. The sublime self-satisfaction of your generation of dissidents is firmly based on an almost total ignorance of all the nations. It is a constant complement of the idealism of the young people of all the generations of history that there has always been a protest against war, against brutality, against killing. . . . I cannot say whether or not I approve of men fleeing to Canada and Sweden to avoid the draft. . . . I know that I could not do it that way, because it is pure cop-out. When you think a law or a situation is unjust, and you decide that you are not going to go along with it, then you must prepare yourself to accept the penalty involved. Thoreau did not run to Canada when he decided not to pay the head tax. He went to prison. When Emerson visited him in prison and said, "Henry, what are you doing in here?" the answer was "Ralph, what are you doing out there."

John D. was irascible in his views, but not all of it was just a middle-aged slide into the realm of the curmudgeon. His irascibility had a real foundation; beginning in 1967, every day was clouded with pain and numbness in his feet and legs. He wrote in October of that year:

The first vague symptom appeared in July. I noticed that when I got up in the morning and brushed my teeth, bending at that angle seemed to pull at a nerve that runs down my left leg, on the outside, down to the ankle area, and it was eased by merely standing with my weight on my right leg., and lifting my left heel off the floor. It became more evident, and a bit more painful as weeks went by, and then I began to awaken early in the morning by pains in my left hip and thigh. When I moved the pain would go away and I could get back to sleep. When I would first get up the leg would be sore, but as I moved around it would ease. At last, after waking up earlier and earlier, finally there came a time when I could not find any position comfortable enough so that I could go back to sleep. It was then that I went to Dr. Matthews who sent me for X-rays. That was in early September, I believe. They were X-rays of the lower back. While there I asked the girl to also take pictures of the left hip, as that seemed to be where the trouble "felt" as if it was. The discs looked thin but okay and [the doctor] sent me to [a specialist]. He had me strip and move this way and that, and found movement restricted by pain when I had to move the left leg in certain ways. When I was doubled up like an Arab on a prayer rug, he thumped the area of my back just above the tailbone and it did not hurt, and he said it was not a disc, and I might add that my back has not hurt for a moment throughout these weeks. I have been going along doing the recommended exercises without noticeable improvement. I find that I can get back to sleep by taking aspirin and using a little bolster pillow to rest my left leg on. Ten days ago I noticed that the underside of my middle two toes had become semi-numb. Then this extended to the ball of my left foot, so that it feels somewhat as if there was an alien substance there, like a lump in a shoe. The leg suddenly seemed worse. More pain. Night before last I tried to work it loose by walking up to the Stickney Point area and back, a distance of 2 1/2 miles. I found myself "clumping," slapping the sole of the left foot. I could control it with an effort akin to walking on tiptoe. Also on uneven ground there was a tendency of the foot to turn outward. The pain that wakes me now seems to be a hard, dull ache in the ankle bone on the outside. This morning the numbness has extended to the outside edge of the big toe, and to a lesser degree across the instep. The motor restrictions seem to be in lifting the foot with the heel on the floor, pulling the toes upward. I now realize I have been clumsy lately, tripping on stairs, and unable to balance on the left leg when putting my pants on. I do not know what could be constricting the nerve system as my back feels relaxed and flexible, without pain or tension. With absolutely no reason to back me up, I keep thinking of something in the hip or groin that is pressing on the nerves.

John D. continued to limp around for about three months, and then went back to the doctor:

I went to the hospital December 21st for tests and, they thought, a probable operation on my back for a herniated disc. But after all the tests they decided that I had, a couple of months ago, an attack of the toxic neuritis brought on by a virus-bearing mosquito, and the reason my left foot and ankle are numb and do not work well is because of the nerve damage caused by the neuritis. So it is a post-polio kind of therapy now to see how much recovery of muscle control I get, and how far the numbness will decrease. When I got back from the hospital on Christmas Eve I had to stay sacked out on the couch a couple of days because in one of the tests they remove spinal fluid and you have to stay flat until the pressure builds back up to normal.

The neuritis was the first of a series of illnesses that would plague him for the rest of his life. But all of his maladies weren't physical. He suffered a sort of social vertigo, as he made clear in a letter to Don Farber, his New York lawyer. Farber wrote MacDonald and suggested dinner and drinks the next time John D. was in New York. MacDonald declined:

Look, my good friend, I must herewith pledge you to a kind of secrecy that falls quite outside the client-attorney relationship. Perhaps I am being a bit stalwart about it, but I would far rather maintain the big stalwart image and depend upon a lot of shifty foot-work than come out with the truth of the matter. So here is the truth . . . The New York scene, for many and obvious reasons, places a large strain upon me, but I do not respond to it as I should. For several years now it has been imperative that I use up my days there in the necessary ways, run them into the cocktail hour, and then quit all socializing scenes. I have to refill the lamps. Otherwise I arrive at an unpleasant condition called (by me) the Whips and Jingles. The medics call it latent acute anxiety syndrome, and it is nothing I can talk or reason myself out of. And, believe me, nothing I want to take the risk of arousing. It cuts a trip damn short. So be a good fellow and have a daytime drink with me, and keep my dreary little secret from those whom I wish to think I am impregnable, insurmountable, and indefatigable.

Despite all the problems, John D. and Dordo finally moved into their dream house in August 1969. The architecture resembled that of an 1800 Florida fish house. It was nine feet off the ground and rested on forty-nine pilings of Florida pine. A tin roof covered the building, and there was a four-foot veranda all around it. The house was made of rough-cut cedar boards, inside and out. The pilings went right through the house and looked like telephone poles in the living room. "It is the kind of place where you can hammer a nail into the wall and nothing is harmed," John D. wrote.

But the angst of MacDonald's encounter with the 1960s was not over. He still had to settle a lawsuit with American Express. In late 1967, John D. got a letter from G. Foley, a customer representative from American Express. It was addressed to F. M. MacDonald and thanked him for calling about a $10.50 billing error. John D. wrote back and said he knew nothing about the matter. He added prophetically: "I have the eerie feeling that this little dandy is NEVER going to get straightened out." He was almost right.

Then it got worse. MacDonald disputed a $7.20 bill for gasoline and another for a $130.46 airplane ticket. Meanwhile, another customer service representative wrote him and said his bill was past due. John D. answered:

Whether or not my account is past due, sir, is a matter of interpretation. At least, I have had no such notifications from your establishment. And you have heard from me. Ah, yes, you have heard from me time and again, a detail which mayhaps the Great Machine overlooked when it upchucked my card in your "in" basket. I would be bedazzled, humble and grateful indeed if you would inspect the attached copies of certain documents and not only write me a prompt, personal, and thorough and thoughtful answer, but also unravel and eliminate the ancient, unadjusted, semi-corrected charge of $7.20 dating back, so help us all, to December of 1967.

Six days later, when he got no response, he wrote again:

It must be a new age of efficiency there at Big Ex. No more fussing about with first, second, third notices. Send the final notice first! I think we can both safely agree that it would be distressing for both of us were the brute electronic equipment to start assessing delinquency fees before I even have a chance to get that prompt, personal, thorough and thoughtful answer you promised me.

Then came the threat:

Of the 35 million copies of my thirty-odd books which have sold all over the world, several million have involved the adventures of a character I named Travis McGee. It is often very difficult to dream up brand new torments and handicaps for a fictional character. . . . I now realize I have been over-looking an affliction which even Mr. McGee might not be able to overcome. I am now thinking of, in the next novel, gifting him with an American Express Credit Card! It would make Poe's bit about the pit and the pendulum look no more distressing than diaper rash.

American Express answered by canceling John D.'s credit card. Then came the lawsuit. John D. asked for $600,000 in damages. American Express got a restraining order to keep MacDonald from mentioning the progress of the suit. John D. went to New York, where depositions were taken. It was, he said in a letter to Dan Rowan, almost a moral crusade: "I want to know if a huge corporation can damage me with utter cynical impunity merely because it is big and I am small, and I want the Court to clarify this little point of citizenship rights, damages etc. in a computer-cold world." Eventually, on another trip to New York in late 1969, the suit was settled. Part of the agreement was that MacDonald agreed never to write a novel about credit cards. For John D., it was a victory for the little man. Through his attorneys he issued a statement under the heading "Victory Claimed for Humans." "I would hope that I have had some part in acquainting them with the imperatives of human contact and communication," he said. Ultimately, of course, it was a hollow victory. In a little more than two decades, long-distance operators and bank tellers and travel agents would be machines. Money would be plastic. Stores would be screens on computers. They would not really exist at all. And the people? They never even noticed as they zipped through the cyberspace of their brave new world. But MacDonald tried.

On December 18, John and Dordo left Florida for Mexico. He put the problems of civil rights, of the Vietnam War, of American Express, and of his numb leg and foot all behind him. And for the first time in years, he relaxed.

"I did not realize how uptight I had gotten—how many extraneous things were taking the time I should be putting into the books," he wrote in a letter to a friend. "Anyway I have eliminated a whole jumble of things that were keeping me from my work and am now set to go at full steam, and shall finish four books this year."

CHAPTER 12

John D. MacDonald had a strange ambivalence about Hollywood. He was like a confused socialist who curses the rich and yet wants to be invited to their parties so he can turn them down. He had a proprietary feeling about his work. MacDonald wanted his books and short stories to be true to the way he had written them, and he complained or refused to sell the rights to producers he felt weren't literary enough.

It was a different attitude from that of other writers who came from the pulps. Both Raymond Chandler and Dashiell Hammett worked as Hollywood screenwriters. For Hammett at least, that experience wasn't a happy one, despite the money he earned. Warner Brothers tried to keep the creator of Sam Spade from using that character again, because they believed the rights they had bought to *The Maltese Falcon* meant they owned Sam Spade. Hammett eventually won, but it took an appeals court to give him the right to use Spade again. Chandler, on the other hand, was a man of Hollywood and enjoyed writing screenplays. He saw motion picture work as a meal ticket for a less than prolific novelist. "You beat the [publishing] racket by having so many books around," Chandler wrote. "I can't beat it because I'm such a slow writer."

That, of course, was never a problem for John D. It was just that to him, Hollywood seemed a little greasy, a little too concerned with money. It was a feeling writers had had about motion pictures since the 1930s. To work for the movies was to sell out. And MacDonald, the great moralist, was not about to sell out. At least not right away. The production of *Cape Fear* in 1962 had been a success, although MacDonald felt the script was too simplistic. MacDonald never wrote screenplays, but in 1963 he tried turning the screenplay for a Judy Garland film, *I Could Go On Singing*, into a novel. It was a flop. During the heyday of live television, a number of his short stories and novels were adapted for the major dramatic programs of the era—*Robert Montgomery Presents, The Schlitz Playhouse of Stars, The*

Kraft Suspense Theater, Studio One, and *Alfred Hitchcock Presents.* He also worked as cowriter for a two-part adaptation of his novel *Cry Hard, Cry Fast* that appeared on the NBC series *Run for Your Life.*

John D. was a loner who liked total control. Novels let him be that way. Hollywood—movies and television—would have meant collaboration, and he despised the idea of working with someone else. Still, everybody else who was a popular crime writer in the 1960s seemed to be making big money from movies, and for all his standards, John D. would have liked to share some of the gravy. The big money, of course, went to Ian Fleming and the James Bond series produced by United Artists. Then there was the Matt Helm series starring Dean Martin that was based on novels by Donald Hamilton; the Len Deighton books like *The Ipcress File*; and, of course, the never-ending Perry Mason television series based on Erle Stanley Gardner's novels. Even Ross Macdonald was having some success with film. Two of his Lew Archer novels, with his detective renamed Harper and played by Paul Newman, were on the screen. Things seemed right for Travis McGee to appear either in the movies or on television. But John D. said no. And he explained why in a 1967 letter to Dan Rowan:

I put so many restrictive clauses in the option agreement [for McGee] they've had problems peddling the merchandise. One item is that the serial television rights are completely escrowed, sequestered, or whatever you call it. The McGee books are to keep me in boats and baubles during my declining years, and I have said to those who would have him on the TV screen that it isn't very likely right now that any huge swarm of people would run to their favorite newsstand and snap up new novels featuring Ben Casey. Or Sgt. Bilko.

The people I had the most trouble explaining this to were a sort of matched set of about four fellows from [Mark] Goodson–[Bill] Todman [television producers]. They jollied me up [in New York] at the Oak Room at the Plaza, phones on the table amid the raw meat, etc. Seems some overconfident type on the coast had conned them into thinking he had the lock on the television rights, and so they had gone ahead with script and contracts with sponsors and network folk and all that, and had, bless my heart, signed one Chuck Connors. All this was two years ago. . . . They kept saying, "How much?" and I kept saying I wasn't going to talk price because he wasn't for sale. . . . They had those pained little half smiles, half frowns and they were wearing those giant cuff links that must be full of helium or they couldn't get a hand up to their mouth to take a tranquilizer. You know, I feel like a pretty standard true-blue middle-aged American boy until I get with these types and then somehow I begin to feel like some very stupid broad must feel in a hotel bar lounge when three or four salesmen are trying to talk her into coming up to the suite, honey. Later it was Mr. G. or Mr. T., I forget which, told my agent . . . that it was extremely difficult to find the right approach to a writer who doesn't believe in television. He was wrong. I believe in it. One per cent of it is very very good. . . . And 99 per cent . . . is schlock. I just don't want Trav to undergo that simplistifying (new word!!) change which the series tube requires, nor do I want the angle of approach wrenched this way and that when the ratings don't move and everybody starts to get frightened and they start trying this and trying that.

But Hollywood kept waving money at John D. and ultimately he gave in. First he tried a pilot for a series he called *Bimini Gal*, which was produced by Warner Brother–Seven Arts. Filming started in September 1967. To save money, Warners decided to produce it as a made-for-TV movie rather than a thirty-minute or one-hour pilot. However, there were some other changes Warners made as well. Originally, Robert Mitchum was to play the male lead, an old thief who operates a tramp steamer for an older woman, played by Joan Blondell. He was replaced by Richard Boone. The script was set in the Bahamas, but it was shifted to Hawaii. Then there was the matter

----

of the title. No longer would it be *Bimini Gal*. Now the producers were considering *Kona Coast or Hula Gal*. The winner was *Kona Coast*. It was a flop. "The few people who have seen that pilot on the tube—in random places, usually very late at night—have thrown up," John D. wrote a few years later. But financially, he did all right. "I came out reasonably well on the whole thing," John D. said, "and it is probably my first and last adventure in Fantasyland." It wasn't, of course.

Within a few months he was working for Tom Tannenbaum at 20th Century Fox, knocking out a treatment for something called *I'll Find You*, the story of Jake Olson, who, MacDonald wrote, "faced the special problem of portraying a time of fundamental change in what has been called the inner climate of the soul." The treatment sounded like television:

> Everything always came too easily [for Jake Olson]. Sun-brown, brawny, mature, he was a welcome addition to all the guest lists at Palm Springs, Puerto Vallarte, Sun Valley or on a Mediterranean cruise. Maybe sometimes he got a little too smashed, but held it well. He knew all the tricks of the amusing chit-chat of the In group. . . . It was inevitable that he should marry a lass with a good fat inheritance. . . . But life has a funny way of busting us out of the pattern. . . .

And so on. Fox passed. Other offers came and went. He was offered a chance to write a sequel to *In the Heat of the Night*. He turned it down. Wolper Productions wanted to buy the rights to *Please Write for Details*. Not enough money, MacDonald said, and a contract was never signed. He made a little money in 1968 by selling the rights to his novel *The Girl, the Gold Watch, and Everything*. It was supposed to star Jack Lemmon and be a movie for the theaters. It ended up as a movie for television staring Robert Hays.

Back to McGee. Although John D. did everything in his power to keep Travis off television, he was willing for him to be in a theatrical movie. In 1966 he signed a deal with Jack Reeves and Walter Seltzer of Major Productions Corporation, an independent production company, giving them the right to film the McGee books, but only for motion picture theaters. The plan was to make a McGee movie every eighteen months, much the way the James Bond books were being filmed. Still, though, John D. said in a letter to Harry Ackerman, vice president of *Screen Gems,* it was not money that motivated him:

I said [to a producer] that I would not sell [the McGee television rights] for $10 million on a ten year spread. He looked at me as if I had turned into a Thing from the Great Swamp. Maybe it *is* quaint in these times not to give a damn about the big money. I just never have and never will. If I were in this business for the purpose of making big money, I would probably be Harold Robbins or Irving Wallace, and I envy them not, financially or professionally. . . . I am just a plain, stubborn eccentric who constantly goes around making the mistake of saying just what he believes.

MacDonald liked Ackerman, something he never felt for producers. "He is that rare bird out there, a man who actually reads books," he wrote to Max Wilkinson.

But the Travis hype continued. In 1969, Eagle Shirtmakers planned, with MacDonald's blessings, the McGee shirt. Originally, it was to be called the John D., but MacDonald felt that was an invasion of his privacy. So it became the McGee, available in eighteen colors, a short-sleeve number with two breast pockets. Many of the colors were taken from MacDonald titles—Plain Wrapper Brown, Deep Goodbye Blue, Cupcake Brass, Nightmare Pink. An old friend of John D.'s was now the president of Eagle Shirts, and MacDonald agreed to let him make the product and to never take any royalties or percentage of shirt sales. John D. hoped the shirts would help promote the new McGee movie that Major Productions was filming,

Darker than Amber, and maybe sell a few more books. He also might have wanted to cut into the James Bond merchandising that was flourishing at the time. The shirt promotion was kicked off with color advertising in *Playboy* and *The New Yorker.*

Shooting for *Amber* was scheduled to begin in Miami on October 13, 1969, and John D. was beginning to feel like an anxious parent. Even though Jack Reeves had bought the rights to Travis McGee, MacDonald would not let him go. Originally, Robert Culp was to play McGee. Culp was a hot actor in the sixties. He had starred in *Bob and Carol and Ted and Alice* and, along with Bill Cosby, played a lead in the hit television series *I Spy.* But Culp fell through. "Culp was a disaster," John D. wrote. "No comprehension of the touch needed. Glad he will not be McGee. Suspect he is in a stage of self-importance where he will not take direction. . . . I find that Rod Taylor is going to be McGee. Dorothy and I went to see him in a [movie]. . . . He looked a bit jowly, seemed to be in good shape, but the part did not give him any chance at the light touch. Culp too wispy and elegant, and this one maybe too squat and hairy and direct." Rod Taylor had appeared in more than twenty movies before he was signed to play Travis McGee, including *The Birds,* directed by Alfred Hitchcock, and *Zabriskie Point,* directed by Michelangelo Antonioni. He had been a sort of romantic hero in such fluff movies of the 1950s and 1960s as *The Glass Bottom Boat* and *Do Not Disturb.*

More than the casting for McGee, there was the matter of the script. John D. hated it. Jack Reeves mailed him a copy of it and MacDonald found it "cheap, ordinary, vulgar and impossible." He took a weekend off from his novels and rewrote the first forty pages of the film and sent it to CBS. "Max Wilkinson, my agent in New York, who had a couple of years as right hand man to Sam Goldwyn, pronounced it as just about the worst script he had ever read," Mac-Donald wrote in a letter to Dan Rowan.

Jack could write Max off . . . but he could not write me off. . . . So he came down here [and] in five or six hard hours

of talk, I shook him. . . . Somehow all the people involved . . .
were looking at the script but they were seeing my book and
not the perversion of my book. Jack kept saying in defense of
the horrid lines that it is a director's medium, and I kept saying that a script has to stimulate directorial creative ability,
not quash it by being so goddamn ordinary. . . . Anyway,
though I do not have script approval I won my major
point. . . . Now Reeves is embarking on "one last major final
revision" which should eliminate, I hope, a great deal of the
vulgarity and illogic and trite characterization. For example,
they turned Meyer into a fat clown, clumsy and dumb.
Degrade a man's closest friend and you do not enhance him
by comparison—you only degrade him too.

A few weeks after the meeting, he wrote Jack Reeves a six-page
single-spaced letter that told him more about how to handle Travis
McGee:

From what you have told me *now* of the script, I feel you
may indeed be able to put together a picture. You needed, as
you said, another touch on the dialogue and on the intimate
scenes to delete that kind of gratuitous vulgarity in characterization which soured the first versions.

As I told you, if you stay with the bones of plot and locale
in each book, I think that the writers should be free to sim-
plify and alter the intricacies of construction which I use, not
only to find cinematic equivalencies, which will do the same
thing in visual form, but also to leave more room for a constant characterization of McGee, one that will make people
want to see him again. . . .

Now let me give you the reasons why I cannot approve that
change in our agreement which would enable you to retitle
the first motion picture of the series and call it *Travis McGee*:

1. You should attempt to get the maximum benefit out of

the tie-in with Fawcett Publications, and their willingness to reissue in quantity a print order of *Darker than Amber* to coincide with your release date on the picture. I have control of the covers on the Fawcett editions, by contractual clause. I certainly would *not* approve retitling one of the books in the series to fit this curious notion, nor do I believe Fawcett would want to upset the pattern and success of the series by any title experimentation at this time. Also by contractual arrangement, I have control over the text of the advertising by Eagle Shirtmakers, and I would not wish to approve copy which established that sort of notion. This same situation also exists with Lippincott, who will bring out *Amber* as the first in their projected program of putting all the books in the series into hard covers. As I explained to you, if you have a tentative release date of June, then by November the Cinema Center or CBS people should get together with the editorial and sales people of Fawcett and Lippincott, to arrange covers and dust jackets which would help the exposure, and this should occur about November of this year at the latest.

2. You said there would be an additional 500,000 ticket sales using the title *Travis McGee* instead of *Darker than Amber.* You base this, apparently, on the appeal to non-readers. And the figure is, of course, plucked out of thin air by someone. I cannot see why, to a non-reader, *Travis McGee* would have any more allure than *Homer Feep.*

3. You told me several times that *Darker than Amber* would appear along with my story board credit. So? Jack, I think if you all desire, quite reasonably, to lay heavier emphasis on the name Travis McGee, then this is a problem that falls quite logically and naturally into the provinces of advertising and promotion people already assigned to the project by the distributor. I hardly think the audience acceptance years ago of *The Lady in the Lake.* would have been enhanced by retitling it *Philip Marlowe,* nor calling *The Maltese Falcon,* incidentally, *Sam Spade.*

4. You and I and CBS are all hoping, naturally, for a taste-

ful and highly successful picture. Suppose this odd retitling were used, and the picture became the smash we hope for? Can you imagine the pressure that would then be generated to retain some version of the same thing for the second picture? You could not then return to the color concept, one that has been proved valid and profitable in a marketplace just as unpredictable as the motion picture marketplace. The title change would *not* have been responsible for the success, and would leave you all in a dead end insofar as future titles would be concerned, but, like the manager who won't launder his shirt while the team is winning, you would be stuck with some of the more unfortunate mythology of the industry.

5. I must be a little bit brutal in my thinking, Jack. If high hopes and investment money and hardworking talent inevitably resulted in success, no plays would ever close after a couple of nights. I would naturally hope for a winner in *Darker than Amber.* If it turns out to be a dud, then it seems reasonable that according to our contractual agreements there would be, in time, a reversion to me of all the rights which you now own, and which you would not keep current through inability to swing the second one. I would then expect that because the books are uniquely successful on a geometrically increasing basis, someone in the misty future would take another crack at a motion picture. Were you to use the title *Travis McGee* I don't think this would *ever* come to pass. Additionally, I hope I made myself clear on the question of any peripheral commercial exploitation of the public recognition values in the name McGee, Busted Flush, Manequita and so on. You said that CBS felt that I may have made some sort of mistake in proceeding with Eagle Shirtmakers in the shirts and beach wear areas. As they are quite aware, I was quite careful not to divest myself of any of the commercial exploitation rights in the characters and the series. I would not care to have them think I am some sort of casual idiot who goes about giving things away thoughtlessly. . . . Eagle will tastefully and cleverly promote a first

class product, and has given me the rights to preview the advertising to be certain it remains consonant with the lasting image and the status we seek. . . . Does CBS and Cinema Center believe, perhaps, that all authors are dangerous, unpredictable, foolish fellows who should be left totally in the dark?

No father of the bride has ever been more suspicious of the man who was coming to take away his little darling. And no groom has ever shown such disdain for his future in-laws. A sales executive for Fawcett asked MacDonald in September if he could help get some dealers cast as extras in the movie. John D. scoffed at the idea. "It is always a serious risk in personal relationships to try to set something up with the cinematic pricks. They do not really care—or know— whether anybody ever sells a book to anybody. They will make promises, and then screw you, and leave you red-faced in front of your dealers."

And then, suddenly, everything changed. The movie stars came to town and MacDonald was charmed. He was like a giddy teenager after his first major league baseball game. Here's what he said in a letter to Knox Burger, of Fawcett Publications, written in late October:

Because you have been my editor on all these Travis McGee books, I guess you have the right to know what happened and what it felt like to go over to Fort Lauderdale and spend one full day watching them in the process of turning my book *Darker than Amber* into a motion picture.

"Them" means Major Pictures Corporation, which means Jack Reeves and Walter Seltzer, using a production crew from Ivan Tors Studio in Miami, for a film to be released to the exhibitors through Cinema Center. But I suppose when I say "them," I am really thinking more about Rod Taylor as ol' Travis McGee, and Theodore Bikel as Meyer, and Suzy Kendall playing a dual role—good girl, and a sort of rotten girl. (The one they drop off the bridge in the first sentence of the book.)

I spent my days at Bahia Mar, where the company was on location. They had come in there with a whole convoy of those big silver-colored Tors trucks, and boom trucks, and portable dressing rooms, and several billion dollars worth of gear and gadgets. Because Trav has been parking his houseboat, The Busted Flush, at Bahia Mar for a few years now, I've become friendly with the manager, Irv Delbert.

Irv was walking around with a slightly glassy look and he was developing a twitch. He sort of expected the movie people to come in with some hand-held cameras, and a shy smile. But there they were, laying track down a long pier, laying cable as big as your wrist around everywhere, and running monstrous generators, and turning the area into something resembling a truck depot in Newark.

My first impression was of such vast confusion nobody could possibly have it under control. But I found out that Bob Clouse, the director, Frank Baur, the unit manager, and Andy Costikyan, the cinematographer, knew what was going on all the time, and along with Jack Reeves and Walter Seltzer, kept it all moving in the right direction. Ever see a good infantry battalion on the move, setting up bivouac, tearing it down and rolling again?

Reporters kept asking me questions. Dumb questions, some of them, like, "Do you think Rod Taylor will make a good Travis McGee?"

I was apprehensive about meeting Rod Taylor. Why should an actor be expected to relate to the fellow who wrote the novel? I hadn't written the script. But we hit what is called instant empathy. I like the guy. He has a face that looks lived in, and he projects a masculinity that can glaze the young female eye at seventy paces. But what matters to me is that he understands what McGee is all about—the anti-hero, tender and tough, with many chinks in the armor. The motion picture McGee will be, I am confident, the McGee of the novels, altered to the extent to which Rod Taylor will add his own dimensional interpretation. The final effect will be the amalgam of *my* McGee and *Rod Taylor's* McGee, and I trust Rod's wit, irony and understanding to make the whole greater than the parts. We talked maybe three times, totaling maybe an hour, and I think we are friends, which is a valuable thing anywhere.

He will be right in the role of McGee as Theo Bikel is right for the role of Meyer. And Bikel *is* Meyer, a large hairy gentle watchful thoughtful man. They told me he thinks Meyer is McGee's conscience, because too often McGee in anger and impatience will throw out the valid conventions along with the false ones.

Suzy Kendall has a fine, sensitive face, and a very clear light of intelligence in direct and lovely eyes. Do you know—had you ever realized—that *all* these people are awfully bright, with quick perceptions, humor, a knack for sorting out what is real and what is unreal? I should have guessed. You cannot do a good job of portraying someone else until you have discovered who *you* are.

Well, old friend, the rest is a jumble of vivid—and startling—impressions. It is very very weird to invent a big houseboat in your mind, write about it in eleven books, and suddenly walk onto a dock and come upon it in the flesh, so to speak. Big and solid and fast. And that bathtub aboard is exactly what you think it would be. . . .

That day they did a big party scene aboard the big boat owned by the Alabama Tiger. How do you visualize him? I know, I know. Would you believe Jane Russell? So help me, that's who it is. We were sort of hunkered down on the aft deck behind dozens of lovely little extras clotted along the rail in party clothes, as the Flush went by over and over with cameras aboard, and Rod Taylor at the top side controls. I know now how it would be to be held captive in a Barbie Doll factory.

Maybe I will catch up with them again to take another

look. But it isn't fair, really. Everybody from gaffer to star knocks himself out to be friendly and helpful, and to explain things to this ignorant writer. It takes too much of their time and attention.

Best to stay out of the way and let them do their complicated job. And, you know, I think they are going to do it. I think they are going to come out of this with a good picture.

At first, during sneak previews, it appeared that MacDonald's optimism might be justified. "I kept hearing from curious sources that the whole thing was a disaster, but last Sunday Jack phoned me after a sneak preview in Tucson and Phoenix to report an apparent mild commercial success," MacDonald told Harry Ackerman in a May 1970, letter. "[There was a] quiet audience, some applause during the film, with gasps and laughs in the right places." The optimism was wrong. *Dress Her in Amber,* as the movie was titled, was a flop. Gene Siskel of the *Chicago Tribune* called it "opaque." Siskel was not as hard on the movie as John D., who told Clarence Petersen, a television critic for the *Chicago Tribune,* that the movie was "feral, cheap, rotten, gratuitously meretricious, shallow and embarrassing."

Nevertheless, Jack Reeves and Walter Seltzer started planning for a second McGee film, *A Deadly Shade of Gold.* "If I had it to do over again I would never let Mr. McGee out of my hand," MacDonald told Petersen. "Not for a movie, not for television. If I had it to do over again, I wouldn't even sell stereopticon rights to McGee." But, of course, a contract is a contract. "They can go ahead and make any kind of a deal they want, as long as it does not interfere with my deal with them—revision rights, front money and everything else. . . . I expect nothing, and if it's a little bit more than nothing, I'll be pleasantly surprised."

MacDonald got what he expected. The deal fell through, the McGee rights reverted to him, and the movie was never made. But then, in 1979, as the McGee rights lay dormant, John D. had intimations of mortality. In a conversation with his accountant he discovered that there could be a major problem with inheritance taxes from

McGee books that were never made into movies, and so a deal was set up with Warner for all the books featuring Travis McGee, both the ones that had been published and those yet to be written. In a letter to Tom Bethancourt, MacDonald describes what he calls "a horror story."

> I had refused to sell McGee to the movies (after the *Amber* fiasco) or to TV. [My accountant] told me that when I die the estate tax experts will take the average price I have received for motion picture rights and multiply it by the number of books published where the rights have not been sold, and add that to the value of the estate. And in the case of McGee at that time it came to something like eight million dollars. I said they couldn't DO that, and he said that they could and they would. . . . So I told [my agent] George Diskant to make a deal, and he made one with Warner Communications, real quick. My stipulation was that the contract should make it so horribly expensive for them to go the TV route instead of the motion picture route that they would never be tempted. You can guess the rest. They had a couple of scripts done and didn't like them. They had paid me some substantial front money, and if they didn't do something by this year, the rights were going to revert to me. I wish they had. . . . Anyway, times change and inflation screws the currency, and what was too expensive five years ago is apparently okay now.

So Hollywood, specifically Warner Brothers, decided to make another Travis McGee movie. This one would be based on *The Empty Copper Sea*. Sam Elliott, an actor who specialized in strong silent heroes in westerns, was cast as McGee. But there would be a few changes. Just a few. The title was changed to *Travis McGee*. The location was shifted from Florida to Los Angeles. The *Busted Flush* was junked and Travis now lived on a sailboat called the *Bequia*. It was all written by Sterling Silliphant, who had worked on TV hits like *Naked City* and *Route 66*: He had won an Academy Award in 1966 for the screenplay of *In the Heat of the Night*. "Those portions of the Travis McGee movie which stayed with his original script were the only parts which held up," MacDonald said years later. The movie got good ratings, but the producers at Warner Brothers waited too long to decide if it should be a series. When they made up their mind, it was too late. Sam Elliott already had other work. John D. was disgusted. "I have never met or talked to any studio people," he wrote, "but they must really be congenital incompetents. I should never have peddled McGee. . . ."

There was never another Travis McGee movie, but that didn't mean Hollywood stopped pushing. In 1986, Warner Brothers gave it one more try. Their actions disgusted John D, and he said so in a letter to a friend in Hollywood:

I am a little more irritated than usual with Hollywood . . . Now they have a script of *The Lonely Silver Rain*. Pretty good script. They want to make a two-hour pilot to lead into a weekly one-hour television show. They have turned Meyer into a kid. An electric, electronic whizzy kid, twenty-five-inch waist, high style hair, and he has filled Meyer's cruiser with gadgets so he can sell French francs on the Tokyo exchange at three in the morning, our time. I hate it. It is like losing an old friend. But they mumble about demographics. If demographics and all that shit is so terribly important, why is the overall TV audience going down and down and down? The friends of Meyer will not rise up and crush the scoundrels because people who watch TV use books as door stops.

So McGee, who sold books in the millions, couldn't make it as a movie hero. Actually, he was not alone. It took three tries to turn Dashiell Hammett's *The Maltese Falcon* into a good film. It only worked when John Huston, the director of the third version, decided to follow the book. Mickey Spillane's Mike Hammer was the protagonist in four films, but only one, *Kiss Me, Deadly*, directed by Robert Aldrich, is memorable. Only the adaptations of Raymond Chandler's Philip Marlowe novels, *The Big Sleep, Murder, My Sweet*, and *The Lady in the Lake*, were first-class films. And, just as for Hammett, it took more than one try to make it right. The novel *Farewell, My Lovely* was first adapted for the screen as *The Falcon Takes Over*, and Chandler's book *The High Window* became a Michael Shayne mystery, *Time to Kill*. Traditionally, Hollywood is a factory, an assembly line. And on that assembly line it is a simple story, conventional characters, and a standard location that makes work easier. So that's what most films are made of.

With McGee, there was another factor at work. Travis McGee, more than any other fictional detective with the possible exception of the porcine Nero Wolfe, was bound by the printed page. Rex Stout's Nero Wolfe had an abbreviated cinematic career that matched McGee's. He was in two movies in the thirties and one aborted television series in the seventies in which the running gag was to see if the fat man could stand up.

In the Travis McGee novels, there is all the inner dialogue, all the conversations with Meyer, all the arcane details about stamp collecting or Mexican history or Florida development. These are the elements that make the books treasures to readers. And then there's the sex. McGee doesn't hop in bed with all the girls, and when he does seduce a woman, there are often some sort of healing psychological overtones. These facets of a McGee novel are as important as the plot, which often doesn't really amount to much. Nero Wolfe's readers are fascinated by his food, his knowledge of orchids, his musing on language. The plot doesn't really matter. If you like Nero Wolfe, you'll read more about him. If you like Travis McGee, you'll buy the next book in the series. But, with the exception of *My Dinner with André*, movies about two people sitting around and talking don't make much money or generate much interest. That is the stuff of literature. Movies and TV "dramas" are about car chases, hot sex, and explosions. Hollywood shrinks from the cerebral, and so they shrink from McGee. The way most movie and television executives see it, who wants to watch an obese gourmet eat Duckling in Flemish Olive Sauce and cut orchids or a middle-aged beach bum spout philosophy when they could be seeing the jiggle and squirm of *Charlie's Angels* or *Baywatch* and the explosions and car chases in *Rambo* or *Die Hard*?

Yet there were television variants of the McGee formula that worked. The best one, of course, was *The Rockford Files*, in which James Garner played a McGee-like character who lived in a rusted mobile home rather than a houseboat, and whose Meyer was his father. It worked, but it wasn't very cerebral. Rockford was John D. MacDonald's favorite television detective. "In believability, dialogue, plausibility of character, plot coherence, *The Rockford Files* comes as close to meeting the standards of the written mystery as anything I found," MacDonald wrote in *TV Guide*. "[It has] good tight dialogue, good pictorials, and a strong emotional evolvement [that] keep the story afloat. . . . And it is heartening to a book writer to note the success of the series that most nearly fulfills our scriveners' standards."

In the eighties, Burt Reynolds starred in a series of made-for-TV movies called *B. L. Stryker* which was about a private eye who lived on a houseboat in Miami, had a sidekick, played by Ossie Davis, solved crimes around the bay, and fooled around with Rita Moreno. It was the acme of diversity, a paean to political correctness—a white man, a black man, and a Puerto Rican woman hanging out together. It was also a McGee knockoff, and it didn't last very long.

Yet all the problems with bringing McGee to the screen cannot be blamed on Hollywood. MacDonald was no help. He carped, whined, bullied, and demanded changes. Usually he was right, but his moralism must have been distracting. John D. admits his problems and acknowledges his lack of understanding of screenwriting in an article for *TV Guide*:

Script writing is a specialized technique. I would have to learn how to do it. Learning would take time. What time I have I want to use learning how to do what I do better than I am now doing it. Secondly, making movies is a group activity. They have conferences. They make conference-type decisions. I hate trying to work with other people. I would rather make my own mistakes than help them make theirs.

The result of all that was that John D. MacDonald's great hero never made a successful transition to the screen. Whether it is his fault, the fault of film directors, of the fault of Hollywood executives doesn't matter. It may be that Travis could never have been a screen idol. He is, after all, a middle-aged man in a land of youth, a moralist in a sea of hedonism, a philosopher in a world where thoughts run no deeper than a thirty-second commercial.

Tain't funny, McGee.

CHAPTER 13

Ohn D. MacDonald was on his way home from a bank meeting on September 18, 1970. It has been a particularly unpleasant meeting, and he saw in it the first signs of corruption that would plague the financial institution a year later and end with its president being led away by the FBI. On the way home he felt chest pains and had trouble breathing. He tried to ignore it. The meeting had been bad-tempered, and he dismissed the pains as anger and stress. But they would not go away. The next morning he went to Doctors Hospital. Diagnosis: coronary. He stayed in the hospital for two weeks.

In earlier years, MacDonald had scoffed at Borden Deal's constantly referring to his heart attack. He felt Deal was using it as some kind of badge of honor. But now it was *his* heart and he felt differently about it.

The medical problems MacDonald faced did not end with that first coronary. On December 2, Dordo was hospitalized for two days so a pacemaker could be installed. Two days after Christmas, John D. was back in the hospital being treated for flu and strep throat.

Six months later, he got ready to go under the knife for a disk operation to address the back problems that had begun in 1967. But he balked. He went to the Department of Neurology and Neurosurgery at Columbia Presbyterian Hospital in New York, where the doctors laid out their plan for him. They would freeze four vertebrae and then lock them in place with bonemeal from his hipbone. Recovery would involve twelve weeks in the hospital and then a minimum of five weeks in New York before he could go home. "Screw them," he said in a letter to Rowan. "I'd rather hurt now and then. . . . All of a sudden the right leg felt better, and then better, and then better again. I think I am going to do nothing at all, exercise as much as I can."

That summer John and Dordo lived at their camp at Piseco Lake. It had been seven years since they had been there in the warm weather. It was a tonic for him:

The alders, swamp maple, berry bushes, etc. have turned the lake front into jungle, and up the long road, our woods are full of fallen birch and beech. Every day I quit work about four to four thirty and spend a couple of hours cutting brush and stacking it, to clear out all our old paths and picnic places. . . . My [exercise machine] came and it is one hell of a lot of exercise. It is great. Dordo loves it. I endure it. I would rather cut brush. That is exercise which you can look out the window later and see what you have done.

Those two weeks in the hospital in December and the slower pace he was forced to live after that gave him time to think about his mortality. He wrote to Dan Rowan:

Have been sort of marking time in some kind of professional personal sense, a fallow period of thought, appraisal, redefinition, a kind of delayed byproduct of the little coronary, and a definite product of my years, I suppose. A process of closing out all random noise and saying: What in the hell am I *doing* here, and what the hell do I *want* to be doing here? I am beginning to think that it is irrational sentimentality to try to impose on oneself this shit about walking slowly and pausing to smell the flowers. I am a worker and work is my pleasure and my nature and my way of life. So I think that what I shall do is wind myself up one notch below the spring tension of before, and get some of the exercise I despise, and stay off the weed. I shall try to stay out of doing things that bug me, but if I have to do them, if I get trapped into them, I shall extract from them the maximum amount of cash money and squirrel it away in a separate place and call it blood-sweat-and-tears money, and let it reproduce and support me in the style I would like to become accustomed to.

The first half of the 1970s brought MacDonald more tragedy than just his failing health. He had to face two major deaths in his family. In 1974 it was his sister, Doris. The alcohol got her. A few months before she died of cirrhosis, John D. visited her:

> She was in a coma for nine days. What she is right now . . . is a creature of certainly no more than 70 pounds, skeletal, with a terrible restless energy, strange starey eyes, and a whole set of delusions. One doctor says it is his belief that her irrationality will persist, that the brain damage is permanent. Another expects her to recover her wits in six or seven weeks. The first doctor believes she will go once again into kidney failure and will not survive. My mother is in her eighties, has an apartment and, because of two bad falls, a part-time nurse-housekeeper. She and my sister, Dorie, were very close, talking each day. . . . My mother is in complete despair at this turn of events. [Dorie has] two adopted children, age 20 and 22, neither of them sufficiently mature to be of any help coping with events here. I am handling monetary affairs for my sister.

Doris died on October 12, 1974. MacDonald was the executor of her will and was named guardian of her children. A year later his mother died. The two deaths made John D's continuing health problems seem minor—he had hives and pieces of his teeth were falling out. Finally, he developed "some sort of skin crud." He had to sleep with his hands in baggies, rub ointment on himself seven times a day, and stay out of the sun. "I am going to go around tinkling a little bell and crying, 'Unclean! Unclean!'" he said in a letter to Rowan.

MacDonald's writing in the early seventies was only a fraction of what it had been in the days before the heart attack. He wrote one McGee book, *A Tan and Sandy Silence*, in 1972; two more in the series, *The Scarlet Ruse* and *The Turquoise Lament*, in 1973; no books in 1974; and only one, *The Dreadful Lemon Sky*, in 1975.

Yet John D. stayed busy, even if he was not behind the typewriter.

For most of the decade he was on the board of trustees for both the Ringling School of Art and New College, a small, progressive liberal arts college in Sarasota. New College was his favorite. He began his association with the school in 1969 when he was elected to the board of trustees. In 1972, in the midst of a financial crunch, MacDonald acted as executive head of the college for a month. In 1973 he taught there as part of a creative prose seminar. Although John D. studied business as an undergraduate and then got an M.B.A. from Harvard, he had changed his mind about what education should be. Over the years he had begun to believe that the best schools were based on the liberal arts. He talked about his ideas in a letter to Al Mittal:

> I am a trustee of New College . . . which has become in eight years one of the best small liberal arts colleges in the country. I have been deeply involved with it, and have come around to an elitist attitude re education. Of 600 of the brightest young people in the country, we can provide the resources for one out of fifty to hone his own mind to an edge of sharpness he could not achieve by himself. . . . The brain is a muscle in the sense that the more demanding use made of it, the better it functions. In a time when intellectual discipline cannot be imposed from the outside, only an inner motivation will create a mind of sound pattern, structure and capacity. In the colleges of a hundred years ago, no one was *permitted* the luxury of drifting. That is why the spoken and written language of a hundred years ago, as used by small town lawyers, doctors, and merchants, had dignity and force, depth and persuasion. We can turn out one out of fifty. It is a waste. A total permissiveness is a luxury which is ultimately paid for by those who relish it most—by their developing far below their capacity.

The heart of a liberal arts education, MacDonald believed, was reading. He talked about that with Jean Tribbi on a radio program called *Library Edition*:

I've been thinking about this for a few weeks, ever since I tried to have a conversation with a nonreader some weeks ago. Now, you're a reader, I'm a reader. . . . We stand in the middle of a landscape that we're familiar with. We know about those great swamps and marshes which are all of the religions and philosophies and all of the psychological identifications of what's going on in the bottom of man's mind. . . . Let's say there are rivers running through our landscape. Those would be the arts, literature, painting, all of the things that you learn from books that sharpen and enhance your mind. . . . A nonreader is somebody standing there in a blindfold. They don't see the history of anything. All they have to talk about is vacations and food and drink and automobiles and movies and sort of trite little anecdotes about what is happening and what has happened to them lately. One cannot carry on any kind of a conversation that gets away from the anecdotal without them saying a whole bunch of absolute, grotesque, absurd misconceptions of what the world is like. They don't *know* what the world is like, because they haven't read what history is, what geography is. They don't know Lima [Peru] from lima [bean]. It's interesting to try to have an argument or a discussion with a nonreader. It really is bothersome. And so, what the reader has to do is kind of just smile politely and swallow his irritation and say, "Yes, that's right, that's right, un-huh, yeah, I agree with you." That's about the only way you can get out of it, because [to] a nonreader, you cannot possibly explain where you're coming from, because he hasn't, or she hasn't, been there. . . . Right now the schools are raising a good batch of consumers and maybe that's what they're there for. These people, they can find their way around supermarkets and they can find their way around showrooms . . . they know how to run their credit cards. Maybe if we have too much useful education we're going to get a community of people who are too questioning of everything that's going on. Maybe we need a bunch of people who just accept the world as it is and say, "Hi, wow, it's wonderful, baby." . . . There's no way that you can take a complicated thought, really complicated, and transfer it . . . into someone else's mind, with words, spoken words, with body English, with dancing about, with drawing pictures. There's no way! . . . You'll get it from a book, where you can turn back and figure out what you didn't understand the first time and then turn again. . . . [The idea that if something is complicated it's not worth the effort to understand is] the great American thing, almost our national natural heritage. . . . "If I can't understand it, it must be wrong." You know? Which is a kind of arrogance that we have as a nation.

MacDonald's efforts to promote a liberal arts education, particularly at New College, didn't bear fruit. The Ford Foundation gave the college an annual grant of $1 million a year. The school, in turn, had to raise another $1 million. John D. tried selling personally signed first editions of his books to readers of the *JDM Bibliophile*. It wasn't enough. Finally, New College gave in. The school's physical plant was sold to the State of Florida and the college became a public institution—an honors college. And yet New College continued to try to raise an additional $600,000 a year to assure the kind of education it was known for. "The egalitarians in state government raise hell with us," MacDonald said. By 1978 he had resigned from the board. "I think the public service phase of my life is over," he said.

The heart attack, the long, brooding thoughts about himself, and his immersion in New College changed the way he wrote. When Travis McGee returned in *A Tan and Sandy Silence* in 1972, he was aging. As he entered middle age, the legendary ladies' man, brawler, and adventurer begins to have doubts that never plagued him in the first twelve novels:

I'm overdue. That's what Meyer says, and that's what my gut says in a slow cold coil of tingling viscera. Overdue, and

scared, and not ready for the end of it yet. The old bullfight-
ers who have known the famous rings and famous breeds
despise the little country corridas, because they know that if
they do not quit, this is where they will die—and the bull
that hooks their steaming guts out onto the sand will be a
poor animal without class or distinction or style. . . . Maybe
it isn't just the women. . . . Or a passing of time. It is the
awareness, perhaps, of the grasshopper years, of always pushing all the pleasure buttons. The justification was a spavined
sense of mission, galumphing out to face the dragon's fiery
breath. It had been a focus on the torment of individuals to
my own profit. Along with a disinterest in doing anything at
all about those greater inequities to my own profit. Oh, I
could note them and bitch about them and say somebody
ought to do something. I could say it on my way to the beach
or to the bed.

Who will know you were ever around, McGee? Or care?

These are not the thoughts of a beach bum. They sound like the
intimations of mortality that spring from a fifty-five-year-old author
who has suffered a coronary, has a bad back, and is undergoing
tobacco withdrawal symptoms. MacDonald talked about McGee's
aging in a letter to Marion Poynter, a columnist for the *St. Petersburg
Times:*

I have established [McGee] in a fairly static environment,
peopled with friends and transients. In the beginning, I knew
that ,I wanted to have him grow older, without defining his
precise age. . . . So it would be grotesque not to have some
passage of time. But out of enlightened self-interest I did not
want him to age as fast as all the rest of us. Maybe one year
every three or four? He began in 1964. I mentioned, in an
early book, Korean war service. So that would make him
about 35? I wouldn't know. Eleven years later, is he 38? Who

knows? Maybe he was 33 and is now 36. I don't really *want* to know. Chronological age is no great problem. The problem is, as I have tried to state, an emotional and psychological one. I have had to involve him deeply with people and then I have killed those people off. If I repeople his world with new intimates, and make him the same jolly-boy of yore, then I am saying, indirectly, that this is a shallow and trivial man. If I make him a shallow fellow, I shall tire quickly of him, and there will be no more books, because when they stop being fun I stop doing them. Guaranteed. So, realistically, I must induce a malaise (without getting it mixed up with mine own) and understand why he has it. . . . Life *does* become smaller and more cautious because identity becomes more difficult to ascertain and maintain. The dwindled circle of intimates becomes aware of being survivors. Loss is more sharply felt because more acutely understood, but at the same time the pang is dulled by the pre-awareness of its inevitability. So what can I do to keep McGee and Meyer from becoming too withdrawn and morose? I can move them about more. Or I can go back and pick up on the casual contacts and bring those people back into a more intimate and valued focus within their home turf. I favor the latter. . . . What I guess I am saying . . . is that a fictional hero has to be real to whatever possible extent I can make him real. And in order to make him real, I have to apply to him those same jolts and shocks of reality I have felt myself. Humor fades from slapstick to irony, and who can say which is better? There is more tolerance of error, and of the more gross of human vices. There is more skepticism of the concept of justice. There is more value in gentleness.

Travis McGee was facing changes beyond just the ravages of age, however. In 1973 the fifteenth McGee novel, *The Turquoise Lament*, was published in hardcover by J. B. Lippincott. Suddenly, after all those years on spinner racks in bus stations and drugstores, the iconoclastic beach bum had a new home in the front shelves of respectable bookstores. McGee did not rise to the best-seller lists with *Turquoise*—that would come later. But he was running in better company. The move to the upper literary classes seemed inappropriate to the snobbish vision of John Skow, who wrote in his review in *Time*, "The experiment of issuing MacDonald in hardback . . . is not progress. Few artifacts are as needless as hardback crime stories." And Dick Datchery, writing for *The Critic*, also lamented the passing of John D. MacDonald and Travis McGee from the world of paperback originals. "As it must to all successful paperback writers, immortality has come to Mr. MacDonald in the form of his first cloth publication. . . . All accomplished without the help of critics. . . . Travis seemed more at home in paperback with a come-on cover." And MacDonald himself wondered about the transition from paperback to hard cover. "*The Turquoise Lament* . . . is an alternative Book-of-the-Month Club selection . . . and it is the choice of the Detective Book Club . . . and is a selection of the Book Find Club . . . So McGee is a bit more respectable than I would like to have him, for the nonce," he wrote.

At first glance, it seems that McGee in hardback meant a step up for MacDonald. But what it really meant was survival. Publishing had changed drastically since 1950, when *The Brass Cupcake* hit the stands. Slowly, over those twenty-three years, the market for paperback originals had dwindled. For an author to survive, certainly for him to get the publicity and book reviews he needed, he had to have hardback sales. The Travis McGee series probably could have continued to sell as paperback originals, but the business and its new distribution system was making that more and more difficult. Publishing became a hardback game.

The change in publishing began in 1968 when an insurance company called National General bought Grosset & Dunlap, a hardback publisher that owned half of Bantam Books. It was the first time a non-book publisher had come into what had been a clubby, old-boy industry, and it signaled a conglomerate takeover. That same year a company called Intext acquired Ballantine Books. A year later, CBS took over Popular Library. In 1972, Warner Communications, which until then had been a film studio and recording label, bought Paperback Library and renamed it Warner Books. But the swallowing of one company by another was not just a takeover by non-book corporations. The next year Ballantine books went on the market again, and this time it was scooped up by Random House. And the buyouts and selloffs continued. Harcourt Brace Jovanovich took over Pyramid Books, Gulf & Western devoured Simon & Schuster, Filmways acquired Ace Books, and Doubleday engulfed Dell. Fawcett, John D.'s publisher, became a part of CBS in 1977.

With all of the prominent paperback houses now owned by companies that had no interest in books, the emphasis shifted from literature to the bottom line—all that mattered was profit. The biggest profit, the conglomerates believed, came from segmenting the market. It was no longer a *mass* market, it was a collection of segments, like special interest magazines. The executives of the paperback houses no longer talked about books, they discussed product. "Product is the only fair term to describe the current output of the paperback industry," Kenneth C. Davis wrote in *Two-Bit Culture*, his history of paperback publishing.

> The paperback business . . . is characterized by a failure of nerve and creativity. The result is . . . artless imitation, a frightful lack of imagination, crass pandering to lowest common denominator tastes, and a slavish adherence to supposedly sound management practices that limit creativity and risk taking. . . . All this has led to a fearfully homogenized output from American publishers. Always an imitative field, publishing—paperback publishing in particular—has become dominated by me-too-ism and an alarming dependence on ephemera.

With this change in paperback publishing there came a reliance on the blockbuster. No longer did a publishing house want a solid line of books and a reputable stable of authors. It wanted a big hit. It wanted Arthur Hailey and novels like *Airport*; James Michener and his massive historical epics *Centennial* and *The Covenant*; Mario Puzo and *The Godfather*; and Stephen King, whose *Carrie* was published in 1974.

And no longer were paperback publishers dependent on hardback houses for their manuscripts. Take the case of *The Exorcist* by William Peter Blatty, who was a screenwriter. First it was a script for a movie. Bantam bought the rights to it and Blatty converted it to a novel. Then Bantam leased the hardback rights to Harper & Row. Everything was topsy-turvy. This was the publishing world when John D. MacDonald's Travis McGee went from paperback to hardcover.

Actually, MacDonald was a small part of this topsy-turvy world before *The Turquoise Lament* was published. Beginning in 1967, McGee novels that had previously been published in paperback by Fawcett were issued in collections by some better-known hardback houses. Doubleday published *Three for McGee (The Deep Blue Goodby, Nightmare in Pink*, and *A Purple Place for Dying)* in 1967, and another volume, *Shades of Travis McGee (The Quick Red Fox, Pale Gray for Guilt, Dress Her in Indigo)* in 1970. In the early 1970s, J. B. Lippincott began publishing the Fawcett McGee novels in hardcover including *Darker than Amber* (1970), *Dress Her in Indigo* (1971), *Pale Gray for Guilt* (1971), *Bright Orange for the Shroud* (1972), *The Long Lavender Look* (1972), *The Girl in the Plain Brown Wrapper* (1973), *A Deadly Shade of Gold* (1974), *The Quick Red Fox* (1974), *The Deep Blue Good-by* (1975), *Nightmare in Pink* (1976), *A Purple Place for Dying* (1976), *One Fearful Yellow Eye* (1977), and *A Tan and Sandy Silence* (1979). So when *The Turquoise Lament* appeared first in hardcover, and not as a mass market paperback, it was an extension of a program started by Doubleday six years earlier. MacDonald continued to submit duplicate manuscripts to Fawcett and Lippincott, however.

In April 1972, John D. MacDonald added the Grand Master award from the Mystery Writers of America to his honors. He had already been awarded the Grand Prix de Littérature Policière for the French edition of his novel *A Key to the Suite*. And Syracuse University had presented him the George Arents Pioneer Medal, its highest honor, for "contributions to American literature." MacDonald had been president of the Mystery Writers of America in 1962. Although he had written, at this point, more than fifty books, he had never received an Edgar, the award for best novel of the year. Now his peers were rectifying the omission with the Grand Master award for "[his] entire body of work in the mystery field." In some ways, it was like the Lifetime Achievement Award presented by the Academy of Motion Picture Arts and Sciences—an award to a master craftsman who had been overlooked. MacDonald, still gripped by his fear of New York, didn't go to the ceremony. He had Fawcett pick up the award for him.

The Dreadful Lemon Sky, the sixteenth Travis McGee novel, was published in 1975 by Lippincott, and for the first time a MacDonald book hit the best-seller lists. It was on *The New York Times*'s best-seller list for twenty-three weeks, rising to a high of number three. On the *Publishers Weekly* and *Time* lists it got to number two. It was gratifying to John D., but he took it in stride. "One old friend had an explanation," he said. "He said that it worked like the Chinese water torture. I had dropped so many books on their heads one at a time, over the years, I had established a conditioned reflex."

With the hardcover and best-seller status, *The Dreadful Lemon Sky* began to receive the critical attention MacDonald never got when he was relegated to paperbacks. What's more, his books were not banished to Newgate Callendar's "Crime" column in *The New York Times Book Review*. He was reviewed by a respectable author—Jim Harrison—in the front pages of the magazine. "MacDonald could never be confused with the escapism that dominates the suspense field," Harrison wrote. "You would have to be batty or ignorant or a masochist to read a MacDonald novel for pure amusement. . . . All sorts of poets and novelists . . . readily admit that MacDonald is a very good writer, not just a good 'mystery writer.' He far surpasses the critical conventions of the suspense category. . . . More purely literary writers admire MacDonald's fertility, his ease of producing at great speed works within a specific genre that don't seem at all limited to that genre." *The New Yorker* praised MacDonald's "usual keen depiction of the moral grubbiness of contemporary American life" and commented on "McGee's oddly appealing and highly unfashionable integrity." Even a political magazine got into the act. *The Progressive* said, "MacDonald does not neglect his customary shafts at the moral decay and the environmental deterioration that characterize much of the American scene in our time."

But perhaps more satisfying than any of these reviews was a letter from Paris he received in July. "Dear Mr. MacDonald, Would you please send me Travis McGee? I have read all the books you wrote and I am desperate because there are no more. . . . I am distributing your books here in Europe and everybody is deserting everybody because nobody will sleep with anybody when they have a new book of yours." It was signed "Marlene Dietrich."

MacDonald was philosophical about his new status. "The hard-cover publication does give the reviewers a chance to write something," he told Rust Hills in an interview published in the August 1975 issue of *Esquire*. "But I think the attention comes mostly as a result of my having written a lot of stuff over a long period of time. There have always been people interested in what I do. Besides, you know, there's a lot of academic interest now in what they call pop culture. . . ." Then John D. reached into a filing cabinet and pulled out a list of academic papers. One was called "Figures of Evil: Simile in the Travis McGee Novels," and another was "Travis McGee and the Underdeveloped, Unactualized Self in the Detective Hero." MacDonald called the authors of these papers "English department addicts." By 1978 the academics were so interested in his writing that the University of South Florida sponsored the John D. Mac-Donald Conference on Mystery and Detective Fiction.

Still, for all the success, all the fame, all the accolades, there was something missing in the novels about the aging Travis McGee. David Benjamin put his finger on it in a review he wrote for *The New Republic:* "One senses a certain ennui creeping into Travis's soul. He seems to be more remote with his friends, his women, even his enemies. . . . Perhaps Travis and John D. both need a vacation, a time for McGee to savor his putative retirement, and a chance for MacDonald to work on a different type of novel for a while, to freshen his extraordinary narrative gifts."

It was a good idea, and MacDonald considered it. But first things first. Right now there was a company making plans to build an eight-story condominium for old folks next to his house on Siesta Key. And he needed to do something about it.

CHAPTER 14

In mid-June 1973, John D. was confronted with a development company that wanted to build an eight-story condominium next door to his property on Siesta Key. Being part of an urban development was not what he and Dordo had envisioned when they moved into their new house. For decades, Siesta Key had had a reputation as an artists colony, and it was quiet and congenial for a man who wanted privacy above everything. When he wrote the specifications for his new house, MacDonald talked about privacy over and over again. His first requirement was "total privacy"; he wanted a "private vehicle gate" that would assure that no one could get into the house; he insisted upon a sort of foyer where uninvited guests would not be able to look "either into the inner privacy area, nor at the view toward which the house will face"; he demanded an "opaque fence" on the side of the house facing property once owned by the Out of Door School. As early as the mid-sixties he feared "eventual multiple dwellings" there. Now all of those precautions were for naught. An eight-story building would be next door, and people could stare at him and at Dordo all day and into the night.

MacDonald began to fight. First he wrote his lawyer, William Korp, and suggested that the proposed condominium project didn't meet zoning requirements. That didn't stop the Schroder Company. They continued with plans to build the development they called the Penthouse. By November, John D. had been given a copy of the condominium site plan. He was horrified. In a November 7 letter to Korp he expressed his fears:

> Do you think you can throw enough of a roadblock or a series of roadblocks in the way of this venture so that it will be given up as unfeasible? I do not want it to happen. I would rather take a chance on the next promoter developer who eyes it being subjected to rather more stringent rules and restrictions than this one. Also, the next developer might

be one who, unlike Schroder, takes a continuing interest in
management and service, rather than selling it and dodging
back under a wet rock. . . . I do not need a year of construction next door, and the Key does not need another 100 people and a further encroachment of multiple housing. . . . I
want you to ride ahead, my friend, fearlessly and tirelessly
poisoning the wells, chasing away the game, burning the tall
prairie grasses and making horrid sounds by night until they
give up at last and turn the wagon train around and head
back to Little Theater, Nebraska. . . . And one more [thing].
If we TRY to block them and fail to do so, and they get rancid
about it, can they bitch me up any more than they are already
doing? Like paving the existing easement in use, and using it
for the whole development? Like lighting the tennis courts
for night use?

The gauntlet was tossed, the line drawn. But it would not be the
first time. Six years before, in 1967, MacDonald had begun a long
and involved fight to stop the Arvida Corporation from reclaiming
land from Sarasota Bay. The philosophical underpinnings of the
Arvida battle actually began in an article MacDonald wrote for
Tropic, the Sunday magazine of *The Miami Herald*. It was not just
developers MacDonald was against in the article. It was corporations
and computers and the reduction of men to a bundle of statistics
that got him. In the article, he gave his own feelings to Travis
McGee:

McGee resents being processed, programmed, fed through
the machinery by experts trained in handling people rather
than persons. He knows that the dentist, the post office, the
County, the IRS, the airline hostess, the librarian, the highway
engineer, the supermarket, the city government, the census
bureau, the banker, the advertising agent, the automobile
agency, the hospital, and the mortician are all intent in using
him as a statistic, as one atom in a manageable mass, then

studying him, weighing him, measuring him, predicting his actions on some huge probability table. They use manuals and trade journals and computers and statistical methods and psychological testing devices to predict mass reaction, and handle mass demand on a totally impersonal and totally efficient basis. It irritates him to have society take away his face and dump him into the great hopper labeled Standard Operating Procedure. But don't try to tell him that in a densely populated urban culture it has to be that way, that people *must* be turned into a commodity or we would have chaos. Don't try to tell him that if the processors tried to measure the uniqueness of each human personality, the wonderful specialness, the delicious inconsistency of every one of us, all the memory banks would start smoking, the sorters would spew out a snowstorm of punch cards, and all the complex technology of our culture would grind to a sickening halt. . . . He reserves the right to resent being sorted and graded on the basis of "sameness" rather than on the basis of uniqueness. It makes him feel degraded, and he reserves the right to do his little bit here and there to startle the processors out of their compulsion to flatten and deaden all human contact. . . . The urban capture of mankind is a contemporary phenomenon. . . . When we look at ourselves as individuals, caged by our own cleverness, each of us is as out of time and place as a tiger on a raft, it is easy to see how desperately hard it is to contain and subdue the wilderness. . . . We call it "the tension of modern life." Chain the primitive part, tie it down, and then it breaks out in despairing ways. Heart attacks, ulcers, nervous breakdowns, addictions, all the psychosomatic woes, perversions, depravities, ugly mischief. . . . Everybody knows *something* is wrong, and everybody has an eerie and formless nostalgia for something he has never known. . . . We have no choice except this neon jungle, this asphalt wilderness. . . .

For John D. MacDonald, however, the nostalgia was not formless. He was nostalgic for the Florida he came to in the late forties. He wanted the Florida he evoked in *The Brass Cupcake, The Beach Girls, The Drowner,* and *Where Is Janice Gantry?* That Florida was gone, covered over by the dawning of the age of Walt Disney World and by the directionless lifestyle created by retired people who had emigrated from the Northeast and Midwest. At the turn of the century, Florida was for the rich who could afford to travel to the sunshine on Henry Flagler's railroad and stay in his exclusive hotels. After World War II the nomadic plutocrats moved farther south to the Caribbean and left Florida to people seeking tawdry fun, a tacky life on the beach and its neon environs, where they wore a patch of cloth, a quart of suntan oil, and a dazed smile. It was a low-rent paradise of sorts until Disney moved in and pulled the tourists away from the beaches to the flat swamps of Orlando. Then Florida became a subtropical nirvana for the beneficiaries of Social Security who left Ohio and Michigan in their Airstream trailers, driving down Interstate 75 to live in pink and lavender and chartreuse subdivisions and stare at their mailboxes in anticipation of a government check, quarterly dividends, or their own death certificate. When MacDonald wrote *The Brass Cupcake* in 1950, the villains were the amateur gigolos, "the tweedy, stag-line, Cannes, horsey, column bait, so-charming chiselers."

But with the coming of grown men in mouse suits and the never-ending stream of elderly "snowbirds" who left the chilly north to take advantage of Florida's warmth and the absence of a state inheritance tax, the enemy changed. He wore a three-piece suit now, not tropical-patterned bathing trunks. And he was not a chiseler looking for a rich and willing dame. He was a real estate developer.

MacDonald knew the type. They worked for Arvida and they moved to implement the corporation's plan to fill part of Sarasota Bay and build a golf course for the newly retired. He started the battle in November 1967 with a letter to the mayor and city commissioners in Sarasota. A spokesman for Arvida, Wallace Minto, accused the opponents of the bayfill of being afraid of change. John D. raged against him:

> I am affronted and irritated to have this Mr. Minto toss in a sticky dollop of philosophy, accusing all of us of some kind of emotional fear of change. "Change," he says, "is the natural

order of all living things; only death is a static state." This is a patronizing and cunning perversion of an elemental truism. It makes the land-grabbers very reasonable, canny creative chaps, and turns everyone else into a throng of screaming, whimpering bird-lovers. And it is total nonsense, and one of the typical devices of the spoilers. "Now now, little man, just let Big Daddy Arvida take care of everything for you in a very tasty manner." . . . The men developing Arvida land have *no* common interest with us. They are charged with processing an asset (submerged land) in such a manner as to return a profit on the operation, and if it is necessary to maneuver public opinion in order to make this landgrab possible, they will. . . .

Two years later, in 1969, he was still fighting. This time it was in the "Letters to the Editor" column in the *Sarasota Herald-Tribune*:

Arvida will hasten the day of crisis without alleviating it. How can that be? Because the luxurious waterfront home is at the apex of a population pyramid. It is like wartime, where for each combat soldier in the lines, there are ten men in the support and supply areas. New contractors, new suppliers, new shopkeepers, new service people, new professional people, new banking facilities, new barbers, new municipal and county employees—they are going to come swarming in to service the demands created by all of Arvida's golden dollars, and they in turn create additional demands which bring in more new resident folk. . . . So let us assume that the 2500 new high-income families actually *will* pay a bit more than the cost of the services they will require, even though *all* recognized taxation authorities state that *no* residential area *ever* pays its own way. . . .

MacDonald continued his fight with his pen. For a column called "Speaking Out" he wrote against corporations as the villain in the fight to save the environment:

The Arvida Corporation, 51% owned by Penn Central, seeks to fill yet another area of Sarasota Bay adjacent to the uplands the corporation owns. . . . [Any] corporation . . . is a monolithic thing, a legalistic invention which thrives and flourishes upon profit, and is made sick, sometimes mortally, by loss. No matter how much feeling of public obligation the executive staff of any corporation might possess, the corporate entity is involved in maximizing short and long run profit and minimizing short and long term loss. . . . Yet this very yardstick, essential to our industrial culture, is responsible for the geometric deterioration of our environment, for the sickening smutch overhanging our cities, for the despoiling of natural wonders, for the stinking acres of dead fish floating belly-up as one by one the last few rivers are being turned into waste disposal areas. . . . This is the way the redwoods disappear, and a great lake dies, and smog kills off the frail and the elderly, and clean pure water becomes even more rare. The controls are scattered, hodge-podge, an illogical patchwork of state laws and county and municipal ordinances. Under these circumstances it becomes the policy of the management people to obstruct enforcement, to weaken existing laws, to deceive inspectors, all to avoid additional expense which . . . comes out of profit. Industry in the least regulated areas has the advantage over industry in places where the codes are stringent and scrupulously enforced. The old [profit] yardstick is deadly but we cannot abandon it because it is what makes out our society function. But it is turning our land, from sea to shining sea, into a sour jungle, noisy, dirty, gritty, and infinitely depressing.

MacDonald wrote letters of protest to the secretary of state of Florida. He pleaded with the state's secretary of agriculture. He sent a letter to the editors of *Look* magazine suggesting a story on Arvida and its plans. Nothing worked. Arvida won. The bay was dredged and filled. The golf course was built. New residents moved in. The streets clogged with traffic. John D. licked his wounds, abandoned politics, and started writing novels again. Then, four years later, the projected condominium was announced. MacDonald didn't want to see change in the neighborhood he loved. He expressed his nostalgia in a letter to Mark DeVoto:

> Three doors away from us on Point Crisp Road [lived] Henry Hill, the only seven-fingered church organist I have ever run into. Wife name of Esther. Old Professor Hill lived [there] in winters during his retirement. A courtly old citizen. Once, as he said to prove "I am also a writer," he brought us an LP record of two of his compositions. The Hills had an old semi-blind dog. . . . Hill was going quite deaf. He used to walk the dog on a lead, up to the busy Midnight Pass Road. It made Esther nervous to have them on the narrow shoulder of that road. Right across from Point Crisp, on the Gulf side, was a more elegant development called Siesta Club Properties. Esther went over and spoke with one Rita Kip, a lady of great wealth and connections . . . asking if the retired head of the Harvard Department of Music might walk his blind dog on a leash through the quiet roads of their development. Mrs. Kip, after a hesitation, said, "Of course, my dear. Provided he won't try to . . . ah . . . *mingle*."

This was the Florida John D. feared would vanish with the construction of an eight-story condominium. The suit of rusting armor came out of the closet again. The battle was joined.

This time he won. The Sarasota County Commission refused to approve the condominium. At the meeting, Commissioner William Muirhead, who called himself a conservative, said that "property rights are not absolute," and he said he feared that allowing the Penthouse to be built would amount to "destroying the very things we came to Sarasota for."

The victory was sweet, but it was short-lived. The developers went before the Board of Zoning Adjustments and said that unless their project was approved they would simply change the building from a condominium to an apartment building. An apartment complex, they said, would not violate zoning standards. William Korp, John D.'s lawyer, protested. Then the lawyers for the Penthouse went to court, and in October 1974, the judge wrote a temporary court order that required the Sarasota County Commission to issue a building permit. The commission appealed and lost. MacDonald and his lawyer would try again to thwart the development, but it didn't work.

John D. didn't give up. He had tried fighting Arvida with a pen and lost, and he had tried fighting The Penthouse with a lawyer and done no better. When he settled his lawsuit with American Express, part of the deal was that MacDonald would never write about credit cards. Fine. But he had never made a deal with the condominium developers. So he started writing what would be the longest novel of his career. He called it *Condominium*.

Most of MacDonald's novels are about sixty thousand words long. *Condominium* was nearly triple that. When he sent the manuscript to Lippincott, in July 1975, it was 168,000 words, 560 pages. In *Condominium*, "I bring in a hurricane name of Ella and destroy a Florida key and probably the future of condominiums on these sandy spits," he wrote to his friend Jack Lord, the television actor who starred on *Hawaii 5-0*. "The publishers are all set to do the big promotion, so it will either make me fat, rich and nervous, or it will disappear without the slightest trace."

It never disappeared. For twenty-seven weeks in 1977—from March through August—it was on the *New York Times* hardback best-seller list. *Condominium* was a selection of the Book-of-the-Month Club and had a first printing of fifty thousand. A year later it came back for twelve more weeks on the paperback best-seller list. MacDonald might have lost to the developers in the course of the legal battle, but he would have the last word about condominiums.

The book has more than twenty main characters, and, of course, they all become involved in the end when the hurricane strikes—disaster is the thing that brings them together. In essence, it's sort of a windy version of the film *Grand Hotel*. But it's also in keeping with a mania for disaster—both literary and filmed—the American public had in the 1970s. There was a fire in a skyscraper that was immortalized in *The Towering Inferno*, an ocean disaster in *The Poseidon Adventure*, a volcano eruption in *When Time Ran Out*, an aviation Armageddon in *Airport*, an aquatic death trap in *Jaws*, and amusement park carnage in *Rollercoaster*. A hurricane would seem to be a natural, and in the bookstores it was. John D.'s luck ran out in Hollywood, however. A producer named Dino De Laurentis decided to cash in on the disaster craze with a film called *Hurricane*. It was a box-office disaster, and Hollywood shied away from another wayward wind. Instead of a becoming a theatrical blockbuster, *Condominium* was filmed for the cable television network Home Box Office and shown in two four-hour segments.

The reviews of the book were mixed. There was, of course, the usual praise for the facts—MacDonald consulted a friend who was an engineer to get details of the construction business, and his own business school background let him write knowledgeably about financial minutiae. Sometimes all that knowledge got in the way of telling a good story. "Although *Condominium* purports to be fiction, its apparent intention isn't so much to explore character, plot or theme as it is to compile every conceivable fact about condominiums . . . [and] every chapter ends with a lengthy weather report that allows the author to demonstrate once more his considerable skill at research," wrote Michael Mewshaw in *The New York Times Book Review*. "He seems to have lost sight of what he learned from the detective genre—economy, taut structure and pace. . . . If you hope to build a tight case, you can't waste time tracking down useless information." Across town at the New York *Daily News*, Pete Hamill said the novel showed that MacDonald was "the best novelist in America. . . . [his] muscular style, with its swift pace and ability to describe technical details in plain words, is displayed at its best in his new novel, *Condominium*. If Zola were alive now, he would write this kind of book." *The Washington Post* took the middle ground in a review by Stephen Zito. "[It is] a substantial work—long, solid, and written with a desperate irony. It is a very personal novel . . . a brief against the rape of

Florida. MacDonald writes with outrage. . . . [It] is in many ways a remarkable achievement. . . . His style is as hard-boiled as a thirty minute egg. . . . MacDonald is a genius at the instant creation of a believable character. . . . He mints people as fast as Mattel turns out Ken and Barbie dolls."

Of course, he denied that the fictional development, called Golden Sands in the novel, had anything to do with the real development, the Penthouse. "I have not patterned any of my fictional characters upon any individual characters I have known in the banking, construction, real estate, legal, development, or service businesses," he said just after the novel was published. But consider some coincidences. Both the real and the fictional condominiums were eight stories tall. The Penthouse had forty-five units, Golden Sands had forty-seven. The Penthouse was on three and a half acres, Golden Sands on four. Both, of course, are on barrier islands. Mac-Donald talked about *Condominium* in an interview with Jonathan Yardley in a 1977 story in *Tropic*, the Sunday magazine of *The Miami Herald*:

> MacDonald is reluctant to concede that *Condominium* is an angry novel, even though corruption of several kinds is chief among its many concerns; he says only that it was inspired in part by "a certain amount of irritation with the social structure—a tax structure which encourages the debasement of the environment rather than protects it." He prefers to describe it as "a story about the retired people" in which they are treated as "persons rather than symbols," and when he is asked to summarize the novel's theme he says: "The book is *basically* about the problems of the geriatric ghetto and also about how the disasters of nature tend either to enhance or solve the problems of mortals."

Or, as John D. said in a letter to Mark DeVoto, "[In *Condominium*] I try to show that retired people will be happiest in the known communities where they have assembled enough brownie points to warrant recognition and respect."

It was these retired people that MacDonald worried about. He cared about their empty lives as they sat doing nothing all day long, living with only a memory and a mortgage. In *Condominium* one of the characters ruminates about the days before she and her husband came to Florida:

The first few months at Golden Sands were kind of fun, getting the apartment fixed up the way we want it. Of course we brought too much stuff down. You pay a fortune to have some slobby men smelling of beer throw your furniture around, but when it gets down here in the tropics, it doesn't look the way it did in Warren, Ohio. The light is brighter, or something. It looks all shabby and tacky. We sold a lot of it. I don't really know why I say sold, because we practically gave it away. When the man made that offer, I actually broke down and cried. But Jack said we better take it, so we took it. The new things were very costly, and they're not made as well as the old things were, but I must say they look a lot nicer in the apartment. The thing that is driving me out of my skull is having Jack around every living minute of the day. I am even . . . getting my hair done oftener than I should because it is the only way I can get away from him, and even now I'm not really away from him because he is right out there roaming around in the parking lot, or roaming around in the drugstore or the hardware store, or he is sitting in the Buick rattling his fingernails on the horn ring. The thing about my husband, everybody knew him in Warren. It isn't really a very big place. Jack had the lumberyard his father started way back, and the building supply business. He was in the Rotary and the Kiwanis and the VFW. He was on the board of directors of Ohio Savings and Loan, and he was chairman of the Community Chest a lot of times. And he was on the hospital committee. And he was on the house committee at the country club. He'd walk down the street and about half the people he met would know him by name and he'd know their names. He isn't used to people not knowing who he is. But it's more than that, I think. He had a lot of things going on all the time. . . . It was the way he lived for years and years and years, and all of a sudden there isn't enough going on to use up all that energy, so he is just about to drive me crazy.

And, of course, throughout the book, there is the great storm chugging its way from the coast of Africa, like the finger of God inching closer each minute. It was not the first time John D. had written about hurricanes. After twenty-eight years in Florida he knew the big storms that came swirling in from the Gulf. One took the roof off his office when he lived on Point Crisp Road. Another caused him and Dordo to evacuate, and they drove north to safer ground with two pets, a goose and a duck, that swam in the bathtub in the Howard Johnson's motel while the rain and the wind thrashed about them outside the double-occupancy room. He wrote about hurricanes in two earlier novels, *Murder in the Wind* in 1956 and *Dead Low Tide* in 1953. In the earlier novel he predicted the things to come in *Condominium*:

And you pray, every night, that the big one doesn't come this year. . . . One year it is going to show up, walking out of the gulf and up the coast, like a big red top walking across the schoolyard. And the wind isn't going to mess things up too much, because people have learned what to do about the wind. But that water is going to have real fun with the made land, with the sea walls and packed shells and thin topsoil. It's going to be like taking a good kick at an anthill, and then that local segment of that peculiar aberration called the human race is going to pick itself up, whistle for the dredges, and start it all over again.

Condominium is about the old people, and it's about the great storm, but it is also an elegy to the Florida he loved. *Condominium* is dedicated to 144 people, "those people who were part of the good years in Sarasota and were washed away." They were not literally washed away, of course. "That dedication covered the people on the Sarasota scene who died from all manner of things since we first came here in '49," he told Mark Devoto.

For MacDonald, the good years in Sarasota were in the past. Now it had become a distortion of the town he loved. He talked about the change in a letter to Jordan Crandall:

> It is too pricey for the young writer or artist. There are lots of cheaper places that are just as warm in winter. Also, Sarasota has this culture lag which seems to invite poseurs and phoneys to our area. Their attitudes are just too precious to be believed. They gather in little groups and honk and gush at each other, and stare coldly at anyone who does not have an artistic soul as inexpressibly delicate as theirs. I think a tract house in Yoohaw Junction with a three mile walk to the 7-11 would be a better environment.

John D. seemed to feel Sarasota needed to be cleansed and returned to the way it was when he moved there. Otherwise, it was just another paradise lost. You can see it in the closing pages of *Condominium* when the hurricane has passed and the survivors see what is left. It is like a new Eden, with the sins of the past washed away:

> There is a sort of green fuzz beginning to show above the high-water line. . . . Things are beginning to grow again. It will be nice here, you know? I wish there would be huge lush vines growing up these condominium towers someday, like some giant kind of ivy so that it would all be like those old Mexican ruins in Yucatán. A park can be a memorial to . . . I

can't say greed and stupidity, really. There was something else, wasn't there? A kind of autohypnosis.

The autohypnosis began as part of Flagler's dream; it became a dream he shared with John Ringling, and then with the slightly shady sun worshipers. Now it was a nightmare of greed and the heartbreak of old age and loneliness.

CHAPTER 15

In the spring of 1977, John D. MacDonald began thinking seriously about religion. He had been brought up in the Congregational Church, an upper-class denomination, and had abandoned it when he left home. He retained its Calvinism, but he never returned to organized religion. His new interest in religion wasn't to save his soul but to understand the new electronic church populated by preachers like Jim and Tammy Bakker, Jerry Falwell, Jimmy Swaggart, and Garner Ted Armstrong. With the growing popularity of cable television, it seemed like these preachers were everywhere: praising the Lord, shouting victory, urging their flock to be born again, and pulling in countless millions of dollars.

The new electronic pulpit both fascinated and repelled MacDonald, just as did the idea of aggressive evangelism. He wrote his young friend Al Mittal about his feelings:

> I used to get very frustrated trying to rationalize my own dislike for the great born-again brotherhood. I finally realized one very obvious truth. A true nerd who becomes born again becomes merely a born-again nerd. His smarts, his social adjustments, his empathies—none of these things are changed. They are merely put into a new frame—one in which he can feel spiritually superior—but in essence he is, intellectually, physically, socially, sexually, the same old misfit he always was—in fact still loaded with the same hangups which led him into the born-again phenomena.

His feelings about the electronic media became more than a quip to a friend in 1978 when he began working on his eighteenth Travis McGee novel. Actually, MacDonald had written himself into a corner. At the end of the previous McGee, *The Empty Copper Sea*, Travis falls in love and brings the woman, Gretel, home with him. If these were real people, the fact that a confirmed bachelor finally fell in love and wanted to live with one woman and not just have a series of drop-ins on the houseboat would be a cause for celebration. But for MacDonald, it meant gloom. How could his adventurer have escapades as exciting as what he had known before if he had to turn down women for the wifey, or had to put aside Boodles martinis to buy a gallon of milk on the way home? Besides, the last few McGee books had spent too much time ruminating on the pains and trials of middle age. So he decided to do something about it. He wrote about his problem in a September 5, 1978, journal entry:

> One factor will be different, of course, and that is the prob-
> lem of Gretel. She is sort of an overlap. In prior books the
> lady was disposed of—in one way or another. This is a left-
> over lady, and at the time I introduced her I chose to vary the
> pattern and keep her alive and loving at the end of the
> book. . . . So, as I do not want the books cluttered with too
> many leads—McGee and Meyer are aplenty—I shall follow
> my plan to somehow get rid of Gretel in this untitled eight-
> eenth book.

The book—ultimately known as *The Green Ripper*—would return McGee to unattached bachelorhood. MacDonald said he wanted this book to be "closer to the original patterns, rather than seek a further deviation." But he needed a new villain. He had used up thieves, con men, chiselers, and land developers. That's when he turned to the electronic church. He wrote in his journal:

> As to the general area of hanky-panky, I want to take a
> closer look at TV religious demagogues. There are bland
> men about, who support themselves in a life style of fantastic
> elegance by playing upon the fears and hopes of the elec-

tronic congregation. . . . For some years a reader in California has been sending me great sheafs of material on the Worldwide Church of God. Some of the rules imposed upon the congregation are almost beyond belief. Herbert W. Armstrong, the patriarch-founder, recently tossed his controversial son, Garner Ted, out of the church, and Garner Ted immediately founded his own religion called The Church of God, International, and began broadcasting from a San Antonio radio station. . . . I do not think I can proceed by using a thinly disguised Worldwide Church of God. I cannot understand why the faithful enriched father and son to the extent of $65 million a year, and thus I find it hard to write that story convincingly. So the religion will have to be an amalgam. Scientology has been in the news lately. Ron Hubbard started it when he wrote a book called Dianetics. [MacDonald had known Hubbard when both were pulp writers.] He had previously said that the only way to become a millionaire in these times is to start a religion. . . . It is astonishing the way the Reverend Moon has turned thousands of young Americans into a devoted, humble, funny-looking money machine. And, though not as prevalent as a few years ago, the Jesus freaks are still stomping and extorting, and parents are paying money to kidnappers to go steal a child back from the programmers and deprogram the child. . . .

MacDonald started the book in August and finished it in December, but was beginning to consider ending the McGee series. "At the moment I'm trying to decide if this should be the end of the road [for McGee]," he wrote to Leona Nevler at Fawcett, "but I am hampered by having a pretty good idea for number 19." Then he wrote a letter of self-doubt to his editor at Lippincott that arrived with his manuscript:

Here it is. I feel neither confident of it—nor despairing. I have just absolutely no opinion at all. I tried to bring him

back to the status of the middle books of the series. I was
sliding off with TURQUOISE, LEMON, and COPPER, moving too
far away from my concept, so I needed some spasmatic kind
of thing to bring him on back. So if it works, it works. If it
doesn't, we are all suddenly bums.

It worked, of course, but not without more self-doubt from Mac-
Donald. This time he was questioning the use of sex in the novel. He
wrote to Leona Nevler about it: "I keep worrying about the final
resolution of the scene between Travis and the girl. It seems ever
more gratuitous, and out of character." His editors left the sex in.
The book hit the best-seller list for fourteen weeks, and MacDonald
and his publishers were never bums. In a way, *The Green Ripper* was
the postwar combat novel he was unable to write in the 1940s. But
now, more than thirty years later, he won an Edgar for the best novel
of the year and the National Book Award for the best mystery of the
year. Still, MacDonald was not really satisfied with the book. "*Green
Ripper* was, in retrospect, a mistake," he told a professor at a German
university in a 1980 letter.

A Travis McGee novel with religious zealots as villains did not
satisfy MacDonald. He wanted to do more with the subject. But it
would have to wait until after two more McGee novels were written—*Free Fall in Crimson* and *Cinnamon Skin*. Like *The Green Ripper*, neither of these two adventures is set in Florida. Of course, they
begin there, on the *Busted Flush,* but they go somewhere else for
the action—to California for *The Green Ripper*, to Iowa for *Free Fall
in Crimson*, and to Mexico for *Cinnamon Skin*. MacDonald always
said that writing a detective series was like a folk dance—there had
to be the same theme but there could be variations around it. It was
as if *Condominium* were his last Florida novel. The state had changed
so much it was easier, and more interesting to him, if Travis left the
Busted Flush for his adventures. As John D. said in a letter to a
friend, "Florida is getting so damn tacky we are beginning to think
of moving elsewhere. Wistfully. But too many roots are down, I
guess."

Travis had been out of town before. He spent a frigid winter in

Chicago solving a crime, some time in the Western desert, and made an occasional trip to New York. But it was different now. Now many of the McGee adventures coincided—not surprisingly—with Mac-Donald's own traveling. On one trip to New Zealand to see Johnny and his family the MacDonalds stopped over in Pago Pago. In *The Turquoise Lament*, Travis stops off there, too. But there had always seemed the promise of a homecoming. Before, the trips were just diversions. Now, it seemed, home was less important.

Of course, part of the reason might have been that MacDonald was out of town so much himself. Ever since the opening of the McGee movie, *Dress Her in Amber*, John D. and Dordo had been crazy about cruises. At the premier, a public relations man offered to give them a trip on his cruise ship from Europe back to Miami. They considered it, but were unable to go. However, beginning in 1975, the two of them took regular ocean voyages—the first one was from April through June aboard the *Monterey*, and it covered almost every port of call in Europe. Two years later, they were back on board again, this time on the *Mariposa* for another three months at sea. A few years later, MacDonald wrote about cruising for *The New York Times Magazine*.

If you are jaded by traveling by land or air, the thought of a sea voyage may amuse you. I myself have traveled 256,000 nautical miles on ships and, if time permits, I will run up as many more again. I am fond of this mode of travel because, primarily, it saves a lot of packing and unpacking and allows one to avoid the broad, plastic, glassy squalor and the institutionalized anxiety of international airports, along with the drugged ennui of jet lag. . . . But too often the potential passenger thinks of life on cruise ships as being an unspeakable elegance of Champagne, caviar, and ballroom dancing. It isn't. Take Champagne. Unless you have the wine steward bringing the stuff to your table at $24 to $35 a pop, all you get is what you can take on at one of the captain's receptions, where too few harassed waiters try to serve too many thirsts.

If you have the agility of a broken field runner and the voice of a hog caller, you might get one of those little shallow glasses filled enough times to give you a remote buzz.

In 1981, MacDonald was the star, of sorts, on a murder mystery cruise. Mystery fans had a chance to talk to him and try to solve a mystery committed on board the Norwegian-American Lines' *Vistafjord* on a two-week cruise to Italy. The trip was organized by Dilys Win, the owner of Murder Inc., an all-mystery bookshop in New York. You would expect MacDonald—or, at the least, McGee or Meyer—to have some sarcastic rumble about this. But they never did. Cruising became his love away from the typewriter, and no matter how hokey, he adored it. He would go back again and again. Traveling, particularly on the big ships, was his real hobby—not the things he told reporters about, such as boating, collecting netsuke, or singing "A Bicycle Built for Two" backward in Hindustani.

Cruises became such a passion MacDonald decided to write a book about them. He would not just put Travis on a ship, nor would he write a thick blockbuster about life and love on the high sea. That had been done before by Katherine Anne Porter in *Ship of Fools*. This time he would try nonfiction again and combine his observations about the trips with the memoirs of John D. Kilpack, captain of the last passenger ship to fly an American flag. The book was titled *Nothing Can Go Wrong*. But everything did. "The non-fiction cruise book, *Nothing Can Go Wrong*, seems to be shaping up," he wrote to a friend. "I am finding it a bit dull and heavy going, but maybe the reader will be understanding." It would have to be the reader who was understanding, because nobody in the publishing business was. When he finished writing the 160,000-word manuscript, he sent it in. Everybody hated it, including his agent and his editor. While waiting for his publisher's verdict, MacDonald wrote a friend:

Max hates it, says it will hurt me. Peg Cameron hates it, says it will hurt me. Now I await Ed Burlingame's opinion.

Dorothy loves it. So does my trust officer and his wife. What is this shit about hurting authors? Only, I think, when they write shit like *Fools Die*. I never got hurt by doing a low volume book (*House Guests, No Deadly Drug*). Why do all of a sudden people want to keep me from hurting myself? Do they mean themselves, perhaps?

The critics ignored it, the booksellers didn't stock it, and the public didn't buy it. "Where are the sales figures?" he asked in a letter to Ed Burlingame.

I was dismayed to learn that no copies were purchased by the four stores in the Brentano's Beverly Hills area. I took two copies aboard The Royal Viking Sea [a cruise ship], loaned them only to people who promised to buy a copy on their return, and left my two in the ship's library when we got off. They all liked it. Cruising is a big thing, even during this recession.

Yet the book sank. After a year, it had sold only a little over three thousand copies. Of course, he was such a big seller, he could get anything published as long as he promised to keep writing McGee novels. Books like *Nothing Can Go Wrong* were just a cross his publisher had to bear.

Between cruises, John D. and Dordo spent months at a time in Mexico. Ever since they were first married, Mexico had had a hold on them. They loved it when, just after World War II, they lived there as John D. sharpened his craft. And they loved it when the family went again to Mexico, this time with Johnny studying archaeology. Beginning in 1979, they returned to Mexico, only this time it was not to the Cuernavaca of their youth. It was to Akumal. They drove down there in a van, just before Christmas. Akumal is on the Caribbean coast of Mexico, about an hour and a half from Cancún. He wrote to a friend about it:

Akumal is very quiet. If you can't find what you need at a little store outside the gate, then it is a 120 mile round trip to Cancún. Food wasn't as good as in prior years. Fantastic construction along that coast, with government help and encouragement. . . . They still want to trap the Yankee dollar any and all . . . possible ways. Though we had three nights on the road in Mexico, both coming and going, and traveled in the worst time of the year for Mexican tourism, everything crowded, we made out just fine without reservations anywhere along the road.

In late 1980, they were back again, this time with Johnny and his wife and five children. It was fine, if not memorable. In their third year, Mexico began to change.

There is terrible feuding down here. Now the management has cut off all power to the casitas and to the Villa Mayas and the houses along the road, sending it just to his hotel and our dining room and kitchen and to our bungalows which he rents. So, in order to be able to work down here, and have some refrigeration, I bought a little 1500 watt Honda gasoline generator, and it is hooked up outside the back door and it is running the typewriter, our lights and refrigeration and water still. The owner of the Operadora, Ken Morgan, must be losing his wits. In effect he is refusing to sell us power or even name a price for it, when he is bound under contract to supply us.

Even though conditions got more primitive, the MacDonalds' ardor for Mexico did not cool. In 1982, just before they left for Akumal, they were as excited as ever. "I have been invited to be honorary grand marshal of the Christmas parade of 150 boats at Fort Lauderdale, standing on a replica of *The Busted Flush*, beaming and waving like your garden variety chamber of commerce asshole and I have sent regrets. If all goes well we will be within three days of Akumal on December 17 when they put on their parade. . . ." The Mac-Donalds considered Mexico their third home, after Sarasota and Piseco. "Any sensitivity we may have [toward Latin America] comes from living in Mexico, once for a whole year, once for three months, and lately in Yucatan on the beach a little while every winter," he wrote to a friend. "We speak kitchen Spanish, and always keep trying to improve it, but never do." Mexico was the setting for six of Mac-Donald's books—*The Damned, The Empty Trap, Border Town Girl, Please Write for Details*, and two of the Travis McGee novels, *A Deadly Shade of Gold* and the recently completed *Cinnamon Skin*. But their love had waned by 1984.

He explained what happened in a letter to Mr. and Mrs. Richard Livingstone:

> The three months we spent at our place in Yucatan were not so great this year as it has been other years. We got back from there last month with no need to go back there for a long time. Unsanitary situations on food and water. Dordo was very pooped when she got back. On April 6 she passed out when I walked her out of a local restaurant to get some air. She was feeling woozy. So I followed the ambulance and she was in for five days while they found out that one of the heart medications she was taking had stopped working. . . . But that did not account for the weary feeling and after she got out we found out that she has hepatitis and has evidently had it since the first month or so in Mexico. . . .

Nothing had been the same, really, since 1981, when Dordo had what appeared to be a heart attack near their cabin in Piseco. She was seventy years old. One morning, August 3, she had the classic symptoms of a heart-attack—a sense of doom, pain, ashen color, weakness, breathlessness—and John D. rushed her to the hospital. A doctor there said there had been no heart attack, but the wall of the left ventricle was weak. A cure? "Some people get worse, some people get better, and some stay the same," said the doctor. "But there's no cure."

The circumstances with Dordo's heart and his own advancing age made John D. think seriously about death, a subject he hadn't wanted to face. He told Dordo about it in a June 1982 letter:

I had an experience that made a profound impression on me, and I guess I should have told you about it long ago. . . . It happened that summer Margie died. In between our umpteen trips to Utica I went walking one day, perhaps two weeks after she had died, and I wondered that I did not feel *more*, in fact *a lot more*. I had not felt much when [my father] died, I thought. But there was an anxiety thing that felled me for a time. And not much when Bill and then Dorie died— that being understandable I guess because of the helplessness of their plight and the uselessness of trying to help them in any way. My God, I felt so desolated when [the cats] died! What was this about me and people? So I stopped on the outlet bridge and there were some swallows flying and I tried, really hard, to imagine myself totally alone in the world, without friends or heirs, relatives or wife. . . . I could see how I could survive without relatives, heirs, possessions, places to be—but not without you. I knew then at that moment I couldn't cut it without you around—that any continuing existence would be pointless, and there would be no end to my despair. . . . I certainly haven't told you how much you do mean to me when I really should have. All this heart thing with you has made me very very edgy. Sort of like a room with a mirror that you don't want to look at but you have to look at it. . . . I have been thinking about it a lot. I don't know if I should give you this or just let it ride. I don't want to depress you by letting you understand that I feel as if I was walking around and around the edge of a pit. You said the other day there was a twenty to one chance now that I would survive you. I always thought and believed . . . that I would die first. I can handle that. I can leave everything in good order for everyone, mostly you. But ever since my walk to the bridge—was it five years ago?—I knew it *had* to be me first.

MacDonald worked himself out of his funk by writing, the therapy that had always worked. It was time to return to that electronic pulpit. He went over his journals and notes, fleshed out a story, and then wrote his publisher, Edward Burlingame, at Harper & Row, his new publisher since that company swallowed Lippincott, about the new-time religion.

I have one book, among others, in progress that is concerned with a sect which I am calling, so far, the Global Church of the Lord. It is patterned after the Worldwide Church of God in California because that is the only group soliciting TV donations which has had enough internal litigation so that the mechanics of it are public knowledge. I have been collecting materials on this strange operation for years. . . . I have moved the fictional operation [from Atlanta] to Florida and I am making it the story of a "prodigal" son who comes back at about 35 after seventeen years of tacky living, to try to insert himself back into the family of imperial daddy, young stepmother, elder brother and sister. They have 2000 acres of rolling country in central Florida, forty miles from Orlando. They have a time-share piece of a satellite, a professional television and radio broadcasting studio, a mainframe computer and sophisticated data base access, with word processing programs, to their thousands of followers across the sun belt. Because the hard core 30,000 of the followers of the Global Church [come up] with 10%, the cash flow to headquarters is nearly $5 million a month. They have a college, an auditorium, private aircraft, legal staff, etc. Okay, I have been dubious about this project *only* from the point of view of possible litigation. I will try to keep it as far away from their operation in every possible detail. I am not a complete idiot. I am not writing a book *about* the Armstrongs, merely using them as part of my research into the whole area of electronic religion, Falwell included. . . .

What MacDonald wanted was to be included in the umbrella libel insurance Harper & Row had for authors. Burlingame was hesitant. Harper operated differently from a lot of other publishing houses, he said, and relied on in-house attorneys. They didn't have libel insurance, it seems. And Burlingame was a little queasy. About religious fanatics he said, "They are quite fanatical and react savagely to criticism, understanding well the principle of their chilling effect," then added, "All of this is not to suggest that we are in any way timid about publishing a book by you or any other author about these groups."

John D. walked. He wound up at Random House, Inc. Or, more precisely, at Alfred A. Knopf, the most prestigious of its subsidiaries. Part of the reason for choosing Random House was its willingness to publish *One More Sunday*, as the religion book was called, and to put MacDonald under its blanket libel insurance. But another part of the move to a Random House company was Leona Nevler, who had been MacDonald's friend since the early days of paperback originals at Fawcett, which was also a Random House company now. He explained all that to Burlingame in a letter:

My personal and professional relationship with Leona Nevler began back in the middle nineteen fifties, a very few years after Fawcett published my first book. We survived the CBS episode, and I believe I played some small part in her finding safe harbor at Random House and bringing the Fawcett list over. . . . I have not been aware of any overt effort on her part to bring me under the Random wing, lock, stock, and barrel, but she is pleased that I am making the move. It will facilitate the coordination of the hard and soft cover on-sale dates, the advertising and promotion efforts, and also the financial aspects. I have not made a spur of the moment move. I began to think of it toward the end of 1982, at the same time as I began to realize that I would have to find a new literary agent for future work. The need to make simultaneous necessary changes can become mildly compulsive, but in the end, refreshing.

MacDonald gave a more detailed, less formal explanation in a letter to Elmore Leonard, another crime writer:

I was held back by feelings of loyalty. I was reluctant to leave Ed Burlingame at Harper and Row and to leave my agent of a few decades, Max Wilkinson. But both these relationships unraveled early in 1983. Max had been telling me for three years that each book I wrote was shit and shouldn't be published as it would hurt me somehow. He started that harassment when he was 76 and he is now 79 and we parted amicably when I asked him if he felt up to going to New York [Wilkinson also lived in Sarasota] and disentangling me from Harper and setting me up with Knopf. He said he didn't. I said I would probably ask George Diskant to do it, and Max said that if I had asked for his suggestion, that is who he would have named. Harper was easier because Ed said they would not fit me under their libel umbrella for the new book *One More Sunday,* as it would set a bad precedent. And Knopf had already said they would—in a press release in [*Publishers Weekly*]. I was given a great deal of money in front for the completed *One More Sunday* and then for the next two McGee books. I worry about that. If the books bomb and the money is really big, then it gets to be like the motion picture shit—the word gets around people took a bath on your product, and it is a handicap from then on. But I will keep enough of that money to soothe any bruises from any quarter.

One More Sunday was published in 1984. It is a sort of literary docudrama. Although it's fiction, it was based on fact and seems to be a true account of the television evangelists who were at their height of power and influence. It was before their fall in the 1980s, before Jim and Tammy were arrested, before Jimmy D. Swaggart picked up a hooker on Highway 61 near New Orleans.

Reviews were mixed. David Shaw, writing in the *Los Angeles Times*, said of MacDonald and the book: "The more he writes, the angrier, the more skeptical and the more judgmental he seems to become. . . . In *One More Sunday* virtually everyone—and virtually everything—is villainous. . . . It is an ugly story about mostly ugly people." Jonathan Yardley was more charitable when he reviewed the book for *The Washington Post:* "MacDonald is no mere knee-jerk critic of the evangelists. He realizes they can often be ruthlessly exploitive . . . but he is quick to acknowledge that they seek, out of whatever motive, to fill a genuine longing among their followers. . . . He is willing to acknowledge the humanity of his evangelists and their henchmen even as he deplores their ideas and actions." And in *The New York Times Book Review*, Caroline Seebohm said that *One More Sunday* "shows all the right signs. . . . [He does not] fall into any simplistic traps, nor does he dismiss all of the religious work as worthless. His description of the Church's organization . . . are brilliantly done, and the question of conscience comes vividly to life. . . . What we lack is a character strong enough to identify with."

The book got more reviews than any other book MacDonald ever wrote. But at the bookstores it was not the raving success Knopf had hoped for. *One More Sunday* was on the best-seller list for only nine weeks (*Condominium* was there for twenty-seven) and never got higher than sixth place. For anyone else, that would be magnificent.

But for the author one critic called "America's Wordsmith," it was less than expected.

But never mind that. Now MacDonald was up to his ears in new intrigue involving an investigative reporter and a Russian detective. And it was all for real.

CHAPTER 16

Bob Sherman, a thirty-five-year-old investigative reporter who worked for Jack Anderson, was on the train in mid-July 1983, traveling from Washington to his home in Montgomery County, Maryland. Before he boarded the train, Sherman picked up a copy of MacDonald's McGee novel *The Dreadful Lemon Sky* from a newsstand in Union Station. Sherman was a voracious reader, and he read mysteries on the train home every night.

There was something about this *Dreadful Lemon Sky* that sounded familiar, he thought. The account of a woman's death from a fictitious newspaper was just like something else he'd read. Only he couldn't remember the title. When he got home he went through his bookcase and found *Nevsky's Demon* by Dimitri Gat. He checked one book against the other. They matched, at least in the plotline and characters. The words were not always the same. Sherman was fascinated. He bought more copies of each book and pasted up the pages next to each other. The two books were so similar that Sherman felt cheated. For a while he thought MacDonald was using Dimitri Gat as a pseudonym and recycling the Travis McGee books. Always the reporter, Sherman called MacDonald and asked him about the pen name theory. MacDonald denied it, but he was intrigued and went out and bought a copy of Gat's book. It was plagiarism. Sherman called Gat's publisher, Avon, and complained. Then he called Fawcett, which got in touch with the lawyers at Random House. The lawyers cited thirty-two instances of copyright infringement. Avon recalled sixty thousand copies of Gat's book.

Gat was a forty-five-year-old procedures analyst for a company in Connecticut. He had written another book in the Yuri Nevsky series, *Nevsky's Revenge*. Of course, in Gat's book the hero is not a Florida beach bum but an American of Russian extraction. He had also written two other books, *The Shepherd Is My Lord*, a science fiction novel, and *Some Are Called Clowns*, the story of a black baseball team. MacDonald told Gat he wouldn't sue if Gat did three things—made sure all sixty thousand copies of *Nevsky's Demon* were destroyed, made sure the plates for the book were destroyed, and sent MacDonald a formal apology. The books and plates were pulverized, and in a day or two John D. got a letter from Gat in the mail: He apologized and said plagiarism was never his intent. "I thought I had massaged all the Travis McGee out of it, and went on my own way with it," Gat wrote, referring to *Nevsky's Demon*. "I changed characters around, used new ones, put in different love interests. As a longtime reader of Travis I certainly didn't want to get in where I didn't belong or *ever* pass your works off as mine. This isn't the way I'd first hoped to communicate with someone whose books I've enjoyed for years."

MacDonald issued a one-sentence statement: "It is very difficult for me to understand how Mr. Gat could have written *Nevsky's Demon* without direct and frequent references to my novel, *The Dreadful Lemon Sky*." He didn't sue.

In private, however, he had more to say about the matter. In a letter to his friend Richard Glendinning he wrote:

> You were quite right to guess that something was missing from the epic story about Dimitri Gat. His first novel in the genre, *Nevsky's Revenge,* was patterned quite closely to the plot structure and plot incidents of *The Empty Copper Sea*. So what happened to him? Kudos. He got a splendid mention in *The New York Times* and also a nomination for best first novel from the Mystery Writers of America. Nobody caught it. Not Avon or the NYTimes nor the MWA. And it was only by chance that Bob Sherman [saw] the similarity in *Demon*. I suspect that it could have gone on and on until by the time somebody did catch it he would have cannibalized lots of the McGee books. I read *Revenge* and found that, though it is very close, especially in the beginning of chapters five and six, it did not lend itself as readily [to a] point by point comparison as did *Demon* and *Lemon*. Okay, so the guy had one juvenile and one non-book before he began . . . the series. Because nobody caught him up on it the first time, I can eas-

ily see why he could decide he had been right. If you change the characters, the sex of the characters, the locale and the dialogue, all is well. And he told Bob Sherman on the phone . . . "but all of those books are full of that kind of stuff." I don't think he really knew how much trial and error, patching and changing, adding and deleting, is necessary to hammer out a structure that will hang together and be satisfying to the reader. There was no point in going after both books. I could have confused the point at issue—which was to make him stop. I suspect that because publishers are such notorious cowards, Mr. Gat has been forever removed from public print. And that, I think, is too bad. He writes adequately, and obviously enjoys writing. With the contemporary moral standards being what they are, it is difficult for a fellow in his forties, new to the business, to realize that publishing is an old-fashioned trade.

While Dimitri Gat was writing plagiarized MacDonald thrillers, John D. was putting the stamp of approval on the first biography of him. It all began in 1977 when an English professor from the University of South Florida named Edgar Hirshberg approached him about writing a biography for the Twayne Publishing Company's U.S. Authors Series. MacDonald knew Hirshberg. His brother was a former sportswriter in Boston who moved to Sarasota and became a member of the Friday writers' group. His younger brother, Ed, followed him to Florida after he got a Ph.D in English from Yale. Ed also became a regular at the Friday meetings.

Edgar Hirshberg had the trappings of an academic but the soul of a fan. He had reviewed every Travis McGee book MacDonald ever wrote, he would eventually become publisher of *The JDM Bibliophile* when Len and June Moffatt gave it up, and he organized the John D. MacDonald conferences, meetings of academics and fans who would gather to present papers and talk about Travis McGee. He offered to split any money he made from the book with MacDonald in return for his cooperation. "The amount of money would be minimal," he said in a letter to John D., "since the books in this series are scholarly." He asked for John D.'s help. "Your involvement would mean, first, your consent, second, your cooperation in a couple of taping sessions, . . . as well as your critical gems and something about the way you write."

MacDonald agreed, but said he wouldn't have time to be interviewed for several months. In the meantime, he said, Hirshberg should go to the University of Florida library and peruse its special collection department. "*All* of my papers are there, Ed," John D. told him. And then he made a proposal. "I would like to trade off my share of any monies from this venture to you in return for the right of approval of the final manuscript. Okay?" It was fine with Hirshberg. In 1984, seven years after he started the project, the book was ready to be published. MacDonald read the manuscript and asked for twenty-five changes. Hirshberg made them. Later, in 1986, two years after the book was published, he wrote to a friend about it. "Should you read Ed Hirshberg's tome, you will find some obvious discrepancies here and there," the letter said. "That is because he is such a nice, gullible, trusting chap, I just can't keep from lying to him. I know it is a bad habit, but I keep wondering how far I can go before he realizes it's a put-on. This is a strange basis for a bio."

In 1984, MacDonald sent the manuscript for *The Lonely Silver Rain* to Knopf. It was the twenty-first McGee and it would be the last one. The truth is, he was getting tired of Travis, and he had always said that when it no longer amused him to write about his fictional detective, he would stop. In February 1984 he told Leona Nevler he was ready to end the series. "Today I will reach page 120 on the new untitled [McGee]. I am a bit dubious about the way I have laid waste Travis' Lauderdale landscape and disbanded his friends and associates, but I can see now that I'm aiming for an end to the series with the 22nd installment."

Nevler tried to talk him out of it: "I am . . . appalled that you would ever *think* of aiming toward an end to the series with the twenty-second installment. . . . A twenty-third is essential."

A year later, he was working on an untitled McGee manuscript. It would have been the twenty-second in the series. By January 1986, the book had taken form. He discussed it in a letter to Stephen King:

"I have made enough of an inroad on the 22nd McGee to know now it will be twice as long as any which have gone before. It will be two books in one, twenty years apart in time." And in a 1984 interview with Peter J. Heck, he talked about ending the series with the twenty-second book and having McGee move away from Fort Lauderdale. Before the interview was published, MacDonald looked at the transcript and edited out almost all the references to the end of McGee. But before the editing, here's what the interview said:

> I'm gonna end [with] the twenty-second book. I got it blocked out enough to know that if the book goes all right, which I trust it will, he's gonna pull up stakes with a bunch of about five or six other boats, good friends and what not and acquaintances. Well, he's gonna go find the place and then go back to Bahia Mar and they're gonna load up and take off and move to a new marina up in the Panhandle. Up there you can find areas that are as pleasant as Fort Lauderdale was twenty years ago.

For years there were rumors that a secret manuscript existed with "black" in the title. In that book, the story went, MacDonald kills off McGee. He told Peter Heck it was true:

> I've got some materials on it, but not for immediate publication and I don't want to publish it because it would spoil the fun for people who are just now finding McGee and people wouldn't want to read a book about a dead hero, right? So I use that threat and twenty to thirty pages. . . . I've used that as a bargaining base with my publishers. When they get funny ideas how long it takes them to get the royalties. . . . Why, then I start muttering about that book. I say, "You better treat us right, McGee and me, or I'll kill him." That straightens things out. That's practical economics.

Three years earlier he had said to a fan, "There will never be one called BLACK where he is killed off. It wouldn't be fair to the people who are just discovering the fellow."

Even though he never intended *The Lonely Silver Rain* to be his last book, at times it seems to have an aura of finality about it. Here is the beginning of the closing scene:

It is May, early May, a lovely time of the year in Florida. We have taken the *Busted Flush* north up the Waterway to a place where it opens into a broad bay. I have dropped the hooks at a calm anchorage well away from the channel and far enough from the mangrove coast to let the south breeze keep the spring bugs away.

We brought aboard pungent cauldrons of Meyer's Special Incomparable Chili, and enough icy beer to make the chili less lethal. How many of us are there? Twenty? Thirty? Let's say a lot. Jim Ames and Betsy. The Thorners, Teneros, Arthur and Chook Wilkinson, the Mick and Carlie Hooper, Junebug, Lew, Roxy, Sue Sampson, Sandy, Johnny Dow, Briney, Frank and Gretch Payne, Miguel, the Marchmans, Marilee, Sam Dandie with two nieces, and a leavening of beach folks, and two dogs and a cat, dutifully ignoring one another.

We are here, and there is music and there are bad jokes, and so we are all a little bit longer in the tooth and have seen life go up, down and sideways without any rhyme or reason anyone can determine. We laugh at tired old jokes because they are old and tired and familiar, and it is good to laugh.

Physically, writing the final McGee novel was easier than writing the first one. MacDonald started using a computer in 1982, even though Travis McGee often lists computers as one of the modern world's evils. In a letter to his friend William Campbell Gault, he was as enthusiastic as a child with a new toy. "Hey, don't knock the word machines," he wrote. "I have been using one for five years and it is a great crutch for the ageing mind. . . . I am telling you, pal, that as the days dwindle down, we need every crutch we can find. And that's all these things are, crutches. But the end result is better work. And faster. I found the changeover difficult, but I imagine it was just as tough for fellows to drop the quill pen and go to the typewriter."

But his writing, his newfound love of the computer, and even the prospect of world cruises were not enough to lift his spirits in the fall of 1984. Dordo got a mastectomy at Strong Memorial Hospital in New York. He wrote about the operation in a letter to his editor at Knopf, Robert Gottlieb:

> Dorothy did well on the operation. They did not remove any muscle tissue so recovery will be simplified. The lab said that the underarm nodes they removed are not affected, so I am hoping they will not prescribe any chemotherapy. She cannot have radiation in that area as it is too close to her coronary problems. Her attitude is just fine, which I think must be almost the most important thing in this particular operation.

Less than a year later, in July 1985, she was back in the hospital for another operation. The mastectomy was supposed to stop her cancer from spreading to her lymph nodes. It didn't. Her operation was to remove the cancerous cells, and then she would begin chemotherapy. Dordo's health problems took their toll of John D. as well. He wrote to Stephen King:

> I tried to be strong and brave and true and all that shit, and I did indeed take care of her pretty good, but it threw me into a practically permanent migraine. Have had the classic variety

all my life but nothing like this. Anyhow, we got along without a resident nurse because neither one of us like strangers in the house, and I changed dressings and all that. Chemotherapy was rough on her and she finished the course two weeks ago. We have been packing and packing and packing, and we will get on the Sagafjord next Monday, January 6, and go around the world on that old familiar bucket, getting off it rarely—just for favorite places like with the grandchildren in Christchurch and again at Bangkok. The oncologist says that the three month cruise should put her back in trim.

While he was waiting on Dordo and helping her to recover, John D. was taking another chance with seeing one of his books turned into a movie. This time it wasn't a McGee adventure that was going before the camera, it was his 1962 environmental thriller, *A Flash of Green*. And this time it wasn't Hollywood that was involved, but an independent filmmaker named Victor Nunez, a native Floridian who was now a film director living near Tallahassee. When he started work on *A Flash of Green*, Nunez had made one other film, *Gal Young 'Un*, which was based on a Marjorie Kinnan Rawlings story. *Flash of Green* was shot on a budget of less than $1 million and was financed by public television's *American Playhouse,* the National Endowment for the Arts, and some Florida investors. MacDonald was one of them; On July 15, 1983, he sent a check for $30,000 so he could become a member of the Flash of Green Limited Partnership.

Filming took place during 1984 and 1985. In May 1985, *A Flash of Green* was shown at the Cannes Film Festival. It was released in the United States in November of that year. Plans were to show it on *American Playhouse* and then release it to art theaters. MacDonald was opposed to a general release for the film. "I think [commerical release] would be a mistake," he wrote to Sam Gowan, associate producer. "The big distributors feel they have to spend millions on [duplicate prints] and advertising, and I do not think it will or could do well enough in commercial release to equal the amount of distributor's gross you'd get from the art theater release." MacDonald loved the movie. Critics said its pace was too slow. "It's *supposed* to have a slow pace," John D. fumed.

As he worked on the film, he was also crafting another novel, *Barrier Island*. This is the story of a land scam on barrier islands off the coast of Mississippi. "Bob Gottlieb doesn't like the title and doesn't care much for the book," he wrote to William Hart, referring to Knopf's president who was also his editor. "It is only 65,000 words. If I wrote only about McGee, [Gottlieb] would be a happy man, but I wouldn't be." The book never made the best-seller list. It was MacDonald's final novel, but he was involved with one more book: he would be coauthor with Dan Rowan of a collection of their letters. Originally, MacDonald wanted to call the book *When You and I Were Young, McGee*. The final title was *A Friendship*. "Believe it or not, we had to cut it from 150,000 words down to 101,000," he wrote to William Campbell Gault. "There is some funny stuff in there. If they put Rowan on talk shows (he is willing) it should sell pretty good, as he is a quick and witty fellow."

Dordo's chemotherapy ended December 13, and the two of them were home for Christmas and then, on January 9, 1986, got on the ship for their round-the-world cruise. It seemed to help Dordo. They got home to Sarasota in May. This time it was John whose health was not right. On June 16, he wrote Bandel Linn:

> I . . . had a teeny tiny stroke which has left me with but one residual—a constant shimmering, as of a bunch of black and white tiny triangles boiling away like mad over there at four o'clock in both eyes. I have had it since November and so am getting accustomed to having it boiling away over there all the time. I think I would miss it if it quit.

But the flicker in his eyes would not go away, and it was no joke. He wrote his nephew, Dann Robinson:

[I saw] a neurologist about a residual flicker in the corner of my vision from a whole bunch of migraines I had in November of 1985. . . . The neurologist prescribed Inderal to lessen incidence of migraines. I saw him in June. I called the cardiologist to see if it was okay for me to take. He had me come in for a check up. Then more checks and tests. Then into the hospital for a heart catheterization. Then up to Gainesville for a second opinion. And now I must go off to Milwaukee for a coronary bypass operation. Totally unexpected, as I have *no* symptoms at all. But then, neither do thirty percent of the people with coronary artery disease. Silent ischemia, they call it. . . . I go in on the 16th [of September] and they do the operation on the 18th. I'll be in ten days at least, then some rest at the hotel, then back [to Sarasota].

MacDonald's doctor was W. Dudley Johnson of Milwaukee Heart Surgery Associates. He was recommended by Dr. Gene Myers of Sarasota. On July 21, Johnson wrote to Myers. The doctors looked at the film of MacDonald's heart. He was in bad shape. "He has sustained damage to the heart in most areas of the ventricle," the letter said. A bypass was called for. No problem. Routine. Piece of cake. "I would estimate a five to eight percent operative risk for a patient in this situation," Dr. Johnson said.

John D. took the news like a tough guy. "I cannot keep my mind off the horrid fact that I have to be in the operating room at St. Mary's Hospital in Milwaukee on the morning of September 18 for a quintuple bypass operation," he said in a letter to William Gekle. "It fucks up my concentration."

And in a September 1 letter to Elmore Leonard: "I'm winding up this and that in preparation for a trip to a veritable garden spot—Milwaukee—where a Doctor Dudley Johnson is going to do bypass surgery. There seems to be a lot of it going around. Michener just had one. I wouldn't want to feel left out."

MacDonald checked into St. Mary's Hospital in Milwaukee. Johnny came over from New Zealand to be with Dordo. But it was just a routine operation, right? Right. Johnny took pictures of John D. in a surgical green gown walking up and down the halls of the hospital, pulling a rack filled with intravenous fluid behind him. There were also pictures of him lying in his hospital bed while he typed on his laptop computer.

On September 18, John D. MacDonald went under the knife for heart surgery.

After the surgery, MacDonald developed pneumonia. They kept him in his hospital bed for more than three months. For the last thirty days he was in a coma. He died on December 28, 1986. He was seventy years old. The death certificate, signed by Dr. Johnson, says he died from "respiratory arrest with subsequent coma, chronic respiratory failure after coronary bypass operation." He was cremated.

But wasn't this supposed to be an almost routine operation? As MacDonald said in his letter to Elmore Leonard, there was "a lot of it going around." The letter from Dr. Johnson, dated July 21, less than two months before the surgery was scheduled, had estimated only a 5 to 8 percent operative risk.

The doctors got together and issued a statement. It was carried in the *Sarasota Herald-Tribune*. The story was by Kate Murphy:

> Best-selling author John D. MacDonald, who died Sunday of complications following heart surgery, had experienced chest pains before the operation and was at a higher risk for surgery than the typical heart-bypass patient, his doctors agreed.
>
> Dr. Jay Kaufman, MacDonald's cardiologist in Milwaukee, said the mortality rate for the typical bypass patient is low. But the author had a more severe form of heart disease than the typical heart-bypass, placing him at a greater risk for surgery, Kaufman said Monday. MacDonald had complained of chest pains before he entered the hospital last September, the doctor said.
>
> Dr. Dudley Johnson, the surgeon who performed the bypass, told MacDonald that the author was in a higher-risk category, Kaufman said.

For most bypass patients, a bypass graft can correct artery blockages in the heart, Kaufman said.

But in MacDonald's case, the disease went all the way down the artery, and the bypass was more difficult, Kaufman said. Johnson had to reconstruct the artery, which increased the risks associated with open-heart surgery, Kaufman said.

MacDonald died Sunday at St. Mary's Hospital in Milwaukee after he had been in the hospital since Sept. 18. He was kept in the hospital's coronary-care unit after he developed complications from the surgery.

MacDonald, 70, had been a Sarasota resident since 1951.

MacDonald was referred to Johnson because he is one of the few doctors who perform this special type of surgery, Kaufman said.

In addition to this, MacDonald's heart function wasn't normal, Kaufman said. "It didn't squeeze as strong as it should. The contractions weren't as vigorous as they should be," he said.

And he had problems with his lungs before the surgery which led to complications after the surgery. "One of the major organs that the (heart) patients have trouble with is the lungs," he said. "Even with the routine (operations) the problem is that the patient can't get all the secretions out, and they can develop problems."

In MacDonald's case, he developed pneumonia a few weeks after the surgery, and never was able to recover.

When the autopsy was released it showed that MacDonald had suffered from arteriosclerosis, enlarged heart, a previous heart attack (presumably the one in 1970), terminal pneumonia, blood clots to the lungs, a large spleen, terminal kidney abnormalities, partial abdominal blockage with clots, and, after a month in a coma, severe brain injury. The cause of death is listed as bronchopneumonia, but it is difficult to say if this was the cause of death or a complication that resulted from a heart attack.

Dordo would never have to worry about money. MacDonald's estate was worth $9.5 million. But she didn't have much time. Fourteen months later, she was dead. It was cancer.

When he looked back on his parents' deaths a few years later, their son, Maynard, saw a silver lining:

When my dad died he was in intensive care for three months, my mother and I spent ten hours a day with him. After I went home I was struggling to explain to my wife, not just the details, but the feeling, the atmosphere of the experience. At that point it suddenly occurred to me that there was only one other series of events in my life that felt the same way and that was when I accompanied my wife during the birth of our children. There was pain and blood and struggle, and against the odds a new life, something special, was launched through all that difficulty, and then when my dad died it was the same, it was a long, sometimes terrible process, like birth. And in the end, it felt like birth, one had the feeling that a life was somehow launched rather than ended. My mother's death was similar. I was totally surprised by this. Of course I miss them, of course I feel pain, but also I feel that they are not quite gone in the way I expected. I thought they would feel, just gone, vanished, and instead I feel that they are not "gone" as much as they are actually somewhere else. My own experience of becoming very ill and almost dying, sort of having a foot in the door so to speak, and of accompanying my parents while they approached death and passed into it, has given me an unexpected sense that all my assumptions about death were simply wrong or so incomplete as to be useless.

John D. MacDonald was a man who tried to escape his Calvinist background and spent his life affirming it. His detective, Travis McGee, is one of the great additions to hard-boiled fiction. Without

McGee, the form could easily have become self-parody. Instead, MacDonald made his detective a commentator on politics, the environment, and a world that is becoming more impersonal, a world filled with credit cards and computers. McGee, and, of course, MacDonald, fought valiantly against that, but it was like Don Quixote and the windmills, a cause that could never prevail.

Both MacDonald and McGee were men of honor, and it is this honor that keeps the books interesting to read in an era of e-mail and Visa. Few other writers were able to span decades of American popular fiction—from pulp magazines to paperback originals to hardcover detective stories to blockbuster bestsellers—as well as John D. MacDonald did. He was a success in all of them. But his greatest influence springs from the creation of Travis McGee, a moralist who wants to right the wrongs of the world while solving the case and getting the girls. Without MacDonald, there might not have been a Robert Parker or a Carl Hiaasen. And the world would be a less interesting place without them.

BIBLIOGRAPHY

WORKS BY JOHN D. MacDONALD

Novels and Other Fiction

All Those Condemned. Greenwich, Conn.: Fawcett Gold Medal, 1954.

April Eve. New York: Dell Publishing, 1956.

Area of Suspicion. New York: Dell Publishing, 1954.

Barrier Island. New York: Alfred A. Knopf, 1986.

Ballroom of the Skies. New York: Greenberg, 1952.

The Beach Girls. Greenwich, Conn.: Fawcett Gold Medal, 1959.

Border Town Girl. New York: Popular Library, 1956.

The Brass Cupcake. Greenwich, Conn.: Fawcett Gold Medal, 1950.

Bright Orange for the Shroud. Greenwich, Conn.: Fawcett Gold Medal, 1965.

A Bullet for Cinderella. New York: Dell Publishing, 1955.

Cancel All Our Vows. New York: Appleton-Century-Croft, 1953.

Cinnamon Skin. New York: Harper and Row, 1982.

Clemmie. Greenwich, Conn.: Fawcett Gold Medal, 1958.

Condominium. New York: Lippincott, 1977.

Contrary Pleasure. New York: Appleton-Century-Croft, 1954.

The Crossroads. New York: Simon and Schuster, 1959.

Cry Hard, Cry Fast. New York: Popular Library, 1955.

The Damned. Greenwich, Conn.: Fawcett Gold Medal, 1952.

Darker than Amber. Greenwich, Conn.: Fawcett Gold Medal, 1966.

Dead Low Tide. Greenwich, Conn.: Fawcett Gold Medal, 1953.

A Deadly Shade of Gold. Greenwich, Conn.: Fawcett Gold Medal, 1965.

Deadly Welcome. New York: Dell Publishing, 1959.

Death Trap. New York: Dell Publishing, 1957.

The Deceivers. Greenwich, Conn.: Fawcett Gold Medal, 1958.

The Deep Blue Good-By. Greenwich, Conn.: Fawcett Gold Medal, 1964.

The Dreadful Lemon Sky. New York: Lippincott, 1975.

Dress Her in Indigo. Greenwich, Conn.: Fawcett Gold Medal, 1969.

The Drowner. Greenwich, Conn.: Fawcett Gold Medal, 1963.

The Empty Copper Sea. New York: Lippincott, 1978.

The Empty Trap. New York: Popular Library, 1957.

The End of the Night. New York: Simon and Schuster, 1960.

End of the Tiger and Other Stories. Greenwich, Conn.: Fawcett Gold Medal, 1966.

The Executioners. New York: Simon and Schuster, 1958.

A Flash of Green. New York: Simon and Schuster, 1962.

Free Fall in Crimson. New York: Harper and Row, 1981.

The Girl, the Gold Watch, & Everything. Greenwich, Conn.: Fawcett Gold Medal, 1962.

The Girl in the Plain Brown Wrapper. Greenwich, Conn.: Fawcett Gold Medal, 1968.

The Green Ripper. New York: Lippincott, 1979.

I Could Go On Singing. Greenwich, Conn.: Fawcett Gold Medal, 1963.

Judge Me Not. Greenwich, Conn.: Fawcett Gold Medal, 1951.

A Key to the Suite. Greenwich, Conn.: Fawcett Gold Medal, 1962.

The Last One Left. Garden City, N.Y.: Doubleday, 1966.

The Lethal Sex. New York: Dell Publishing, 1959.

The Lonely Silver Rain. New York: Alfred A. Knopf, 1984.

The Long Lavender Look. Greenwich, Conn.: Fawcett Gold Medal, 1970.

A Man of Affairs. New York: Dell Publishing, 1957.

Murder for the Bride. Greenwich, Conn.: Fawcett Gold Medal, 1951.

Murder in the Wind. New York: Dell Publishing, 1956.

The Neon Jungle. Greenwich, Conn.: Fawcett Gold Medal, 1953.

Nightmare in Pink. Greenwich, Conn.: Fawcett Gold Medal, 1964.

On the Run. Greenwich, Conn.: Fawcett Gold Medal, 1963.

One Fearful Yellow Eye. Greenwich, Conn.: Fawcett Gold Medal, 1966.

One Monday We Killed Them All. Greenwich, Conn.: Fawcett Gold Medal, 1961.

One More Sunday. New York: Alfred A. Knopf, 1984.

The Only Girl in the Game. Greenwich, Conn.: Fawcett Gold Medal, 1960.

Other Times, Other Worlds. New York: Fawcett Gold Medal, 1978.

Pale Gray for Guilt. Greenwich, Conn.: Fawcett Gold Medal, 1968.

Please Write for Details. New York: Simon and Schuster, 1959.

The Price of Murder. New York: Dell Publishing, 1957.

A Purple Place for Dying. Greenwich, Conn.: Fawcett Gold Medal, 1964.

The Quick Red Fox. Greenwich, Conn.: Fawcett Gold Medal, 1964.

The Scarlet Ruse. Greenwich, Conn.: Fawcett Gold Medal, 1973.

S*E*V*E*N. Greenwich, Conn.: Fawcett Gold Medal, 1971.

Slam the Big Door. Greenwich, Conn.: Fawcett Gold Medal, 1960.

Soft Touch. New York: Dell Publishing, 1958.

A Tan and Sandy Silence. Greenwich, Conn.: Fawcett Gold Medal, 1972.

Three for McGee. Garden City, N.Y.: Doubleday, 1967.

The Turquoise Lament. New York, Lippincott, 1973.

Weep for Me. Greenwich, Conn.: Fawcett Gold Medal, 1951.

Where Is Janice Gantry? Greenwich, Conn.: Fawcett Gold Medal, 1961.

Wine of the Dreamers. New York: Greenberg, 1951.

You Live Once. New York: Popular Library, 1956.

Nonfiction by John D. MacDonald

Books

The House Guests. Garden City, N.Y.: Doubleday, 1965.

JDM and Dan Rowan. *A Friendship: The Letters of Dan Rowan and John D. Mac-Donald, 1967–1974.* New York: Alfred A. Knopf, 1986.

No Deadly Drug. Garden City, N.Y.: Doubleday, 1968.

JDM and John H. Kilpatrick. *Nothing Can Go Wrong.* New York: Harper and Row, 1981.

Articles

"Interlude in India," *Story: The Magazine of the Short Story,* July–August, 1946.

"From the Top of the Hill." *Clinton Courier,* Clinton, N.Y. Newspaper column by JDM. Thirty-two installments, October 23, 1947–May 27, 1948.

"Professionally Yours." *The 1950 Writer's Yearbook*, April 1950.

"I Protest." *Writer's Digest*, November 1952.

"When You Retire . . . Will This Happen to You?" *This Week*, March 8, 1953.

"He's Not Talking to Me." *Report to Writers*, July 1953.

"What Is Talent?" *Writer's Digest*, October 1953.

"Off the Beat." *The Lookout and Newsmonth*, Sarasota, Fla. Magazine column written under the name T. Carrington Burns. Fifteen installments for Sarasota monthly/bimonthly magazine, November 26, 1959–June/July 1961.

"Glendinning: The Man and the Legend." *Pocket Pete*, March 1960.

"The Sad Case of the Dead Author." *Publishers Weekly*, October 3, 1960.

"So, Boating Is Pleasure?" *Sarasota Herald Tribune*, May 16, 1962.

"Mao in Leech Land." *Sarasota Herald Tribune*, May 23, 1962.

"How to Beat a Drum." *Sarasota Herald Tribune*, June 1, 1962.

"No Time for Gimmicks." *Sarasota Herald Tribune*, June 6, 1962.

"Life with Roger the Cat." *Sarasota Herald Tribune*, June 6, 1962.

"The Weight of Numbers." *Sarasota Herald Tribune*, June 12, 1962.

"A Package of Delights." *Sarasota Herald Tribune*, November 28, 1962.

"A Savory Theme." *Sarasota Herald Tribune*, December 16, 1962.

"Footnotes to Assassination." *Sarasota Herald Tribune*, December 1 1963.

"How to Live with a Hero." *The Writer*, September, 1964.

"On Crimes and Crowding." *Sarasota Herald Tribune*, November 4, 1964.

"Haniku." *St. Petersburg Times Sunday Magazine*, December 1964.

"Authors Like Them, Too." *The New York Times*, January 10, 1965.

"The Everglades." *Venture*, 1965.

"Think You Can Write?" *St. Petersburg Times*, July 11, 1965.

"Report from the Ironic Underground." *Chicago Tribune*, October 24, 1965.

"John D. MacDonald vs. Doc Savage." *Bronze Shadows*, February 1966.

"Xerography and the Writer." *Author's Guild Bulletin*, March 1966.

"Their Favorite Words." *St. Petersburg Times*, March 20, 1966.

"Pulp Perspective Plus." *Bronze Shadows*, November 1966.

"Says U.S. Can't Quit War." *Sarasota Herald Tribune*, September 17, 1967.

"Everybody Knows Something Is Wrong." *The Miami Herald*, October 15, 1967.

"Compulsion and Butterflies." *The CEA Critic*, December 1967.

"Reader's View." *Sarasota Herald Tribune*, January 4, 1968.

"Bayfill: Thrust and Riposte." *Sarasota Herald Tribune*, January 25, 1968.

"The Little Doll and the Mousetrap." *Rudder*, January, 1968.

"The Florida Keys in Hurricane Alley." *Holiday*, December 1968.

"The Creative Person and Some Dangerous Streets." *Writer's Digest*, June 1969.

"Last Chance to Save the Everglades." *Life*, September 5, 1969.

"His Creator Watched McGee Come to Life." *Aloft*, January–March 1970.

"An Answer to Karen." *Family Weekly*, July 22, 1973.

"Creative Trust." *The Writer*, January 1974.

"Quiet Times." *The Conservationist*, April–May 1974.

"A Terminal Case." *New York Magazine*, October 3, 1977.

"Confessions of a Renegade." *Chicago Tribune*, July 9, 1978.

"The Case of the Missing Spellbinders." *TV Guide*, November 24, 1979.

"Economic Dispair Fueled Miami Riots." *Sarasota Herald Tribune*, May 24, 1980.

"Can Presidents Avoid Violence?" *Los Angeles Times*, April 1, 1981.

"Dashiell Hammett's Compulsions." *The Washington Star*, August 2, 1981.

"The Other Florida." *Jacksonville Times Union*, September 5, 1982.

"Why a Quarter-Century of Growth May Not Have Been Progress." *Florida Trend*, June 1983.

"Missionary Stew—A Wild Concoction." *USA Today*, October 21, 1983.

"Afloat, But Not at Sea." *New York Times Magazine*, October 9, 1983.

CRITICAL, BIOGRAPHICAL, AND BACKGROUND SOURCES

Books

Alger, Horatio, Jr. *Ragged Dick, or Street Life in New York with the Boot Blacks*. New York: Signet Books, 1990.

Blum, John Morton. *V Was for Victory: Politics and American Culture During World War II*. New York: Harcourt Brace Jovanovich, 1976.

Cain, James M. *The Postman Always Rings Twice*. New York: Alfred A. Knopf, 1934.

———. *Mildred Pierce*. New York: Alfred A. Knopf, 1941.

———. *Serenade*. New York: Alfred A. Knopf, 1938.

———. *Three of a Kind: Career in C Major, The Embezzler, Double Indemnity*. New York: Alfred A. Knopf, 1945.

Campbell, Frank D. *John D. MacDonald and the Colorful World of Travis McGee*. San Bernadino, Calif.: Borgo Press, 1977.

Chandler, David Leon. *Henry Flagler: The Astonishing Life and Times of the Visionary Robber Baron Who Founded Florida*. New York: Macmillan, 1986.

Chandler, Raymond, *The Big Sleep*. New York: Alfred A. Knopf, 1939.

———. *Farewell, My Lovely*. New York: Alfred A. Knopf, 1940.

———. *The High Window*. New York: Alfred A. Knopf, 1942.

———. *The Lady in the Lake*. New York: Alfred A. Knopf, 1943.

———. *The Little Sister*. New York: Alfred A. Knopf, 1949.

———. *The Long Goodbye*. Boston: Houghton Mifflin, 1949.

———. *Playback*. Boston: Houghton Mifflin, 1954.

Davis, Kenneth C. *Two-Bit Culture: The Paperbacking of America*. Boston: Houghton Mifflin Company, 1984.

Day, Douglas. *Malcolm Lowry: A Biography*. New York: Dell, 1975.

Durr, Mark. *Some Kind of Paradise: A Chronicle of Man and the Land in Florida*. Gainesville: University Press of Florida, 1998.

Eames, Hugh. *Sleuths Inc*. New York: Lippincott, 1978.

Gannon, Michael. *Florida: A Short History*. Gainesville: University Press of Florida, 1993.

Gardner, Dorothy, and Katherine Sorley Walker, editors. *Raymond Chandler Speaking*. Boston: Houghton Mifflin, 1977.

Geherin, David. *John D. MacDonald*. New York: F. Ungar, 1982.

Glassman, Steve, and Maurice O'Sullivan. *Crime Fiction and Film in the Sunshine State: Florida Noir*. Bowling Green, Ohio: Bowling Green State University Popular Press, 1997.

Goodstone, Tony. *The Pulps: Fifty Years of American Pop Culture*. New York: Chelsea House, 1970.

Goulart, Ron. *The Dime Detectives*. New York: Mysterious Press, 1988.

Gruber, Frank. *Pulp Jungle*. Los Angeles: Sherbourne Press, 1967.

Hammett, Dashiell. *The Big Knockover*. New York: Spivak, 1943.

———. *The Dain Curse*. New York: Alfred A. Knopf, 1929.

———. *The Glass Key*. New York: Alfred A. Knopf, 1931.

———. *The Maltese Falcon*. New York: Alfred A. Knopf, 1930.

———. *Red Harvest*. New York: Alfred A. Knopf, 1929.

———. *The Thin Man*. New York: Alfred A. Knopf, 1934.

Hiney, Tom. *Raymond Chandler: A Biography*. New York: Atlantic Monthly Press, 1997.

Hirshberg, Edgar W. *John D. MacDonald*. Boston: Twayne Publishers, 1985.

Hoopes, Roy. *Cain: The Biography of James M. Cain*. New York: Holt, Rinehart and Winston, 1982.

Johnson, Diane. *Dashiell Hammett: A Life*. New York: Random House, 1983.

Jones, Robert Kenneth. *The Shudder Pulps*. New York: Plume Books, 1975.

Layman, Richard. *Shadow Man: The Life of Dashiell Hammett*. New York: Harcourt Brace Jovanovich, 1981.

Lowry, Malcolm. *Under the Volcano*. New York: Signet Books, 1966.

Madden, David, editor. *Tough Guy Writers of the Thirties*. Carbondale: Southern Illinois University Press, 1968.

McCauley, Michael. *Jim Thompson: Sleep with the Devil*. New York: Mysterious Press, 1991.

Macdonald, Ross (Kenneth Millar). *The Blue Hammer*. New York: Alfred A. Knopf, 1976.

———. *The Drowning Pool*. New York: Alfred A. Knopf, 1976.

———. *Find a Victim*. New York: Alfred A. Knopf, 1950.

———. *The Galton' Case*. New York: Alfred A. Knopf, 1959.

———. *The Ivory Grin*. New York: Alfred A. Knopf, 1952.

———. *Meet Me at the Morgue*. New York: Alfred A. Knopf, 1953.

———. *The Moving Target*. New York: Alfred A. Knopf, 1949.

————. *The Underground Man*. New York: Alfred A. Knopf, 1971.

————. *The Zebra-Striped Hearse*: New York: Alfred A. Knopf, 1962.

McElvaine, Robert. S. *The Great Depression: America 1929–1941*. New York: Times Books, 1984.

McIver, Stuart B. *Dreamers, Schemers, and Scalawags*. Sarasota, Fla.: Pineapple Press, 1994.

McShane, Frank. *The Life of Raymond Chandler*. New York: E.P. Dutton, 1976.

————, editor. *Selected Letters of Raymond Chandler*. New York: Columbia University Press, 1981.

Moore, Lewis D. *Meditations on America: John D. MacDonald's Travis McGee Series and Other Fiction*. Bowling Green, Ohio: Bowling Green State University Popular Press, 1994.

Morgan, William James. *The OSS and I*. New York: Norton, 1957.

Nolan, David. *Fifty Feet in Paradise: The Booming of Florida*. San Diego: Harcourt Brace Jovanovich, 1984.

Nolan, William F. *The Black Mask Boys: Masters in the Hard-Boiled School of Detective Fiction*. New York: William Morrow, 1985.

North, Henry Ringling, and Alden Hatch. *The Circus Kings*. Garden City, N.Y., Doubleday, 1960.

O'Brien, Geoffrey. *Hardboiled America: The Lurid Years of Paperbacks*. New York: Van Nostrand Reinhold Company, 1981.

Peterson, Theodore. *Magazines in the Twentieth Century*. Urbana: University of Illinois Press, 1964.

Polito, Robert. *Savage Art: A Biography of Jim Thompson*. New York, 1995.

Prather, Richard S. *Case of the Vanishing Beauty*. Greenwich, Conn.: Fawcett Gold Medal, 1950.

————. *Way of a Wanton*. Greenwich, Conn.: Fawcett Gold Medal, 1952.

————. *The Meandering Corpse*. New York: Pocket Books, 1966.

————. *Kill Him Twice*. New York: Pocket Books, 1965.

Reilly, John M., editor. *Twentieth Century Crime and Mystery Writers*. New York: St. Martin's Press, 1980.

Robeson, Kenneth. *Fear Cay: A Doc Savage Adventure*. New York: Bantam Books, 1966.

Rumm, Herbert. *The Hard-Boiled Detective: Stories from Black Mask Magazine 1920–1951*. New York: Vintage Books, 1977.

Server, Lee. *Danger Is My Business: An Illustrated History of the Fabulous Pulp Magazines, 1896–1953*. San Francisco: Chronicle Books, 1993.

———. *Over My Dead Body: The Sensational Age of the American Paperback*. San Francisco: Chronicle Books, 1994.

Shine, Walter and Jean. *A Bibliography of the Published Works of John D. MacDonald with Selected Bibliographical Material and Critical Essays*. Gainesville: Patrons of the Libraries, University of Florida, 1980.

———. *A MacDonald Potpourri*. Gainesville, Florida: University of Florida Libraries, 1988.

———. *Special Confidential Report Subject: Travis McGee*. Fort Lauderdale, Fla.: Bahia Mar Resort and Yachting Center, 1992.

———. *Rave or Rage: The Critic & John D. MacDonald*. Gainesville: University of Florida, George A. Smathers Libraries, 1993.

Simpson, Lesley Byrd. *Many Mexicos*. Berkeley: University of California Press, 1966.

Smith, Bradley F. *The Shadow Warriors: OSS and the Origins of the CIA*. New York: Basic Books, 1983.

Smith, R. Harris. *OSS: The Secret History of America's First Central Intelligence Agency*. Berkeley: University of California Press, 1972.

Spillane, Mickey. *The Big Kill* New York: Dutton, 1951.

———. *I, The Jury*. New York: Dutton, 1947.

———. *Kiss Me, Deadly*. New York: Dutton, 1952.

———. *My Gun Is Quick*. New York: Dutton, 1950.

———. *Vengeance Is Mine*. New York Dutton, 1950.

Steinbrunner, Chris, and Otto Penzler. *Encyclopedia of Mystery and Detection*. New York: McGraw Hill, 1976.

Symons, Julian. *Mortal Consequences: A History from the Detective Story to the Crime Novel*. New York: Shocken Books, 1972.

Weeks, David C. *Ringling: The Florida Years, 1911–1936*. Gainesville: University of Florida Press, 1993.

Whitfield, Raoul. *Death in a Bowl*. New York: Alfred A. Knopf, 1931.

———. *Green Ice*. New York: Alfred A. Knopf, 1930.

———. *The Virgin Kills*. New York: Alfred A. Knopf, 1931.

Articles

"Dorothy Prentiss to Teach Cazenovia Seminary Class." *Utica Times*, September 6, 1931.

"Willard Teed Is Married In Utica." *Utica Times*, September 6, 1931.

"Retired Deputy in Westchester $250,000 Short." *New York Herald Tribune*, May 9, 1933.

"J. D. MacDonald Named to Tax Research Post." *Utica Observer-Dispatch*, March 21, 1946.

"Utican Writes 300 Stories in 20 months." *Utica Observer-Dispatch*, May 25, 1947.

"Utican Wins Prize for Story," *Utica Press*, January 30, 1950.

"Why They Do It." *What's What in Clearwater*, February 1950.

Alexander, Josephine. "Writer of Popular Mystery Tales Finds Inspiration in Clearwater." *Clearwater Tribune*, March 3, 1950.

"Beach Resident Proves All Writers Are Not Screwballs." *Clearwater Sun*, May 7, 1950.

"Local Fiction Writer Among Top Authors." *Sarasota Herald-Tribune*, May 17, 1953.

Dickensian, Alberta J. "Former Utican Writes Novels." *Utica Observer-Dispatch*, August 1954.

"Local Author Attacks Censorship of News." *Sarasota News*, November 20, 1954.

"Wartime Letter to His Wife Made MacDonald an Author." *Sarasota Herald-Tribune*, November 28, 1954.

"Spillane Creates Mythological Characters, Says MacDonald." *Tallahassee Democrat*, February 20, 1955.

Barker, Eddie. "The 'Prince of the Paperbacks' Writes Easily." *The Atlanta Journal*, January 15, 1959.

Buck, Pat. "Swell Parties 'Swell.'" *St. Petersburg Times*, February 9, 1962.

"Anne Colfelt Bride of John MacDonald." *Sarasota Herald-Tribune*, February 11, 1962.

Parsons, Al. "Author MacDonald Turns from Mysteries to Examine the Menace of Bay Filling." *Sarasota News*, May 12, 1962.

Harris, Phil. "It's a Gabfest Every Friday for Sarasota Writers." *The Tampa Tribune*, January 6, 1963.

Brock, Charlie. "MacDonald, Dallas, and a Man Named McGee." *Florida Times-Union*, May 31, 1964.

Burnett, Clyde. "Two Sarasotans Open Shop for Graphics Production." November 8, 1964.

Burnett, Clyde. "Form and Technique Found Interesting at Art Exhibit." *Sarasota Herald-Tribune*, February 17, 1965.

———. "Dorothy MacDonald's Show Proves Hard to Review." *Sarasota Herald-Tribune*, March 25, 1965.

———. "Variety, Depth Mark Exhibit Now at Hilton Leech Gallery." *Sarasota Herald-Tribune*, March 29, 1965.

Washington, Sally. "Artist Rules Out Patterns for Decorating." *Sarasota Herald-Tribune*, June 20, 1965.

Deal, Babs. "*Man Who Loved Children* Author Draws Praise." *Sarasota Herald-Tribune*, November 27, 1965.

"Authors and Editors." *Publishers Weekly*, January 2, 1967.

"Minto Answers MacDonald." *Sarasota Herald-Tribune*, January 13, 1968.

"American Express Sued by MacDonald." *Sarasota Herald-Tribune*, September 25, 1968.

Jolidon, Laurence. "Credit Cards: A Mystery to Author MacDonald." *St. Petersburg Times*, November 18, 1968.

Hiss, Philip H. "I'm Really (Sock!) a Moralist (Whack!) at Heart (Bam!) Said the Best-Selling Author to the Quivering Blonde." *Tampa Tribune*, April 6, 1969.

Hass, Joseph. "Maestro of the Mystery." *Chicago Daily News*, September 6–7, 1969.

"Seven Who Do the Whodunits." *Newsweek*, March 22, 1971.

Petersen, Clarence. "Another Travis-ty in the Works?" *Chicago Tribune*, July 27, 1971.

Kahn, Justin. "Travis McGee's Life 'Seems Good Theology.' " *The National Observer*, January 22, 1972.

Pace, Eric. "Bang! Bang!" *The New York Times*, February 11, 1973.

Diehl, Digby, "JDM—The Man Behind Travis McGee." *The Los Angeles Times*, July 27, 1973.

Hanscom, Leslie. "The Paperback Revolution." *San Antonio Express News*, September 20, 1973.

Rubin, Valerie. "Siesta Eyes 70 Pct. Population Hike." *Sarasota Herald-Tribune*, January 7, 1974.

"A Line Drawn at Last." *Sarasota Herald-Tribune*, January 9, 1974.

"County Ordered to OK Penthouse Plat." *Sarasota Herald-Tribune*, October 29, 1974.

"The Quiet Prolific Author Behind the Salty Shamus Called Travis McGee." *People*, May 19, 1975.

Hills, Rust. "The Awesome Beige Typewriter." *Esquire*, August 1975.

Benjamin, David A. "Key Witness: J. D. MacDonald." *The New Republic*, July 26, 1975.

Ebert, Roger. "John MacDonald: He's Not Just Popular—He's Also Good." *Chicago Sun Times*, July 28, 1976.

Hamill, Pete. "He Packs Large Themes in Small Books." *New York Daily News*, April 6, 1977.

Burger, Knox. "Everyman Falls Again, and the 66th Time It Hurts." *Village Voice*, April 11, 1977.

Mitgang, Herbert. "Behind the Best Sellers: John D. MacDonald." *The New York Times Book Review*, May 15, 1977.

Yardley, Jonathan. "*Condominium*: MacDonald's Dreadful Lemon Skyline." *The Miami Herald*, March 6, 1977.

"Unwanted Epilogue." *The Washington Star*, April 4, 1977.

Dreffin, Desi. "History of Siesta Key." *Siesta Key Pelican*, July 21, 1977.

Mulligan, Hugh. "Mulligan's Stew." *The Charleston Evening Post*, February 11, 1978.

Oberdorf, Charles. "The Dauntingly Prolific Beige Typewriter Keys." *Macleans*, November 20, 1978.

Rehlmann, William. "MacDonald: A Hit Author by Accident." *The Ledger Star*, August 8, 1979.

Cicero, Linda. "Dirty Deeds on the High Seas." *Miami Herald*, April 18, 1981.

C. F. "Celebrity Interview: John D. MacDonald." *Purrrrr!*, August–September 1982.

Huisking, Charlie. "The Literary Lunch Bunch." *Sarasota Herald-Tribune*, January 2, 1983.

Vassallo, George. "The Pen Behind Travis McGee." *USA Today*, June 13, 1983.

MacNamara, Mark W. "John D. MacDonald: Unraveling the Mysteries of Authorship." *Family Weekly*, January 23, 1983.

Suplee, Carl. "Finding the Real McGee." *The Washington Post*, July 15, 1983.

"Imitation Novel Went Too Far." *San Francisco Chronicle*. August 4, 1983.

McDowell, Edwin. "Novel Recalled After Author Admits to Borrowing Plot." *St. Petersburg Times*, August 7, 1983.

Wilson, Robert. "Purloined Plot? Publisher agrees to destroy book." *USA Today*, July 22, 1983.

Sherman, Bob. "Author Admits Copying MacDonald." *Publishers Weekly*, July 29, 1983.

Cleveland, Carol. "Travis McGee: The Feminists' Friend." *The Armchair Detective*, Winter 1983.

Hynan, Patrick. "Who Says Crime Doesn't Pay?" *MD Magazine*, March 1984.

Huisking, Charlie. "*Flash of Green* Nears Completion." *Sarasota Herald-Tribune*, April 6, 1984.

———. "Writer Borden Deal Dies of Heart Attack." *Sarasota Herald-Tribune*. January 20, 1985.

Gurney, Jack. "Borden Deal Wrote Erotic Best Sellers, According to Widow." *Sarasota Herald-Tribune*, January 22, 1985.

Champlain, Charles. "Elegant Mob Steals Show at Cannes." *Sarasota Herald-Tribune*, May 11, 1985.

Pottler, Marsha. "Film Remains Too True to MacDonald Novel." *Sarasota Herald-Tribune*, November 22, 1985.

Sheppard, R. Z. "Neither Tarnished nor Afraid." *Time*, June 16, 1986.

Holston, Noel. "Profile: John D. MacDonald." *The Orlando Sentinel*, June 29, 1986.

Murphy, Kate. "MacDonald Was as Entertaining as His Books." *Sarasota Herald-Tribune*, December 29, 1986.

———. "Doctors: Surgery Was High-Risk for Author." *Sarasota Herald-Tribune*, December 30, 1986.

Encenbargar, William. "The Writer and His Hero." *Amtrak Express*, February 1987.

King, Larry L. "State of the Arts: The Writers' Colony." *Sarasota Magazine*, December 1987.

Periodicals

The JDM Bibliophile. Number 1 (March 1965)—Number 36 (July 1985).

Theses

Benjamin, David A. "John D. MacDonald and the Life and Death of the Mythic Hero." M.A. Thesis, Harvard University, 1977.

Jackman, Mary Katherine. "Female Voice: Feminine Narratives in John D. Mac-Donald's Travis McGee Series." M.A. Thesis, New Mexico State University, 1993.

Mallory, Margaret I. "The Heroes of John D. MacDonald's Novels of Violence." M.A. Thesis, San Marcos State University, 1976.

Manuscript Collections

The Liar's Club, Sarasota, Florida.

Glendinning, Richard. "A Host of Fridays: Being a Directory of All Those Who Have Made It to Friday Lunch During the First Thirty Years of That Curious Sarasota Ritual" (unpublished manuscript).

University of Florida, George A. Smathers Library Special Collections, Gainesville, Florida

MacDonald, Eugene A. Untitled, unpublished memoir.

Telegram from S. Roy Prentiss to Rita Van Woert, August 10, 1908.

Telegram from Rita Van Woert to S. Roy Printiss, August 10, 1908.

Certificate, McGill University, French Summer School, 1931, to Dorothy Prentiss.

MacDonald, John D. Unpublished European diary, 1932.

The Academician, High School Yearbook, 1933

MacDonald, Doris. "Always a 'Father.'" Unpublished memoir, 1937.

MacDonald, John D. "Winter," unpublished short story, 1935.

———. "Ode to All Your Days," Unpublished poem, 1937.

———. Classroom exercise, 1937.

———. "Three Paragraphs," unpublished short story, 1937.

Wedding announcement, John D. MacDonald and Dorothy Mary Prentiss, July 3, 1938.

Record of Service with Rochester Ordnance District, 1943.

Halprin, Howard J. Commendation for John D. MacDonald, June 28, 1943.

MacDonald, John D. "India Trip." Unpublished manuscript, 1944.

Military Record and Report of Separation for John D. MacDonald, July 12, 1945.

MacDonald, John D. Untitled, unpublished short story, 1945.

———. Untitled, unpublished short story, 1945.

———. "Bon Air Bounce or Leave Me Until I Get the Brass Ring, Mama." Unpublished comedy sketch, 1948.

Advertising for *The Damned*, Fawcett Gold Medal Books, 1952.

MacDonald, John D. "Officer Roop Routine." Unpublished comedy sketch, 1961.

———. "The Window Stripper." Unpublished comedy sketch, 1962.

———. Unpublished journal, January 17, 1967.

———. Unpublished journal, January 19, 1967.

MacDonald, John D. "New House Requirements." 1968.

Willeford, Charles. "Travis McGee and the Big White Smile." Unpublished manuscript, circa 1970.

MacDonald, John D. MacDonald and Prentiss family history. Unpublished manuscript, September 9, 1977.

———. Unpublished journal, September 5, 1978.

Torres, C., M.D. Admission report for Dorothy Prentiss MacDonald, Amsterdam Memorial Hospital, Amsterdam, N.Y. August 6, 1981.

McDonald, John D. Chronological record of sea cruises, 1983.

———. Plot summaries. Unpublished, 1983.

MacDonald, John D. Unpublished family chronology. May 1984.

Record of Autopsy, St. Mary's Hospital (John D. MacDonald), December 28, 1986.

Certificate of Death (John D. MacDonald), State of Wisconsin, December 28, 1986.

United States Estate Tax Return (John D. MacDonald), Case Number 87–196 CP-02, 1988.

Interview Transcripts

July 9, 1979. Written answers to questions from William Ruehlman.

July 11, 1979. Written answers to questions from Bonnie O'Boyle for *Motor Boat and Sailing* magazine.

January 23, 1980. Written answers to questions from Dawn Parsell, high school student.

1980 (?) Interview with Ed Hirshberg.

April 15, 1981. Transcript of interview with Dick Lupoff.

May 12, 1983. Written answers to questions from George Vassallo.

November 11, 1984. Written answers to questions from C. Jordon Crandall.

December 12, 1984. Transcript of interview with Peter J. Heck for *Criminal Intent, No. 2.*

Letters

Dorothy Mary Prentiss to Santy Claus. December 1919.

Charles E. Hamilton to Dorothy M. Prentiss, February 19, 1931.

"Scotty" to Dorothy Prentiss, July 7, 1931.

Charles E. Hamilton to Dorothy Prentiss, April 22, 1932.

John D. MacDonald (JDM) to Dorothy Prentiss MacDonald (DPM) August 28, 1937.

Rita Prentiss to John and Dorothy MacDonald, 1938.

Sam Prentiss to DPM, March 12, 1939.

Marguerite Dann MacDonald to JDM, 1939.

JDM to Eugene A. MacDonald, February 29, 1940.

Tad and Dedi Reid to JDM and DPM, February 29, 1940.

Eugene A. MacDonald to "Colonel," July(?) 1940.

DPM to JDM, June 4, 1940.

DPM to JDM, June 6, 1943.

DPM to JDM, June 7, 1943.

DPM to JDM, July 12, 1943.

JDM to DPM, September 18, 1943.

DPM to JDM, April 6, 1944.

DPM to JDM, April 16, 1944.

JDM to Eugene A. MacDonald, April 15, 1944.

DPM to JDM, May 2, 1944.

DPM to JDM, May 11, 1944.

DPM to JDM, May 25, 1944.

JDM to DPM, May 16, 1945.

DPM to "People," December 2, 1948.

JDM and DPM to "Family," December 27, 1948.

DPM to "Family," January 3, 1949.

DPM to "Family," January 17, 1949.

DPM to "Family," February 8, 1949.

DPM to "Family," February 14, 1949.

DPM to "Family," March 8, 1949.

DPM to "Family," May 28, 1949.

DPM to "Friends," June 18, 1949.

DPM to "Family," July 3, 1949.

John O. Rich to John Prentiss MacDonald, December 17, 1956.

JDM to John O. Rich, January 31, 1957.

Dyckman W. Vermilye to JDM, September 26, 1957.

JDM to Guy Pasachal, November 13, 1959.

JDM to Jack Benny, May 9, 1960.

JDM to Bob Newhart, October 20, 1961.

JDM to Romer and Howard, May 30, 1962.

JDM to the Editor, *Sarasota Herald Tribune*, January 20, 1965.

JDM to Clyde Burnett, January 28, 1965.

Elizabeth Lambie to JDM, April 29, 1965.

JDM to Connie and Al Sessions, May 3, 1965.

JDM to Marguerite Dann MacDonald, May 31, 1965.

JDM to "All Friends and Relatives," Early 1966.

JDM to Waldo, March 23, 1966.

JDM to Borden Deal, September 4, 1966.

Borden Deal to JDM, September 5, 1966.

JDM to Albert Mittal, July 24, 1967.

JDM to Dorie, Bill, Dann, Susan, Dog, Etc., July 31, 1967.

JDM to Tom Tannenbaum, October 5, 1967.

JDM to Tom Tannenbaum, December 8, 1967.

JDM to Honorable Mayor and City Commissioners, Sarasota, Florida, December 31, 1967.

JDM to Albert Mittal, January 3, 1968.

JDM to Harry Ackerman, January 13, 1968.

JDM to Board of County Commissioners, January 26, 1968.

JDM to the Editor, *Sarasota Herald Tribune*, January 29, 1968.

JDM to the Editor, *Sarasota Herald Tribune*, January 29, 1968.

JDM to Maxwell Wilkinson, February 1, 1968.

JDM to the Editor, *Sarasota Herald Tribune*, February 4, 1968.

Harry Ackerman to Maxwell P. Wilkinson, March 13, 1968.

JDM to Maxwell Wilkinson, March 16, 1968.

JDM to Tom Adams, April 10, 1968.

JDM to T. George Harris, April 22, 1968.

JDM to Doyle Conner, May 4, 1968.

JDM to David Maxey, May 7, 1968.

JDM to David R. Maxey, May 16, 1968.

JDM to Albert Mittal, July 11, 1968.

Mr. and Mrs. Krisman G. Neville to Len and June Moffatt, August 10, 1968.

Len and June Moffatt to JDM, August 12, 1968.

Krisman Neville to JDM, August 17, 1968.

JDM to Mr. and Mrs. Krisman Neville, August 15, 1968.

JDM to Krisman Neville, August 31, 1968.

Krisman Neville to JDM, September 3, 1968.

JDM to Krisman Neville, September 7, 1968.

JDM to Maxwell Wilkinson, September 17, 1968.

JDM to Maxwell Wilkinson, September 17, 1968.

Krisman Neville to JDM, September 21, 1968.

JDM to Don Farber, 24 November, 1968.

JDM to Albert Mittal, January 15, 1969.

JDM to Krisman Neville, January 17, 1969.

JDM to John O. Binns, January 18, 1969.

Krisman Neville to JDM, January 19, 1969.

JDM to Marguerite Dann MacDonald, January 27, 1969.

JDM to Dr. John Deiter, March 20, 1969.

JDM to Jack Reeves, May 24, 1969.

JDM to Krisman Neville, June 30, 1969.

Krisman Neville to JDM, July 15, 1869.

JDM to Krisman Neville, July 19, 1969.

Krisman Neville to JDM, 23 July, 1969.

JDM to Albert Mittal, August 17, 1969.

JDM to Sheriff Ross Boyer, August 25, 1969.

Edward E. Lewis to JDM, September 13, 1969.

Tom Todd to JDM, September 14, 1969.

Jack J. Reeves to JDM, September 17, 1969.

JDM to Ed, September 16, 1969.

JDM to Tom, September 18, 1969.

JDM to Doris MacDonald Robinson, September 21, 1969.

JDM to Harry Mines, November 1, 1969.

John O. Binns to JDM, December 20, 1969.

JDM to Susan Robinson, February 28, 1970.

JDM to Harry Ackerman, May 12, 1970.

JDM to John, October 21, 1970.

Walter L. Bruington to Maxwell Wilkinson, November 18, 1970.

JDM to Don, January 21, 1971.

Lucille Jamison to JDM, March 30, 1971.

JDM to Jane, June 29, 1971.

JDM to Walter Fultz, August 17, 1971.

JDM to Roger J. McCarty, August 24, 1971.

JDM to Maxwell Wilkinson, August 20, 1972.

JDM to Mr. Andrews, September 5, 1972.

JDM to Roger, February 7, 1972.

JDM to Albert Mittal, February 15, 1973.

JDM to William R. Korp, June 28, 1973.

William R. Korp to JDM, August 15, 1973.

William R. Korp to JDM, November 1, 1973.

JDM to William R. Korp, November 7, 1973.

William R. Korp to John Saba, March 5, 1974.

Knox Burger to JDM, July 3, 1975.

Stewart Richardson to Maxwell P. Wilkinson, July 16, 1975.

Marlene Dietrich to JDM, July 19, 1975.

JDM to Marlene Dietrich, July 30, 1975.

JDM to Maxwell P. Wilkinson, August 2, 1975.

Marlene Dietrich to JDM, August 4, 1975.

JDM to Marlene Dietrich, August 18, 1975.

Marlene Dietrich to JDM, August 23, 1975.

Marlene Dietrich to JDM, September 23, 1975.

Stewart Richardson to Maxwell P. Wilkinson, September 25, 1975.

JDM to James D., September 30, 1975.

Doubleday and Co. to JDM, October 28, 1975.

Janet H. Baker to John Charles Baker, December 5, 1975.

Jane Prentiss to JDM and DPM, December 13, 1975.

JDM to Leona Nevler (LN), January 3, 1976.

JDM to LN, January 10, 1976.

LN to JDM, January 15, 1976.

JDM to Mrs. Riva, January 28, 1976.

JDM to Marlene Dietrich, June 21, 1976.

JDM to Jack Lord, July 9, 1976.

Bud Klotchman to JDM, February 28, 1978.

JDM to Gerald Weales, April 23, 1978.

Gerald Weales to JDM, May 15, 1978.

JDM to Van and Scottie, August 1, 1978.

Edgar W. Hirshberg to JDM, September 7, 1978.

JDM to Bruce Voeller, November 9, 1978.

Joyce Rimlinger to JDM, November 13, 1978.

JDM to Joyce Rimlinger, December 7, 1978.

JDM to LN, December 13, 1978.

JDM to Peg, December 13, 1978.

John J. Roman to JDM, January 8, 1979.

Sam Prentiss to John Roman, January 29, 1979.

LN to JDM, February 8, 1979.

JDM to LN, February 15, 1979.

LN to JDM, March 27, 1979.

JDM to Mrs. Blizzad, May 11, 1979.

JDM to John J. Roman, May 12, 1979.

JDM to Mark DeVoto, July 5, 1979.

JDM to Ms. DeLong, August 11, 1979.

JDM to Bill, August 16, 1979.

JDM to Mr. Davis, September 1, 1979.

JDM to Jim Harrison, November 6, 1979.

JDM to Peg, November 26, 1979.

JDM to Mrs. Plummer, December 26, 1979.

JDM to Lee, January 27, 1980.

William P. Scandling to JDM, March 24, 1980.

JDM to William P. Scandling, April 29, 1980.

JDM to Nogs, May 11, 1980.

J. Kenneth Van Dover to JDM, June 5, 1980.

JDM to John G., June 6, 1980.

JDM to Dick Kitchen, July 15, 1980.

David Geherin to JDM, September 3, 1980.

JDM to Mr. Barson, December 5, 1980.

JDM to Carol Dinnean, December 27, 1980.

JDM to Friends, February 4, 1981.

JDM to Sam Prentiss, February 15, 1981.

JDM to Ted Sperling, May 6, 1981.

JDM to George Diskant, May 15, 1981.

JDM to Dr. Raymond D. Fowler, June 19, 1981.

JDM to Pam Conrad, June 22, 1981.

JDM to Mr. Jones, July 11, 1981.

JDM to Mr. Bear, July 21, 1981.

JDM to Dr. Gene Myers, August 17, 1981.

JDM to Charles, October 18, 1981.

JDM to Mr. and Mrs. Richard Livingstone, November 17, 1981.

JDM to Tom, October 20, 1981.

Knox Burger to JDM, October 23, 1981.

LN to JDM, February 3, 1982.

JDM to Edward Burlingame, May 3, 1982.

JDM to Elmore Leonard, May 10, 1982.

Edward L. Burlingame to JDM, May 7, 1982.

JDM to DPM, June 7, 1982.

Elmore Leonard to JDM, October 1, 1982.

JDM to Elmore Leonard, October 5, 1982.

JDM to Tom Greenfeldt, February 9, 1983.

JDM to George Diskant, February 22, 1983.

JDM to LN, April 18, 1983.

Sallie Coolidge to JDM, July 8, 1983.

JDM to LN, July 11, 1983.

Ellis Levine to Dimitri Gat, July 11, 1983.

Dimitri Gat to JDM, July 12, 1983.

Harry M. Reeser III to Samuel LePrell, July 15, 1983.

JDM to George Diskant, July 31, 1983.

Edward L. Burlingame to JDM, July 28, 1983.

JDM to Edward L. Burlingame, August 1, 1983.

JDM to Wm. C. G., August 11, 1983.

JDM to Richard Glendinning, August 13, 1983.

JDM to Elmore Leonard, August 24, 1983.

JDM to Dr. and Mrs. Robert Lauderdale, October 3, 1983.

JDM to Mr. and Mrs. Forrest Dagget, October 5, 1983.

JDM to Mr. and Mrs. Morton Q. Peterson, October 5, 1983.

JDM to Dr. Thomas Dickinson, October 5, 1983.

JDM to Mrs. Judson E. Fiebiger, October 19, 1983.

JDM to Elmore Leonard, December 19, 1983.

JDM to Tom Bethancourt, 1983.

LN to JDM, January 16, 1984.

JDM to LN, January 31, 1984.

JDM to LN, February 4, 1984.

LN to JDM, February 10, 1984.

LN to JDM, February 10, 1984.

JDM to Bandel Linn, March 29, 1984.

JDM to Mr. and Mrs. Richard Livingstone, April 27, 1984.

JDM to Dr. John Lott Brown, April 29, 1984.

Jack Lord to JDM, May 5, 1984.

JDM to Jack Lord, May 8, 1984.

JDM to Richard Martin Stern, June 29, 1984.

JDM to Ralph Daigh, June 29, 1984.

JDM to Elmore Leonard, July 4, 1984.

JDM to Robert Gottlieb, September 14, 1984.

JDM to Sam Prentiss, October 18, 1984.

JDM to Professor Edgar Hirshberg, December 10, 1984.

JDM to Gary Mann, June 13, 1985.

JDM to Maynard (John Prentiss) and Lilli MacDonald, July 27, 1985.

JDM to Karsten MacDonald, August 12, 1985.

JDM to William Campbell Gault, August 20, 1985.

JDM to George Diskant, September 14, 1985.

D. Berry to JDM and DPM, October 26, 1985.

JDM to Robert Gottlieb, November 7, 1985.

JDM to William B. Hart, December 11, 1985.

JDM to Stephen King, January 2, 1986.

Richard Layman to JDM, February 5, 1986.

JDM to William Campbell Gault, May 1, 1986.

JDM to John Robinson, May 3, 1986.

JDM to Charles A. MacDaniel, May 7, 1986.

JDM to Marilyn Staats, May 10, 1986.

Elmore Leonard to JDM, May 20, 1986.

JDM to Elmore Leonard, May 24, 1986.

JDM to Bandel Linn, June 16, 1986.

Jack Lord to JDM, June 23, 1986.

JDM to Jim Charlton, July 14, 1986.

JDM to Joseph M. Moxley, July 17, 1986.

W. Dudley Johnson, M.D., to Gene E. Myers, M.D., July 21, 1986.

JDM to Mrs. Wyatt Blassingame, July 28, 1986.

JDM to William F. Gekle, August 4, 1986.

JDM to Joy and Joe, August 12, 1986.

JDM to W. Dann Robinson, August 14, 1986.

John A. McKerricher to George Diskant, February 4, 1987.

L. Howard Payne to John A. McKerricher, February 11, 1987.

Mrs. Erskine Caldwell to DPM, July 27, 1986.

Maynard (John Prentiss) MacDonald to Mrs. Blanche Laube Allen, May 7, 1989.

INDEX